STATE SECURITY IN SOUTH AFRICA

STATE SECURITY IN SOUTH AFRICA

Civil – Military Relations Under P W Botha

JAMES M. ROHERTY

M. E. Sharpe, Inc.

Armonk, New York
London, England

Library of Congress Cataloging-in-Publication Data

Roherty, James Michael, 1926–
State security in South Africa : civil-military relations under
P.W. Botha / by James M. Roherty.
p. cm.
Includes bibliographical references and index.
ISBN 0–87332–877–9 (cloth)
1. Civil-military relations—South Africa—History—20th century.
2. South Africa—National security.
3. South Africa—Politics and government—1978–
4. Botha, P.W. (Pieter Willem)
I. Title.
UA856.R64   1991
322'.5'0968—dc20
91–14446
CIP

Printed in the United States of America

The paper used in this publication meets the minimum requirements of
American National Standard for Information Sciences—
Permanence of Paper for Printed Library Materials, ANSI Z39.48-1984.

MV   10   9   8   7   6   5   4   3   2   1

To Sean, Brian, and Bridget—intellectually courageous all

CONTENTS

ILLUSTRATIONS

Figure

Maps

Treaties

ACKNOWLEDGMENTS

Over the course of writing what is ostensibly one's own book, it is startling to discover how dependent one becomes upon others. It is the most pleasant of obligations to acknowledge this accumulated indebtedness. The first imperative is to thank the Earhart Foundation for indispensable support. In addition, the assistance of the Hoover Institution, the South Africa Foundation, and the Foundation for the Future of Africa is gratefully noted. Among those many whose encouragement was essential lest the writer flag are Adda Bozeman (an inspiration to all who would follow any of the Muses), Peter Spicer, Lewis Gann, Peter Duignan, John Chettle, and Thor Ronay. There are others, both in the United States and abroad, who warrant similar recognition but will not be mentioned here. However, the unfailing courtesy and cooperation of the men and women of the South African Defense Force and the Southwest Africa Territorial Force must be acknowledged. Their professionalism and dedication has had its part in providing South Africa and Namibia with the promise of a new order.

A particular debt is owed those who, having read early drafts of the manuscript, provided much needed commentary. They include, in addition to the above mentioned, Ray Cline, Adrian Hillary, Roy Godson, Neil Livingstone, and Peter Vanneman. As the project proceeded, the growing attachment of graduate students to the subject at hand was a special satisfaction. My genuine appreciation goes to James D'Amato, Bruce Cauthen, E.T. Smith, Edward Corcoran, Maqsud ul Hasan Nuri, Terry Mays, and especially to Herbert B. Allen, Jr. Captain Allen brought to the project a direct acquaintance with insurgency warfare, a much needed discipline in handling word processors, and a facility for searching questions. The secretarial staff of the Department of Government and International Studies of the University of South Carolina has facilitated things from the outset. It is axiomatic that an author must have a supportive editor: Michael Weber of M.E. Sharpe, Inc., is the model.

And finally, always in this corner and most responsible for whatever of value issues therefrom, there is Maxine. My thanks yet again.

STATE
SECURITY
IN
SOUTH
AFRICA

INTRODUCTION

This is a study of civil-military relations in the Republic of South Africa (RSA) in the era of Pieter Willem Botha. That era has come to a close, opening the way for Mr. Frederick de Klerk and an as yet undefined future for a country of immense promise. It is not our purpose to offer a general appreciation of an extraordinary public career extending over fifty-three years, nor to focus on P W Botha as politician or party leader. This book is an account of an imaginative and innovative utilization of military and intelligence assets in behalf of state purposes. Mr. Botha's direction of his security forces, with the South African Defense Force/*Suid-Afrikaanse Weermag* (SADF/SAW) as the centerpiece, was in fact critical in forming the foundation upon which Mr. de Klerk, today, seeks to build the South African future. Such a distinctive civil-military effort warrants dispassionate examination. If achieved in these pages, then some myths should be dispelled, but more important, some understanding of why South Africa's future holds promise should be gained.

No study, however sharply focused on the interaction between civil and military institutions, can be entirely extricated from its "political surround."[1] This is acutely true in the present case. South Africa is engaged today, as it has been from the inception of Mr. Botha's term as Prime Minister (September 1978), in a dramatic attempt to reconstitute[2] itself as a body politic. Nothing as comprehensive in terms of controlled change—social, political, and economic—has been undertaken in our time. These are, after all, the combustible fuels of revolution and civil war, which observers, by and large, do not expect to see governments contain. That P W Botha should be the first South African political leader to commit his government to effecting a sweeping transformation in the lives of all of his countrymen, confident that the enterprise would not collapse into chaos, was greeted around the world with ill-disguised cynicism. Moreover, that he should launch his great undertaking at a time when his country was at war (in all of its contemporary modalities) compounded the cynicism. Indeed, this confirmed for many that the "White remnant" at the cape of Africa was not content to let the tides of history sweep it away, but was bent on accelerating the process.

It was not for Pieter Willem Botha to preside over the actual transition from one power-sharing formula to another: that time was not yet. He launched an irrevocable process: this was his great undertaking. What he achieved as a reformer, over the course of eleven years as Prime Minister and State President (1978–89), has gone essentially unrecognized and unacknowledged.[3] Again, it is not our task to address or redress this aspect of his public career. We assess P W Botha's utilization of SADF and other security elements as guarantors of his reform effort. This aspect, if anything, has drawn greater attention and produced greater misrepresentations. The sources are readily identified. There is a literary genre defined by the thesis that "a silent, bloodless coup," carried out by SADF officers and related "securocrats," occurred in the tenure of P W Botha. The genre is not confined to but includes Gavin Cawthra, *Brutal Force: The Apartheid War Machine* (London: International Defense and Aid Fund for Southern Africa, 1986); Christopher Coker, *The United States and South Africa, 1968–1985: Constructive Engagement and Its Critics* (Durham: Duke University Press, 1986), and *South Africa's Security Dilemmas* (Washington, D.C.: Center for Strategic and International Studies, 1987); Philip Frankel, *Pretoria's Praetorians: Civil-Military Relations in South Africa* (Cambridge: Cambridge University Press, 1984); Kenneth Grundy, *Confrontation and Accommodation in Southern Africa* (Berkeley: University of California Press, 1973), *Soldiers Without Politics: Blacks in the South African Armed Forces* (Berkeley: University of California Press, 1983), *The Rise of the South African Military Establishment* (Johannesburg: South African Institute of International Affairs, 1983), and an update of the latter, *The Militarization of South African Politics* (Bloomington: Indiana University Press, 1986); Joseph Hanlon, *Beggar Your Neighbor* (Bloomington: Indiana University Press, 1986); Robert Jaster, *South Africa in Namibia: The Botha Strat-*

egy (Lanham, Md.: The University Press of America, 1985), and *The Defense of White Power: Foreign Policy under Pressure* (London: Macmillan, 1988); Richard Leonard, *South Africa at War: White Power and the Crisis in Southern Africa* (Westport, Conn.: Lawrence Hill, 1983); and Brian Pottinger, *The Imperial Presidency: P W Botha—The First Ten Years* (Johannesburg: Southern Books, 1988).

Professor Annette Seegers (University of Cape Town) has remarked on the tendency of these authors to put forward a variety of allegations about the South African security establishment (SADF in particular), only to pull back from the full impact of the charges. This hesitation is not out of lack of conviction, but out of recognition of insufficient supporting evidence. Attempts to substitute for direct evidence by forays through the civil-military relations literature (Frankel, 1984) are unavailing.[4] She points to one in particular (Grundy, 1986) as a "representative example of what scholars have been saying about the role of the military in South Africa."[5] Grundy's contention is threefold: (1) that the military has secured the hub of the national security management system, namely, the State Security Council; (2) that "specialists in control, intimidation, and violence"—"securocrats"—now determine the agenda not only in defense, but in "areas only remotely linked to security"; and (3) that South African society as a whole is "militarized."[6] Seegers reiterates that, apart from a lack of historical perspective, Grundy "does not overcome the problem of evidence." "Local and overseas newspaper accounts figure prominently as sources and, while this practice may be preferable to citing no sources at all, the suspicion lingers that we are dealing with high grade journalism. . . ."[7] (The apparent slight to journalists is undoubtedly inadvertent!)

A further "widely held conclusion" of the coupist school is that Pretoria, under military impetus, has "embarked on a regional policy of 'destabilization'."[8] (We deal with this contention in some detail in subsequent chapters.) Barber and Barratt for their part argue that, on the contrary, the South African military was quite aware that "instability and deprivation on the borders could not provide a buffer of security, but rather a source of insecurity."[9] They dismiss as "an unlikely argument" the assertion (Coker, 1986) that not wanting a "successful black government in southern Africa" it was enough for Pretoria merely "to impede their success."[10] Strong interdependence, inadequate evidence, and a persistent thesis are hallmarks of this school; yet we are informed that this is not *sui generis* to assessments of the South

African military. Other dimensions of South African life are treated in similar fashion. In his research on religion in that country, Richard John Neuhaus was "impressed by how few scholars seem to know much about the independent churches." Among the many writing on this subject, he adds, "there is evidence of a somewhat relaxed pattern of borrowing."[11] Such shortcomings notwithstanding, the portrayal of a South Africa "militarized" dominated the 1980s.

Anyone who ventures into the realm of defense and intelligence ("national security"), irrespective of the country under study, does so knowing that there will be special problems of access to primary sources, whether in terms of public documents or the principals involved. In the case of South Africa, one is led to expect something more than the usual difficulties: again, as with so many aspects of that country's affairs, things are not always as they are represented and one discovers this best for oneself. There is a paucity of official documents, studies, and agency reports that detail the organization and functioning of South Africa's security forces (military, police, and intelligence) and its National Security Management System (NSMS). To be sure, Pretoria makes available a body of material—notable for its lack of detail.[12] However, South African officials with whom the author discussed the dearth of hard information acknowledged that too little is known of their situation abroad. They were generally sympathetic and inclined to the view that, from their own standpoint, a policy of limited disclosure could be beneficial. At the same time, displaying their own brand of reticence, they indicated that any review of information policies would not be likely to lead to significant departures. This is hardly remarkable. No nation under attack will be forthcoming in its disclosures of security information, but over and above this constant there is a South African variable. One encounters a wide variety of South Africans, in both public and private sectors, who insist there is basis for their belief that the "onslaught" against their country (*die aanslag teen Suid-Afrika*) is as much by the pen as by the sword.

We have seen that much of the secondary literature on contemporary South Africa complicates the task of scholarship and does much to explain South African chagrin in coping with inquiring journalists and scholars.[13] In the face of such obstacles it was possible to proceed with the present effort on the basis of one factor alone: a salutary cooperation on the part of principals who either constituted the civil-military nexus at the center of the Botha regime or were closely aligned with it.

A unique opportunity to conduct interviews, initially exploratory but increasingly focused with time, extended over the period 1979–90. An appendix lists sixty of some one hundred political, military, intelligence, corporate, and academic leaders, many of whom were interviewed on several occasions. Included are the most senior officials of the defense, intelligence, and national-security management structures (e.g., Generals Geldenhuys, Gleeson, van der Westhuizen, Earp, du Toit, Potgieter; Admirals Putter and du Plessis; and Dr. Barnard). Likewise, senior civilians from the government and the corporate sector directing such agencies as Constitutional Development, Law and Order, Armaments Corporation of South Africa, Ltd. (ARMSCOR), and South African Atomic Energy Corporation are included (e.g., Messrs. Viljoen, Vlok, Meyer, Maree, Adler, and de Villiers). Interviews with rank and file throughout the security establishment, whether at the Cape with the navy (*Suid-Afrikaanse Vloot*), at Waterkloof with the air force (*Suid-Afrikaanse Lugmag*), or in the Far North Command (at the Zimbabwe border) and the Angolan operational area with the army (*Suid-Afrikaanse Leer*), provided much insight into the mind-set of the men and women of *die Weermag*. No one individual provided quite so much, perhaps, as that inimitable professional, Col. Deon Ferreira (*SA Leer*), who would later command the climactic operations in Angola in 1987–88. The author is pleased to underscore his indebtedness to all of them.

The thesis elaborated in this book stands in sharp contrast to now standardized contentions. Our argument is that P W Botha, recognizing that his country had reached the historical juncture when it must establish a new political order encompassing all of its diverse peoples (in South African parlance: "a new dispensation"), moved with dispatch to put in place those *prerequisites* indispensable to fundamental constitutional change. The prerequisites, for the most part, were "stabilization" measures; that is to say, they were directed to the creation of a climate of security in which, alone, the White contingent could be expected to join the great undertaking of Mr. Botha and his National Party (NP). SADF was his prime instrument of choice, an instrument he knew well and in which he reposed great confidence. By 1989 a striking degree of stabilization had been achieved within the Republic and throughout southern Africa. The groundwork for epochal change had been prepared.

In chapter 1 we deal briefly with "the political surround," but above all else attempt to put the South Africa Question in historical perspective. While taking note of the peripheral world, the salience of local factors in determining the destiny of South Africa is stressed. Chapter 2 is a discussion of the viewpoint from which the Botha coterie saw the challenges confronting the Republic and the counterrevolutionary strategy they outlined. Chapter 3 details the management system PW deemed essential for overriding an entrenched bureaucracy. Critical to the formation of this system was the struggle for command of intelligence roles and missions. We turn in chapter 4 to the South African Defense Force and Armaments Corporation of South Africa, Ltd.—the SADF/ARMSCOR team. The salutary discipline of an arms embargo and fighting alone were major explanatory factors in a success story. In chapters 5 and 6 we assess the stabilization effort as Mr. Botha deployed military, police, and intelligence assets throughout the region, placing them as well within the country from the highest bureaucratic levels to the townships. Strains develop between PW and his generals as the latter are called upon to execute a wide variety of missions. These forces prevail militarily in Angola and Namibia and prove instrumental in achieving a negotiated Namibia settlement. Finally, in chapter 7 we note that P W Botha failed to achieve the relationship with Washington that Pretoria had so long sought. Tensions between southern Africa's regional power and the world's only remaining superpower could not be overcome even through back-channel intelligence initiatives. We conclude, nonetheless, that a basis for convergence between the two remains.

Notes

1. This is borrowed from Elting E. Morison's discussion of the "technological surround" in his classic study of inventions. See *Men, Machines, and Modern Times* (Cambridge: MIT Press, 1968), 8.

2. Invariably the term used is "reform." While "reconstitute" far more accurately characterizes the ongoing process in South Africa, to avoid confusion we use "reform" hereafter.

3. Not altogether typical, but telling, as a commentary on South African politics today is Brian Pottinger, *The Imperial Presidency: P W Botha—The First Ten Years* (Johannesburg: Southern Books, 1988). Pottinger is assistant editor of the *Sunday Times* (Johannesburg) and an unreconstructed devotee of the now defunct Progressive Federal Party (PFP). In a markedly ambivalent assessment of Mr. Botha, Pottinger cannot credit the National Party leader as a reformer, even after presenting a catalog of achievements. The distinguished South African political scientist, Hermann Giliomee (University of Cape Town) finds Pottinger's

analysis "flawed" and Botha's reform record "remarkable," given the constraints under which the latter worked. See his review of *The Imperial Presidency,* by Brian Pottinger, *South Africa International* 20 (July 1989): 42–45.

4. Annette Seegers, "The Military in South Africa: A Comparison and Critique," *South Africa International* 16 (April 1986): 192–99; also H V du Toit, review of *Pretoria's Praetorians,* by Philip Frankel, *Politikon* 12 (June 1985): 64–65. (The reviewer is a retired SADF general officer.)

5. See her review in *South Africa International* 18 (July 1987): 61.

6. Ibid., 59–60. See also James M. Roherty, "Managing the Security Power Base in South Africa," *South Africa International* 15 (October 1984): 58.

7. Seegers (1987), 62.

8. James Barber and John Barratt, *South Africa's Foreign Policy: The Search for Status and Security 1945–1988* (New York: Cambridge University Press, 1990), 272. This is a finely balanced study of more than four decades of South African foreign policy. It is free of the agitation that is characteristic of much American work on South Africa—yet another example of British phlegm.

9. Ibid.

10. Ibid., 379.

11. *South Africa: The Religion Factor* (Washington, D.C.: Foundation for Africa's Future, 1988), 33.

12. In addition to parliamentary debates these include Department of Defense "White Papers" and speeches of public officials. They are cited throughout this study.

13. An exception, not widely noted abroad, is the emerging work of South African scholars who have focused on the security sector with obvious native advantage. These include Michael Hough, Deon F S Fourie, H V du Toit, Deon Geldenhuys, and Dirk Kunert. All are in one degree or another in the intellectual debt of the founder of South African strategic studies, Michael H H Louw. The Institute of Strategic Studies, University of Pretoria (ISSUP), is an important source of scholarship on South African military matters.

1 PERSPECTIVE ON THE QUESTION

> South Africa was one of the great "Questions" which strained the ingenuity and conscience of the makers of British external policy throughout most of the nineteenth century. Like the enduring "Eastern Question" or the emerging "Indian Problem," it proved resistant to any enduring or just "solution."
>
> — D.M. Schreuder,
> *The Scramble for Southern Africa, 1877–1895*

History's larger undertakings—ordained by time—require, it would appear, the precipitating action of smaller undertakings—not always ordained. Replete with the latter, the middle years of the 1970s are a watershed in the early history of the Republic of South Africa. In 1974 the Portuguese barrier in the north gives way; in 1975 London abrogates the Simonstown Agreement, severing the naval connection with the former dominion. These tremors culminate in the shock of the 1975–76 Angolan experience and the break with Washington. Such were the small events that combined to set the Republic on a new path—on a journey not yet finished. At this juncture, its historic ties with the West broken, South Africa begins to articulate a concept of itself as an African state (indeed, as Africa's state of the future) and begins an astonishing ascent to power made all the more vivid against the backdrop of the decline of postcolonial Africa. It is in the term of Prime Minister B J Vorster (1966–1978) that Pretoria becomes fully cognizant of the revolution sweeping Africa and of the irreversible passing of what had been White Africa (Africa below the Zambezi). These tides of history are in some degree understood in the West, although most certainly not to the extent that they are grasped in the Republic. A monumental failure of understanding in our time is the West's inability and/or unwillingness to appreciate South Africa's historic response: that response has been to meet revolution with counterrevolution!

On the subject of Africa no greater realists are to be found than among "the Afrikaner cadre."[1] In dealing with the vicissitudes of history, their thinking is nothing if not realistic, nothing if not pragmatic—an enormous mythology to the contrary notwithstanding. Today they affirm that their new republic (born only in 1961) stands not on sand but on rock, able to withstand the gale emanating in no small part from a "league of champions of lost causes"—and already abating. The essence of South Africa's counterrevolution is sharply etched in the minds of the Afrikaner cadre. It consists of two tasks—two interwoven elements: first, to define a new dispensation within the Republic and, second, to establish the RSA's position in Africa. It will not suffice to quell the alien and the inimical in the revolution sweeping Africa—vital though that be; the new republic must at the same time adumbrate its own *novus ordo*. This is the Great Undertaking upon which South Africa is now embarked: daring, imaginative, but above all else realistic. It entails a historic reopening of the South Africa Question—certain testimony to the aforementioned virtues! It is one of contemporary history's larger undertakings, unique and full of portent for all of Africa. In all likelihood it will succeed. Whether success—not yet achieved—portends well for the West is an altogether separate matter.

Reopening the Question

As we begin an extended analytical foray, it is essential to try to "get the question right" at the outset. Americans, by and large, do *not* have the South Africa Question right, with the devastating result that the inordinate attention directed to all things South African, whether on the part of the press, the academy, or the government, generates little more than sound and fury. Most certainly it has provided little in the way of understanding a question as fascinating as it is complex. The matter will not be entirely set straight in the pages that follow; getting the South Africa Question right is a formidable task in which all who share in the concern must join. Nevertheless, we do propose to make such an attempt before proceeding further. If, thereby, we can underscore the importance of the question and provide some degree of illumination, that will suffice for the present effort.

It will startle most Americans, no doubt, to be told that the South Africa Question stems out of the nineteenth century, that it remains fundamentally unchanged in all of its pristine elements, and that the solution ("the dispensation") set in 1895 remains in effect a century later. In his reappraisal of "the politics of partition" (the massive, White partition of southern Africa after 1877), D.M. Schreuder identifies the constituent elements of a question that Gladstone concluded was insoluble and, equally important, the principal determinants of any outcome. In a compelling argument, he defines the dispensation of 1895 as the cumulative result of "the *local contest* for African resources—in terms of land, labor, and minerals" and concludes that "the politics of the (southern African) frontier" outweighed "the imperial politics of Europe" as a determinant of the partition. By the end of the century

> the *local* balance of power had tilted permanently against the authority of the *African* political communities in favor of the Europeans; the peculiar modern economy of the region (based on vast mineral resources) had been formed, and the settlement patterns—particularly those of *territorial* segregation and the right to land were ultimately decided[2] (italics mine).

The cumulative result may be designated political but only by those who are prepared, with Clausewitz, to include the military element in the aggregate. The first great dispensation of the South Africa Question had the seal of war: intertribal African wars, Boer-Zulu wars, Anglo-Zulu wars, Anglo-Boer wars, and, indeed, Anglo-German wars. An early attempt to alter the 1895 partition (i.e., to repartition) failed in the outcome of the Second Anglo-Boer War (1899–1902). At all events, "South Africa entered the twentieth century not merely as a colonial country but as a white man's country."[3]

The colonials (British, German, and Portuguese) are gone from southern Africa; what remains is not precisely the Boers of the high veld, but rather a diverse White contingent striving to coalesce as South African nationals. Multicultural, multilingual themselves (Dutch, English, French, Jewish, Italian, German, Portuguese, and Polish), White South Africans are at the same time "Africans." This contingent—the White tribe of Africa—is the principal beneficiary and guarantor of the dispensation of 1895. The political solidarity necessary to maintain that dispensation is the achievement of those Whites first to name themselves and their language after Africa—the Afrikaners. Indisputably the vanguard element of White South Africa, "the Afrikaner cadre," ever assertive but ever pragmatic, has reached a junction in its long trek. As to the future path it will follow, it has made the grand decision: the destiny of the *volk* will be sublimated to the destiny of a new South Africa. Now, in the final quarter of the twentieth century, this has set in motion two political undertakings: the first is of immense significance in itself and the second is of truly historic proportions. The Afrikaner cadre is striving first to construct a centrist consensus in and among a complex but coalescing White contingent. They are succeeding: not yet programmatic and accompanied by inevitable splintering on the fringes, White consolidation at the center, by any historical standard, is a seminal feature of contemporary South Africa.[4] This is by way of preparing the ground for the Great Undertaking itself, namely, after a century to reopen the South Africa Question. The National Party, under Pieter Willem Botha, concluded that in the course of time a new dispensation for all national groups had come due. The magnitude of the decision to open for discussion a dispensation embedded in the territorial and economic patterns (not to mention the wars) of the nineteenth century cannot be exaggerated. More imperative is that it be understood.

Constitutional democracy has been defined as an undertaking to enlarge the area of protected freedoms consistent with the viability of the state. This is the nature of the effort underway in South Africa (if only incipiently and cautiously), but it contains an African anomaly. A multinational state made up of distinct national groups, among whose prime objectives is the maintenance of their respective identities, will consider the issue of protected freedoms not only from the standpoint of the individual citizen but from the standpoint of each national group as well. As the shackles of apartheid are broken—not by the Black man but by the White man who affixed them to the Black man—and as the area of protected freedoms grows, "the dominant, assertive group"[5] will continue to control critical facets of state policy. No other power-sharing arrangement is plausible in the context of the present-day African polity. Political fusion of distinct national groups is not a practicable objective in the first stages of what is understood in South Africa, if not elsewhere, as an extended evolutionary process. There is no satisfactory nor is there any obvious case to be made for a unitary state (i.e., for an essentially unrestricted, Westminster majoritarianism) in this setting.[6]

In committing the White contingent to again take up the South Africa Question, Mr. Botha did so with no clear map of where the path ahead would lead. He offered an open agenda[7] and at the same time a solemn guarantee: the new dispensation will be negotiated; it will not issue out of revolutionary chaos. In their passage from the old to the new, the White contingent will not be dispossessed nor will it see its achievement squandered. The guarantee is hardly remarkable: neither the Afrikaner cadre nor the White contingent as a whole are in disarray. They will not be simply one of the parties to the discussion (the great *Indaba*); they will be *primus inter pares*. Westerners, by and large, fail to discern that the Afrikaner mind-set has been formed by three centuries of experience in and with Africa. This mind-set continues to dominate in a polity that is an assemblage of groups. Relationships, statuses, and allocations among groups will have a new definition in a new dispensation, but the reality of the South African polity as an association of groups will not change nor, for the foreseeable future, will the identity of the dominant, assertive group.

The Periphery Today

Schreuder did not set out to minimize "the role of the periphery" in the politics of partition at the end of the nineteenth century, but rather to stress the primacy of "local politics." Nor, a century later, do we wish to suggest that players on the periphery will not have their parts once again in the drama unfolding in southern Africa. What is even more evident today is that outsiders are less likely to effect positive outcomes and very likely, indeed, to exacerbate matters. An explanation is readily at hand reducing invariably to the all but complete failure of outsiders to comprehend the complexity of "local factors and figures." Evidence abounds of the baneful impact on Africa of nostrums from abroad, whether from East or West. (It is not demonstrable that this intrinsic difficulty can be remedied.) The United States of America— very much on the periphery—has made of itself an interested party in the affairs of southern Africa (if only from 1975) and in doing so affords evidence in behalf of our contention. During the course of the eighties, the Reagan administration, under the finely etched rubric of "constructive engagement," sought to make the United States a principal player in the region. While seeking to avoid the unproductive tactics and zeal of the Carter administration, the standard-bearers of constructive engagement, no less than their predecessors, failed to come to terms with the dominance of "local factors and figures."

Washington has given little if any indication that it understands that at the root of the South Africa Question is the most profound of all political issues, namely, power sharing ("land, labor, minerals"). Even less does it appear to understand the context in which Pretoria has reopened that question (i.e., as an element in a broad counterrevolution posing new alternatives for the Republic and for the region as a whole). Moreover, Washington was unwilling to concede "primacy of place" to Mr. Botha's government in this undertaking, unwilling to acknowledge the progress achieved to date—even the reality of its counterrevolution. Against some early signs to the contrary, the Reagan administration ultimately subsumed the complex political, military, and economic agenda in southern Africa under a domestically fabricated mantle of "civil rights." It succumbed to the notion that "civil rights" in the RSA (civil rights in other countries on the continent is not a discussion item in Washington) was somehow amenable to leverage from the periphery. That apartheid—even the grand designs of Hendrik Verwoerd—should be construed as the essence of the South Africa Question is lamentable testimony to myopia from afar. The accretion over time (largely since 1948) of legislation designed to achieve *racial* as opposed to *territorial* segregation is a latter-day development in the history of the South Africa Question and at the same time the most easily disposed of facet of the overall question.

Location on the periphery presumptively confers the advantage of detachment on interested parties, but then that may have been a function of the age of literacy, a casualty of electronic implosion in the twentieth century. At all events if there is "common cause" among Western governments to preclude chaos and to foster a climate for negotiations among diverse parties in South Africa (who have no history of negotiations), this is most likely to be achieved, to the extent that outsiders can be a factor, through incentives. The question will have to be reclaimed (especially in Washington) from the protagonists of punitive measures. Such measures are patently designed to carry

South Africa to the abyss; only a convincing declaration from Western capitals that they are prepared to positively assist a negotiation process, taking account of the sensitivities *of all parties,* will restore a badly deranged relationship between the periphery and the center.[8] The loss of momentum in the sanctions movement in the United States during the course of the 1988 presidential campaign may be a harbinger of change. The declamation in the national platform of the Democratic Party branding the Republic as "a terrorist state" was immediately forgotten. Not surprisingly, Congress did not expand on the 1986 Comprehensive Anti-Apartheid Act in 1989.[9] Today George Bush has a new baseline from which to address the South Africa Question.

Devised in the domestic politics of the United States—not in the exigencies of the region—the premises upon which Washington has approached southern Africa have little validity or utility. Steadfastly held, they block understanding of the region generally and of the South Africa Question most particularly. Likewise, this fund of mistaken premises[10] precludes the United States from a necessary and useful role in the region, that is to say from acting effectively in behalf of its own interests. The rebuttal will be made that the argument is naive: the author does not come to terms with the realities of democratic foreign policy—American style. The rejoinder is—as it must be—that we are required to make a choice, a choice among realities, if one likes. We can choose to base our policy upon the exigencies of the region (by far the most important of which is that understanding of the South Africa Question that animates local figures), or we can choose to pursue a policy that is primarily a function of domestic politics. In the latter instance there will be little basis for a constructive role in southern Africa and every basis for antagonism. In the former there is the possibility for effective action. Although the advocates of "global democracy" are at large today, it is entirely out of character (or at least it has been so historically) for the United States to offer institutional prescriptions to others. Our own *experience* argues in behalf of indigenous construction of institutions tailored to local circumstances—a point to which we shall return in our concluding note.

The Leadership Mantle

Political fortune (*fortuna*) in its most excruciating Machiavellian sense placed John Vorster at the helm of the Republic of South Africa in

1966 and in 1978 removed him therefrom.[11] The mantle of leadership in the Great Undertaking passed to the shoulders of the minister of Defense, Pieter Willem Botha (member from George in the Cape Province).[12] Mr. Vorster had directed himself for the most part to establishing the new republic's position in Africa (see chapter 2). In this endeavor he became increasingly conscious of a fundamental requirement, that is, to dismantle the Verwoerdian edifice of apartheid. The impracticality of apartheid from the standpoint of economic growth did not loom so large with him as did its impracticality from the standpoint of the viability of the Republic and its standing in Africa. Over time Mr. Vorster's successor would also develop an outward orientation, but the South Africa Question itself would be Mr. Botha's great preoccupation. Possessing all the stubbornness that Hendrik Verwoerd displayed in behalf of his edifice, Mr. Botha committed himself to a challenge far greater than the mere dismantlement of existing structures. Preparing the way to build anew would be a task requiring stubbornness and much more.

In his long political journey P W Botha crossed the Rubicon more than once, but not without his followers crossing as well. His split with the Right (August 1982), resulting in the formation of the Conservative Party (KP) under the disaffected Andries Treurnicht, while traumatic, nonetheless had the backing of the great majority of NP members. His decision to put a new constitution before the White electorate (November 1983) incorporating "Coloured" and "Asian" constituencies in a Tricameral Parliament was approved by a two-to-one margin. Still, until the May 1987 parliamentary elections, it was not wholly evident that significant "White realignment" was taking place; that is, that a new consensus was building at the center. In the aftermath of those elections, perfunctory analyses (driven by the standard prepossessions) directed world attention to the Right where the Transvaal's "Dr. No" (Mr. Treurnicht) and the KP emerged as the official opposition, displacing a defunct Progressive Federal Party (PFP). Implied in much of this analysis was the demise of the NP and the prospect of a flight to the Right dominated (in the minds of these analysts) not by the KP, but by the *Afrikanerweerstandsbeweging* (AWB)—the Afrikaner Defense League—of Eugene Terre Blanche.[13] While it must be conceded that the AWB is telegenic (what with its horse-mounted riders, brown shirts, and flags of triskelion sevens), it is not a political party nor, more important, are its numbers important. Just as curious was the reluctance of the press to focus on what was happening on the Left of the South African political spectrum, that is to say, the demise of the Left.

A critical electoral shift took place on the South African Left with perhaps 40 percent of the "Progs" (PFP) moving to the center in support of the NP in the May 1987 elections. In the wake of "the Unrest" and the state of emergency (declared in June 1986 and still in effect at the end of the Botha term), this block of voters joined with the "Nats" in endorsing "security first" as the prerequisite of reform. The plight of the PFP was further underscored when Independents (Nationalists such as Wynand Malan and Denis Worrall) refused to join them, insisting instead on setting up their own parties, however ephemeral. Both men are attractive political figures in their own right (Malan was the only Independent returned to the House of Assembly—Worrall losing out in a close contest to Mr. Chris Heunis of the NP). Yet the political Left in South Africa was in disarray after 1987, its various splinters giving little evidence of an inclination toward coalition building. Apart from the PFP, which its new leader, Mr. Zac de Beer, conceded took a bashing from the NP, there was Mr. Malan's New Democratic Movement (NDM)—almost instantly chastened by unfavorable public reaction to a European tryst with the African National Congress (ANC)—and there was Mr. Worrall and his Independent Party (IP) *sans* members in Parliament.[14] Nor must we fail to mention the PFP's own defector, Mr. Frederick van zyl Slabbert, whose loss of faith in parliamentary possibilities and espousal of extra-parliamentary means has perplexed even the most devoted. To Mr. Worrall's credit he succeeded approximately a year in advance of the September 1989 elections in forging the splinters into a single Democratic Party under his leadership—Mr. van zyl Slabbert continuing on his own course. The combination of Messrs. Worrall, Malan, and de Beer also succeeded in somewhat resuscitating the electoral Left. The flurry of postelection analyses that followed upon the September 1989 pollings was predictable in light of what followed the 1987 elections. What was unalterable in the outcome, however, was a White constituency more divided on the question of its leadership than it had been in 1987 and 1988. The Conservative Party was more firmly ensconced as the "official opposition" than two years earlier, and the Democratic Party (DP), while not achieving the Progressive Federal Party's level of support in the early eighties, made a notable showing with 20 percent of the vote. This would not constitute a swing to the Left in spite of Mr. Worrall's best efforts.

This having been said about the Left, it would be illusory to suggest that the "Old Party" (NP) is in any sense free of serious issues. "Old Nats" are among the first to grant that after forty years in power the NP is much in need of rejuvenation—much in need of new blood (i.e., "New Nats"). The NP continues to hold center ground under the aegis of "Nationalist Principles": the electoral results of May 1987 were an expression of *confidence* in the NP leadership, but they were equally an expression of *dependence* and therein lies a unique reality in South African politics. Should NP leadership falter, should it fail to exhibit confidence in its own vision of the future, should it fail to translate Nationalist Principles into programmatic terms, should it fail to bring forward a new generation of leaders to take the baton from the old, thereby forcing the White electorate to cast about for an unfamiliar alternative, the RSA would be in genuine crisis. A political crisis of proportions that would in fact shake the stolid Republic can come in the foreseeable future only from this peculiarly dependent constituency cast adrift by a cessation of leadership on the part of the NP. Consequently, the ultimate success of P W Botha's Great Undertaking turns heavily on whether the historic political instrument of Afrikanerdom can itself evolve from the old to the new.

Two Old Nats with whom the author has discussed this issue for a decade—today located at different points on the political spectrum—are remarkably uniform in their assessments of the Old Party. As one put it, "The NP has spent itself and must be reconstituted." The issue put before the White electorate in the May 1987 parliamentary elections was defined as follows: "We must go along with the NP—move it along the right path" *or* "There is no improving the NP—it is recalcitrant on the issue of change—we must look for alternatives." They agree that the outcome was clearly an adoption of the former and a rejection of the latter—for now. There is not just a leadership issue, one emphasized: "Quite apart from the need to reconstitute the NP we have to find a way to make the bureaucracy more accountable to the Parliament. The bureaucrats can get away with anything; more importantly they can get away with doing *nothing!*" He spoke with feeling about ministers not knowing the business of their departments, directors-general presiding over somnolent clerks, etc. "Here is the great 'drag factor' on the reform movement," he concluded. "Practicalities are driving the situation today," added the other. "Everyone" recognizes the economic necessity to end apartheid. Demographics alone (about which everyone is increasingly conscious) dictate not only economic growth but a new political dispensation. But everyone also understands that these are two different tasks. We can accomplish the first now (with foreign investment help), but *no one* yet has a power-sharing formula. It is not for the populace to produce one; this is the task that awaits a new NP leadership. Here a push from abroad (a pointed reference to the United States) will not help. "You Americans," he concluded, "have poisoned your chances for affecting political outcomes with your sanctions. In any case it is our task."

The corporate leadership in the RSA—both Afrikaans-speaking and English-speaking—is frequently cited as a reformist element. As with so many other general propositions about present-day South Africa, the underlying reality is more complex. This reality is an important but limited one and can be put succinctly: South African capitalism, having concluded that apartheid slows economic growth both by virtue of restricting labor supply and by dampening real demand, is not only prepared but anxious to dismantle the Verwoerdian edifice.[15] This limited reality has led a number of observers to an overdrawn conclusion, namely, that corporate leaders are in the vanguard of the reform process—at the cutting edge, as some enthusiasts put it. Any imputation of political leadership, let alone political sophistication, to the corporate world of South Africa must be charged up to "hopefulness." This sector has never been a fertile field for the development of political leadership; its contribution to the dismantlement of the Verwoerdian edifice, therefore, cannot be expected to extend much beyond efforts to restructure the South African economy.

One of the aforementioned Old Nats has gone through an interesting metamorphosis on this point.[16] Having long espoused the view that business leaders were spearheading reform, he is much more guarded today in his expectations. The high point for Peter Sorour came when he arranged for the June 1985 visit of the Relly Delegation (Gavin Relly was then president of SAF as well as chairman of Anglo-America) to ANC headquarters at Kabwe (outside of Lusaka, Zambia). Nine months later (March 1986) he spent most of our meeting "justifying Kabwe," but even then he was beginning to show misgivings. In a March 1987 discussion it was an altogether different Sorour: "The business sector has a very limited concept of 'reform'; what they are after is an open, 'consumerist' society—they have no *political* ideas." He was disenchanted with the "Kabwe effort" and, it appeared, years of work at SAF. In the June 1985 meeting with ANC leaders, there was the appearance of the business sector taking on a political mantle, of appearing to address difficult political dimensions of reform. Whatever the appearances, the Relly Group found the political agenda anything but tractable. Sorour, the closest observer of this episode, now finds this not insignificant group of business leaders "put off by politics and politicians"; for them "reform" is cutting away the undergrowth of apartheid, lest it strangle the economy. Politicians will have to deal with the political dimensions of the problem.

While it is necessary to take account of such estimates, the corporate structure in South Africa remains an element in the reform process. Moreover, it does contain within its ranks leaders, however few in number, with acute political vision and substantial influence at the highest level of government. One such is John B. Maree, currently chairman of the Electricity Supply Commission (ESCOM), seconded from his managing director position at Barlow Rand, formerly chief executive officer of Armaments Corporation of South Africa, and vice-chairman of its board, and board member of South African Development Bank.[17] Maree has been called upon consistently over the past decade by Mr. Botha to come into government "on a temporary basis to move critical programs forward." Maree's key role, however, was that of confidant and sounding board for the State President—a principal channel between government and corporate South Africa. (The agenda of issues taken up in these discussions was by no means confined to the business sector.) More optimistic about the role of his corporate colleagues than most Old Nats, he contends that "they are ready to move, but they are looking to government for leadership." Maree has little doubt as to where their sentiments lie, whatever view he may have of their political sophistication: "They are rallying to 'the only game in town' (the NP)." But as for the NP, he confided that we are coming to that point where the baton must be passed. "My generation has brought us to this point; now a new generation of leaders must 'carry us over the ridge.' " While it is not yet established that this transition will be achieved, what is clear is that centripetal forces in the White contingent continue to be stronger than centrifugal forces. Alternatives on the Right—and on the Left—continue to lack plausibility. This much at least continues to favor the case for White consolidation at the center under the NP—so long as the party does not fractionate from within.

Maree turned next to "the crisis we are now going through" (1986) perhaps anticipating "the Emergency" in June. "I expect major demonstrations in the biggest cities—there will be a massive effort to 'blow down the walls of Jericho' on the assumption that the Afrikaner is fractioning, on the run, ready to meet Black demands." That this would not in fact happen this Afrikaner leader then made clear: this crisis period is necessary because only by passing through it can we demonstrate that the *Afrikaner is not in retreat!* Progress, breakthroughs, compromise: all of that will come when Black leaders see that the White chiefs are in good order with solid ranks behind them. The African National Congress can easily become the big losers through continuing intransigence when others are ready for compromise. Maree conceded that Afrikaners are, indeed, divergent in their political views:

> There isn't a party from Left to Right that we haven't headed. We are rather unpredictable, especially in this period when apartheid is breaking up more from its own weight than anything else, *but this regime is not breaking up!* . . . We are a Republic of minorities, and all minorities stand in need of protection and they shall have it. Security first: then we shall address the power-sharing issues and in all of that there are only "two no's"—no insurrection and no plebiscitary (Westminster) formulas which your Mr. Mondale put all too simply as "one man–one vote."[18]

In our March 1987 discussion, Maree began by stating that "we are on hold" until the May elections; then the results will be quickly converted into new directions—one way or the other. He then referred to his discussions with the State President:

> "He" (Mr. Botha) launched the elections as a challenge to the Right wanting to put the far-Right into sharp perspective as a distinct minority. But now (in March) they have turned into something else; now there is the possibility of developing an electoral base upon which we can move forward with reform (within the framework of NP principles). Call this "an opening to the Left," if you will, but if the so-called New Nats in the party (estimated at perhaps thirty) can broaden the electoral base for us, PW will act on the basis of the ballots and put the reform process into high gear.

(Maree was exhibiting uncharacteristic excitement at this prospect but then struck a cautionary note.) The State President understands that *basic support* for the NP lies somewhat to the right of center: "He is always looking over his right shoulder." However, he will follow the ballots wherever they take him. Close to the State President, Maree proved an excellent source on "how PW is feeling" (a factor of no small consequence particularly in the relationship with Washington).

The scheduled passing of the baton from P W Botha to Frederick de Klerk (in the elections of September 1989) was to be an occasion for renewing the confidence of the electorate in the NP leadership. The transition could not have been more badly mismanaged. Mr. de Klerk in effect wrenched the baton from Mr. Botha just three weeks in advance of the elections, turning what could have been a celebratory event in the history of the National Party into, at best, an unseemly instance of grasping. Mr. Botha, having already resigned as head of the NP (February 1989) and having substantially recovered from a stroke suffered at the beginning of that year, resumed the office of State President at midyear after a convalescence, during which Mr. Chris Heunis had served as acting president. Pressures from a de Klerk coterie to resign the presidency forthwith (instead of September as announced) mounted suddenly and drew an utterly typical response from a P W Botha evidently very much himself. On August 14, 1989, following a cabinet meeting in which it was suggested he use his health as a pretext for stepping down now, Mr. Botha announced his resignation to the nation. "I am not prepared to leave on a lie," the State President emphasized. Instead he offered the following assessment: "It is evident to me that after all of my years of endeavors for the National Party and the government of this country and *the security of South Africa that I am now being ignored by ministers serving in my cabinet*" (italics mine).[19]

The unhappy conclusion of a distinguished public career of fifty-three years followed by an electoral shock for the National Party dramatically underlined both the need for NP rejuvenation and the precariousness of the Great Undertaking itself. It may be placing too much of a burden on the events of August–September 1989 to contend that the NP had missed a historic opportunity—had failed to build on the confidence expressed in its leadership in 1987. Yet if P W Botha had accomplished nothing else, he had brought about a stabilization both in the region and within the Republic that provided the indispensable prerequisites for power-sharing negotiations. For the first time an adequate security baseline had been established. Mr. F W de Klerk will now negotiate a passage toward a new dispensation with reduced support (ninety-four seats in the House of Assembly rather than one hundred twenty-three), amidst competing and strengthened claims to leadership of the White constituency. The "Old Party" is not in crisis at the end of the eighties—that would be placing too much of a burden on one election—but the future of the party and its purposes had been questioned. This may well prove therapeutic for Mr. de Klerk and his associates.

Toward Coalition?

There are leadership elements in other constituencies who, for their own purposes, wish to see a vital NP leadership at the helm of the reform movement in South Africa. Among the most important of these, although often overlooked, are leaders of the Coloured constituency. Much attention has been given to the problem of identifying those leaders who might most appropriately speak for non-White constituencies. It is just such African leaders, however, who understand that the negotiation of a new dispensation can go forward only when the White constituency is satisfied on the question of its own leadership. This is the beginning point. They sense that the peculiarly *dependent* White constituency once confident on this score will follow its "chiefs" along an uncharted path. They are prepared, therefore, to cooperate with the NP leadership as it reconstitutes the Old Party. This disposition, more than latent among Coloured leaders, is indispensable to the success of Mr. Botha's Great Undertaking. Coloured leaders follow the trend of White political dynamics closely; they judge the White tribe to be engaged today in entirely rational, wholly predictable ethnic behavior. As White consolidation continues (paced by NP rejuvenation) the preparatory process for the great *Indaba* continues. Those who conclude that a new order for South Africa can only stem out of disarray in the White tribe are not to be found among the Coloured leadership.

What ostensibly was to be a discussion of security matters with Mr. A B Williams (member of the House of Representatives for Koeburg in the Western Cape), a major political figure in the Coloured constituency and spokesman on defense issues as chairman of the House Committee on Security Affairs, turned into a discourse on political dynamics in South Africa.[20] (Interviews often take a serendipitous course, especially in the instant case as the writer was later advised!) "The security question must be addressed first; the Afrikaner will do nothing unless he first feels secure," Mr. Williams stated matter-of-factly. "Hard-core elements (in the townships) are being seized; intimidation of Blacks (not Coloureds) by Blacks is the internal-security issue today—Whites are not being killed." The member for Koeburg noted that the Security Forces were much more inclined to put up new police stations in White areas, "not the Black areas where they are needed. . . . But I must concede," he went on, "they are succeeding in what they have set out to do. They have come to understand that in order to get 'movement' they must calm the situation, i.e., calm the Whites. . . . 'Defense' has taken over the internal-security problem," Williams argued; "yes, Vlok (Adriaan Vlok, formerly deputy minister of Defense) has gone to Law and Order (as minister), but 'Magnus' (Gen. Magnus Malan, minister of Defense) is running it all." Defense reached the conclusion that SAP (South African Police within the Ministry of Law and Order) alone could not get the job done. They are right about that and now 'they' are getting the job done! Williams was emphatic in his support of the NP principle "Security first"; it is the *sine qua non* for the White constituency. Only leadership that provides security will take the Whites into a new era. References to "repressive reform," he suggested, come from the Left and academic circles and merely demonstrate that the Left will not be leading the reform process.[21]

This appraisal of the White constituency from a Coloured leader was followed by an assessment of the political outlook of his own constituency that may be of more significance. Williams responded sharply to a question about the "identity" issue among nationalities in the RSA: "The Coloured don't give a damn about 'cultural identity'—what the hell, we don't have any!" He then added, "But the Blacks care—and the Indians care—so that will have to be dealt with." What each group in the RSA wants, first and foremost, is a better socioeconomic deal—beyond that most will settle for "the reality of being consulted." Western notions of voting plebiscites are an abstraction here. Consultation is the key: "South Africans simply cannot accept that anyone other that their own (leaders) will look after their interests. So long as 'their own' are *directly* involved this will do—the process is secondary. This applies to all—Whites, Coloured, Blacks, what have you. For our part, since we don't have the identity problem others have, we are readier to join with 'others' (Williams made plain he was speaking here of the NP) and get on with the business of a new political (consultative) process. It is the readiness of the Whites to negotiate that is critical, and so we are prepared to reassure them." As for dealing with the problem of Black identities, it was apparent that Williams would prefer to take that one on in concert with the Whites.

Among the Black constituencies, the Zulu are paramount. The ubiquitous, oftentimes misused, oftentimes maligned chief minister of the *KwaZulu*, Mangosuthu Buthelezi, stands larger in South Africa if not in the West than "aging Rivonia trialists" or for that matter "bishops who have neither constituencies nor programs." [22] By virtue of countless trips abroad and innumerable speeches and articles, the Zulu chief has cast himself as "political"—as "accommodationist." (Among anti-apartheid activists, both within South Africa and abroad, this results in his being relegated to a marginal role at best.) More relevant is an estimation of Buthelezi garnered from a variety of White leaders—both Afrikaans-speakers and English-speakers. In the relationship between South African Whites and Chief Buthelezi there is much mutual admiration reflecting a more fundamental mutual admiration on the part of White and Zulu developed over time. Adjectives not commonly employed when speaking of other Black identities are used: "dynamic," "intelligent," "proud." For his part Buthelezi clearly respects the Afrikaner as well as the English-speakers with whom he is so familiar in neighboring Natal. The chief is more prepared to deal with the White tribe than any other. "There is one problem, however," cautioned a Zulu-speaking Afrikaner who had grown up in Natal. "The Zulu think of themselves as 'autonomous.' They will cut political deals with us—that is only a matter of time—they understand our place in South Africa." A White-Coloured-Zulu conjunction for *political purposes* is not a fantasy. Today the leadership elements of all "tribes" understand that tribal hegemony is a thing of the past; the politics of the future will consist of building pragmatic coalitions *across* tribal lines. It is conceivable over the longer term, the gentleman from Natal went on, that the Zulu would attempt to dominate any coalition—would attempt to come to the top. But we understand this possibility—it is not a problem *now*. Now our job is to get our own house in order so that we can enter into the new political era.

The Cardinal Thread

Mr. Botha's solemn guarantee to the White contingent—indeed to all South Africans—that the Republic's future would not be forged on an anvil of arms, but would issue from a process of "managed evolution" was a guarantee confidently given. The new Prime Minister was conscious of a powerful resource at his disposal: unlike his predecessors he had become intimately acquainted with and had developed a high appreciation for South African Defense Force/*Suid-Afrikaanse Weermag*. The relationship between Mr. Botha and SADF will dominate his tenure at the helm of government; it will be the cardinal thread running through a rich tapestry. Enlisting the discipline, the management and organization skills, and (above all else) the dedication to the new nation of the military profession, he will place them in the vanguard of his Great Undertaking. SADF will be a crucible in which a new core ethos—a new South African nationalism—will be formed. From its vantage point in the "First World" of South Africa it will be a bridging mechanism to the "Third World" of South Africa. From the outset Mr. Botha understood, if only intuitively, that at his direction (if somewhat reluctantly) SADF would lead the way in securing his Great Undertaking. For his part, as Prime Minister (and subsequently State President), he would continue to devote himself to the enhancement of this vital resource. Undeniably, the hard choice to make SADF the lead-agency, not only in coping with the external threat but in the reciprocal endeavor of crafting a new internal order, stems out of a paucity of alternative mechanisms available to him and will not be without its costs.[23] What Mr. Botha had discerned early on in his career, but which, notably, continues to escape the less discerning, was that the SADF leadership constituted a powerful impetus for change. Realistic, pragmatic, enlightened (*verlig*), PW's generals are the essence of candor in their reasoning: the security of the Republic ("its position in Africa") demands nothing less than the negotiation of a new dispensation. In that undertaking they will assume such responsibilities as are given them by the chief executive.[24]

The South African Defense Force by all professional criteria is Africa's premier military organization; there is no counterpart on the continent today. SADF is subject to civilian control, it is oriented to the external threat, it trains in the field, it strives to stay at the leading edge of technology, it has demonstrated strategic, operational, and tactical acumen, and above all else, it has the will to fight. Yet this force that is so central to the fortunes of the Republic of South Africa is in almost all respects a new force. It is all but born out of the birth pangs of *Operation Savannah,* SADF's first cross-border operation into Angola

(August 1975–February 1976). In this book our endeavor is to provide an interpretation of what is by any reckoning a stunning achievement—the rise of SADF to preeminence in little more than a decade (a salient element in the Republic's ascent to power). It is the achievement of a handful of men, most particularly Pieter Willem Botha working in close conjunction (over the span of a career) with a new generation of young generals.[25] SADF has been described by one of the latter as "PW's greatest achievement." But he then went on to pose a question that is at the center of this study: "Can this superb instrument forged by the State President assist him with what is surely his greatest challenge?"[26] The general was alluding to the political challenge inherent in the reopening of the South Africa Question. He was not optimistic that Mr. Botha could effectively deploy his greatest achievement in behalf of his greatest challenge. However, a more detached perspective provides a basis for a more optimistic assessment of the role of SADF in the Great Undertaking.

Notes

1. The reference is to an approximate three million of the nearly five million Whites in South Africa who trace their origins in Africa to the seventeenth-century Dutch settlers—not all of whom were Dutch. While it is customary to refer to this segment of the White contingent as "Afrikaans-speakers" it must be kept in mind that South Africans of many different ethnic backgrounds are Afrikaans-speakers.

2. Schreuder, *The Scramble for Southern Africa, 1877–1895* (London: Cambridge University Press, 1980) 4, 9, 318.

3. Ibid., 9. For further development of this perspective see Lewis Gann and Peter Duignan, eds., *Colonialism in Africa, 1870–1960*, 5 vols. (London: Cambridge University Press, 1969–1975); Ronald Hyam, *Britain's Imperial Century; A Study of Empire and Expansionism, 1815–1914* (London: Macmillan, 1976); W. M. MacMillan, *Bantu, Boer and Briton: The Making of the South African Native Problem*, rev. ed. (Oxford: Clarendon Press, 1963); and Adda Bozeman, *Conflict in Africa: Concepts and Realities* (Princeton: Princeton University Press, 1976). Schreuder's own "Introduction and Argument," along with his "Select Recommended Bibliography," is an important historiographic essay. While it is not required for our purposes to delve into the bibliography of the Anglo-Boer wars, the following are recommended for anyone who would attempt to capture an atmosphere that is part of present-day South Africa and without which any understanding of present-day South Africa would be incomplete: Joseph Lehmann, *The First Boer War* (London: Buchan & Enright, 1985); Thomas Pakenham, *The Boer War* (New York: Random House, 1979), the best contemporary British account of the "Second" war; and Byron Falwell, *The Great Anglo-*

Boer War (New York: Harper & Row, 1976), again, an account of the "Second" war—this time an American account somewhat more open to Boer interpretations.

4. Evidence that the fissure between "Brit" and "Boer" is closing has accumulated apace with the urbanization of the Boer since World War II. In this connection see T. Hanf, H. Weiland, and G. Vierdag, *South Africa: The Prospects of Peaceful Change* (London: Rex Collings, 1981), and Merle Lipton, *Capitalism and Apartheid* (London: Smith/Gower, 1985). This trend continues to be reflected in the opinion surveys of Prof. Lawrence Schlemmer, currently Director, Center for Policy Studies, University of Witwatersrand, Johannesburg. However, the most compelling evidence is to be found in the returns from the May 1987 parliamentary elections, which we discuss below.

5. I am indebted to Lewis Gann for this phrase. As for the constitutional concept of "protected freedom" (more European than Anglo-American), see Giovanni Sartori, "Constitutionalism: A Preliminary Discussion," *American Political Science Review* 56 (December 1962): 854–60.

6. See, for example, Willem de Klerk, *The Second Revolution: Afrikanerdom and the Crisis of Identity* (Johannesburg: Jonathan Hall, 1984). The former editor of *Rapport,* and for that matter *Die Transvaler,* while not as firmly ensconced in the National Party as his brother (Frederick de Klerk, minister of Education and ultimately State President), will nonetheless contend that definitive political solutions are illusory. The Afrikaner is prepared to accommodate Blacks but is not prepared to accept a unitary state. The State President, himself, has made it plain that Westminster formulas are not on the table. Certain continental European models may have some applicability however. On this point see Heribert Adam and Kogila Moodley, *South Africa without Apartheid: Dismantling Racial Domination* (Cape Town: Longman, 1986). Standing alone as an assessment of prospective new dispensations for South Africa is Arend Lijphart, *Power-Sharing in South Africa* (Berkeley: University of California Press, 1985). Both the State President and his minister for Constitutional Planning and Development (Mr. Chris Heunis) give every evidence of having assimilated Professor Lijphart's work. South African constitutional planners are also responsive to the work of Professor Donald L. Horowitz of the Duke University Law School. See especially his *A Democratic South Africa? Constitutional Engineering in a Divided Society* (Berkeley: University of California Press, 1991).

7. If in stipulating an open agenda (rather than a prescribed government agenda) Mr. Botha sought to avoid contention, then he failed. Anglo-American Corporation, for one, is earnestly about the task of agenda setting, or as they would have it, "scenario writing." A team of "Anglo-futurists" led by Mr. Clem Sunter in scanning market horizons has developed some interesting end-of-century constructs of the RSA economy. The problem comes when they turn to end-of-century political constructs and offer up Progressive Federal Party gruel for the palates of the Nationalists. Mr. Sunter and his associates, in attempting to do an end run around what Mr. Heunis insists is "the reality of the multicultural nature of our society" and arrive at a polity based on the individual, demonstrates our point that centrist consensus in South Africa is not yet programmatic. "The scenario—the book—the video" from Anglo-American is Clem Sunter, *South Africa and the World in the 1990s* (Johannesburg: Argus, 1987). See as well the recent

Argus journals, *Leadership* and *The High Road,* for discussions of the Sunter scenarios. In the April 1988 issue of the latter, that minister of Information, Mr. Stoefel van der Merwe, forcefully argues the case for establishing "a composite majority" across ethnic lines.

8. A longtime British observer of the South African scene writes that "the international community should clearly be prepared to pay a price for a stable, just, and prosperous South Africa. This is obviously preferable to violence, chaos, and lasting hostility." See William Gutteridge, "The South African Crisis: Time for International Action," *Conflict Studies* 179 (August 1985): 22. Gutteridge reflects the views of British Prime Minister Margaret Thatcher, a staunch opponent of sanctions against South Africa throughout her term in office. On the other hand, the Eminent Persons Group (EPG), an outgrowth of the 1985 Nassau Meeting of Commonwealth Ministers, could not be held in check. In an extended conversation with Mr. Malcolm Fraser, former Prime Minister of Australia and member of the EPG, the author had an opportunity to discover the distinctive proclivities of Mr. Fraser on matters South African and why, perforce, Mrs. Thatcher should take such exception.

9. In the high-water years (1985–86) of the Sanctions Against South Africa movement in the United States, Congress provided the nation and the world with a dramatic example of seizing a foreign-policy issue and thoroughly domesticating it. At the same time it underlined the inherent dangers in such transgressions when even the foreign-policy leadership of the president's party in the U.S. Senate (Dole, Lugar, Danforth, and Kassebaum) capitulated to the orchestration in the streets. By 1988 the aforementioned had more or less regained their balance. In these years the U.S. press (almost none of which had any direct exposure to South Africa) was busily engaged in Boer bashing. While this particular sociology lies outside our purview, the following example will be offered. Columnist Jeff Greenfield, noting that the 1986 Comprehensive Anti-Apartheid Act would deny South African Airways landing rights in the United States, was pleased to point out that this would "help to reduce the flow of . . . politically naive tourists from the U.S. and Western Europe who travel to South Africa," their direct experience serving only to complicate the dialogue in the United States. *The State,* Columbia, S.C. June 30, 1986.

10. A summary of these will be found in U.S. Department of State, *A U.S. Policy toward South Africa,* The Report of the Secretary of State's Advisory Committee on South Africa (Washington, D.C.: GPO, 1987).

11. Reference, of course, is first to the assassination of Prime Minister Hendrik Verwoerd in September 1966 and second to the "Information Scandal" that issued in Mr. Vorster's resignation in September 1978. (He would subsequently serve for eight months as State President.) On the Information Scandal see M. Rees and C. Day, *Muldergate: The Story of the Information Scandal* (London: Macmillan, 1980); LES de Villiers, *Secret Information* (Cape Town: Tafelberg, 1980); and Deon Geldenhuys, *The Diplomacy of Isolation: South African Foreign Policy Making* (New York: St. Martin's Press, 1984).

12. The National Party caucus had to choose among three candidates: Mr. Botha; the now somewhat sullied Information minister, Cornelius Mulder; and a newcomer to the cabinet, Mr. Roelf F "Pik" Botha, who had replaced Hilgard Muller as foreign minister. Winning on the second ballot, PW then asked Mr.

Mulder to resign from the cabinet and asked Pik to stay on as foreign minister—the portfolio he occupies to this day. Professor Geldenhuys quotes the longtime minister of Transportation, B J Schoeman, as indicating that Mr. Verwoerd had to be persuaded that PW had something more than "the party organizer's mentality" before making him minister of Defense shortly before his death (*Diplomacy of Isolation*, 264). It must be noted that Mr. Pik Botha was the leader in public-opinion popularity polls in 1978 and continued to be so a decade later. Once again it did not translate into higher office.

13. In a June 1988 public-opinion survey conducted by the Afrikaans newspaper, *Rapport*, the AWB received a "favorable" rating of 3.4 percent along with an "unfavorable" rating of 90 percent causing one wag to observe that this merely demonstrates once again that the perceptions of benighted Afrikaners and enlightened Western observers are widely divergent!

14. The writer has found Mr. Worrall at all times to be the most pleasant of hosts—but then, is it Professor Worrall, or is it Ambassador Worrall, or is it aspirant-President Worrall, as his critics would have it? The Cornell Ph.D. in political science has an identity problem within the maelstrom of South African politics!

15. "What is apartheid? It is not as many people seem to think, the extreme right wing of the political-economic spectrum. Quite the contrary. It is more accurately described as *ethnic socialism*, a regressive and primitive system, which necessarily involves state interference in every aspect of economic activity (in behalf of, quite mistakenly, the Afrikaner)" (italics mine). From a speech by the British historian, Paul Johnson, before a East Daggafontein Mines seminar in Johannesburg, October 8, 1987. Corroboration of this was provided the author by an Afrikaner luncheon host at the Rand Club (Johannesburg). "The whole business has been a great mistake. Leave it to us Afrikaners to put into statute what the British had the better sense to leave as custom and practice! Now, of course, we shall have to eliminate apartheid, *de jure*, if only out of economic necessity, but that will do nothing about *de facto* apartheid." (Incidentally, the fact that one will hear Afrikaans spoken today in the Rand Club is evidence at least of the dismantlement of Brit–Boer apartheid!) It is not uncommon to hear from Afrikaners the laconic view that their passion for survival has led to mistakes but that apartheid is just that—a mistake, nothing more—and in view of the fact that it doesn't work, we'll fix it. Again, the seminal work is Lipton, *Capitalism and Apartheid*. For a remarkable misinterpretation of what is taking place in South Africa today, Prof. Robert Rotberg could write as late as September 1984 in the *Boston Globe* that South African Whites "are not prepared to dismantle the trappings of apartheid"! (Reprinted in *The State*, Columbia, S.C., September 9, 1984.) They are doing precisely that and at the same time raising questions as to its pertinence to the larger question.

16. Peter Sorour, recently retired director-general of the South Africa Foundation (a privately funded, Johannesburg-based foundation closely tied to the RSA corporate structure). Two other sources with impeccable Old Nat credentials (the first in the academic community and the second in the Ministry of Foreign Affairs) provided the following assessments of the political sophistication of the corporate world: (1) "Afrikaner businessmen don't like politics—they don't understand politics—Jaap Marais tried it to his chagrin; Fred duPlessis will stay out

as will Mike Rosholt. English-speaking business leaders still don't have much influence on the NP." (2) "Our businessmen, when they think about Africa, do not think beyond 'mere trade issues'; insofar as they have a foreign policy it consists of opposing (RSA) 'giveaways' to neighboring countries who engage in strident rhetoric against us. It is extremely difficult to 'sell' them on a realistic foreign policy."

17. The author has met regularly with Maree since 1979 prior to his secondment to ARMSCOR. In our first meeting he was particularly interested in the transition of Mr. David Packard (chairman of Hewlett-Packard) from business to government (a process he was about to go through), having read a piece by the author on the subject. See James M. Roherty, "The Office of the Secretary of Defense: The Laird and McNamara Styles," in *New Civil-Military Relations,* ed. John P. Lovell and Phillip S. Kronenberg (New Brunswick, N.J.: E.P. Dutton, 1974), 229–54. Reprinted in *American Defense Policy,* 4th ed., ed. John E. Endicott and Roy W. Stafford (Baltimore: Johns Hopkins Press, 1977), 286–89. A meeting between Mr. Maree and Mr. Packard was arranged.

18. Maree was referring to the talks held by Prime Minister John Vorster and Vice President Walter Mondale in Vienna in May 1977, talks that Mr. Vorster fully vetted in Parliament the next month. It is difficult to exaggerate the adverse impact of the Mondale prescriptions on South African opinion. It was understood in almost all quarters as interference. (See chapter 2.)

19. *The Wall Street Journal,* August 15, 1989. Press commentary in the United States on the resignation again demonstrated the long-standing bias against a man who admittedly had a temper not altogether compatible with the press. Nothing approaching a dispassionate analysis of fifty-three years of public life appeared in the aftermath. One might find it instructive to repair to Barbara Tuchman's account of the last days of Arthur Balfour as leader of Britain's Conservative Party in 1911. Balfour, confronted with a challenge to his leadership, which strikingly included a BMG movement ("Balfour Must Go"), instead of fighting as many expected, chose to allow matters to devolve upon those prepared "to be politicians and nothing but politicians." See her *The Proud Tower* (New York: Macmillan, 1966), 402–3. In a reflective interview with the author (October 3, 1990), Gerrit Viljoen, minister of Constitutional Development in the cabinet of F W de Klerk and minister of Education under P W Botha, was prepared to give PW his due. Mr. Botha, according to Viljoen, found it difficult to let go of the security issue and turn to a political agenda. However, he added, it was Botha's security achievements that produced the climate for a political agenda in South Africa "that cannot be taken from him."

20. Interview with Mr. Williams. Cape Town, RSA. March 11, 1987.

21. A fashionably Left point of view circulating among both Afrikaans-speakers and English-speakers in the posh northern end of Johannesburg prior to the May 1987 elections proved in the outcome to be a minority view but is worth summarizing here. I am indebted to the late Tertius Myberg, then editor of the *Sunday Times* (Johannesburg), for his exposition over dinner, which I paraphrase: Peace will come only after passing through the catharsis of violence. There is spontaneous rage in the townships; youths are out of control there. To be sure the ANC is trying to exploit this, but they cannot control spontaneous rage. In any case ANC pragmatists will gain the day over the hard-liners. The *gravitas* of the situation in

the townships is not being communicated to the top level of government. Today the townships can be addressed only in terms of a salutary lesson—it is too late for negotiations. After the catharsis we will be ready for some sort of Fifth Republic solution putting behind the anarchy of the Fourth. (We shall take up below the reaction of the chief of South African Defense Force when the gist of this viewpoint was communicated to him!)

22. The characterization, in the first instance, of Nelson Mandela and co-conspirators of the fifties and sixties and in the second instance of Desmond Tutu (and Dennis Hurley), is offered in South Africa to sort them out from "genuine political figures" such as Chief Buthelezi.

23. Annette Seegers suggests that SADF has been converted from a frontier army to "a service institution" by the Botha regime. See her "The Security Establishment's Response to the Emergency in South Africa" (a paper delivered at the Biennial Conference of the Inter-University Seminar on the Armed Forces and Society, Chicago, October 8–10, 1987). In a highly tendentious study, Miss Seegers misses entirely the seminal fact—rife with implications—of tension within SADF stemming from the requirement to be at one and the same time a modern conventional defense force and a service institution.

24. SADF's dual role presents a variation on the general hypothesis that militaries can make a major contribution to development (modernization) especially where civil services are either nonexistent or inefficient. In the South African variation, our contention is that SADF is a vanguard institution in the reform/restructuring process both in terms of maintaining stability and of internal program development. In this connection allusions to the Brazilian case are frequently made. Writing about the Brazilian military's decision to restore civilian rule in 1985, Stanley Hilton notes the extent to which external stimuli contributed to the "return-to-the-barracks" process. He suggests that Brazilian officers saw "an implicit incompatibility between the exercise of direct political responsibility and reorientation of mission toward external defense with its resultant heightened demand for professionalism." See his "The Brazilian Military: Changing Strategic Perceptions and the Question of Mission," *Armed Forces and Society* 13 (Spring 1987): 346. Hilton's analysis underscores our own in which we argue that, far from staging a "silent, bloodless coup," SADF, anxious to orient itself to the external mission, questions its lead role in fashioning a new dispensation. The tensions this produces within the SADF leadership are evident to anyone well acquainted with its members.

25. The allusion is to South Africa's "Age of the Generals" following the Second Anglo-Boer War (Louis Botha, Jan Smuts, J B Hertzog, et al.). Unlike the earlier generation that went on to political prominence, the "young generals" of today are categorical in their rejection of the netherworld of politics, preferring to retire to the refuge of "the farm" instead. See, e.g., D W Kruger, *The Age of the Generals* (Johannesburg: Dagbreekpers, 1961).

26. The judgment, given to the author in a private conversation, is that of a prominent general officer. It reflects at one and the same time the high esteem in which the State President was held by the SADF officer corps and the tension in their ranks concerning appropriate roles and missions for SADF. (See chapter 4.)

2 THE ONSLAUGHT, 1975–1984

There is, on the whole, nothing more important in life than to find out exactly the viewpoint from which things must be regarded and judged, and then to keep that viewpoint, for we can only grasp the mass of events in their unity from that standpoint.
—Karl von Clausewitz, *On War*, XXI

. . . because it is a total onslaught (*die aanslag teen Suid-Afrika*) the only counter strategy with any hope of success is also a total strategy.
—Adriaan Vlok, member for Verwoerdburg, South African Parliament, March 21, 1980

Prelude

The Portuguese Armed Forces Movement (MFA) under the leadership of an improbable liberal, Gen. Antonio de Spinola, set off a year of political turbulence in Lisbon with its coup of April 25, 1974.[1] During the course of the ensuing year, the more ebullient members of the MFA, having dispensed with the Marcello Caetano regime, turn on their own general in a breakout to the Left. This is sufficient signal to Pretoria that the Portuguese Empire in Africa had ended. South African Intelligence (the new Bureau of State Security—BOSS—and the not yet full-blown SADF Intelligence) had been monitoring the Angolan insurgencies for years. Now a much enhanced effort (including increased interaction with Washington) would be required to sort things out.

The Popular Movement for the Liberation of Angola (MPLA), led

34

by Agostinho Neto (described by one observer as "a psychotic poet"), was the principal object of attention because of its known contacts with the Soviet Union. The MPLA, moreover, was the prototypical Leninist cadre with roots in the educated, urban elements of Luanda. Both the National Front for the Liberation of Angola (FNLA) and the National Union for the Total Independence of Angola (UNITA) better exemplified the peasant revolution model, each having a rural, ethnic base: the FNLA in Bakongoland in the northeast stretching back into Zaire, and UNITA among the Ovimbundu people in the southeast with convenient lines into Zambia. FNLA leadership was nearly as suspect as that of the MPLA. Holden Roberto had little taste for field command, and Daniel Chipenda (an MPLA fallout) had a variety of nonmilitary preoccupations. Dr. Jonas Savimbi, rebuffed in his attempt to obtain an FNLA commission, establishes UNITA in 1966. This is the same year in which John Vorster becomes Prime Minister of the RSA (following the assassination of Hendrik Verwoerd) and P W Botha, minister of Defense. While maintaining contact with FNLA, Pretoria from this point on (well ahead of Washington) identifies UNITA's charismatic and accomplished *commandante* as the preferred option in Angola. It is not possible on the basis of currently available information to fully detail the roles of John Vorster, P W Botha, Hendrik van den Bergh (boss of BOSS), Kenneth Kaunda (president of Zambia), and, for that matter, Henry Kissinger in the rise of UNITA and Jonas Savimbi. It is evident that these roles were—and in certain instances continue to be—interactive.[2]

In January 1975, at the height of the turbulence in Lisbon, the government (or what passed for one at that point) brings the three insurgency leaders to the Portuguese Riviera to arrange a transfer of power in Angola. There is little discussion: the hosts dictate the terms of the so-called Alvor Agreement to their visitors, affirming that upon withdrawal they will supervise free, open elections of a new national government. The Alvor assurances (reminiscent of the Paris Peace Accords of the day) would go down as among the most short-lived in history! Dispatched to Luanda to oversee the transition, Adm. Rosa Coutinho of the Portuguese navy brings word that, of course, there will be no election in view of the impossibility of an MPLA victory at the polls. The admiral's sojourn in Luanda is short; he is recalled to Lisbon and this time dispatched to Havana. The MFA has opted for an MPLA military victory in lieu of the unattainable electoral victory—with the proviso, to be sure, that increased fraternal support from Moscow and Havana will be forthcoming. The Soviets had terminated their pre-independence assistance to MPLA in 1972 out of exasperation with the ineptitude of their preferred Angolan option, but now in the spring of 1975, it was again in full flood as the result of the new developments in Lisbon. A U.S. State Department representative, Bruce Porter, "could not believe his eyes" as he observed the accumulation of arms on the Luanda docks bound for President Neto's army (FAPLA).[3] The candor of Admiral Coutinho evidently had not been convincing! The first contingent of Cubans is in Angola by April, presaging a June decision by Fidel Castro to commit a full-scale expeditionary force to the side of his newly found comrades in Africa. The rush of the East bloc to fill the Angolan vacuum is blatant; Prime Minister Vorster sounds out the Ford administration as to a collaborative response.

It is not the best of times in Washington. Gerald Ford, selected by Richard Nixon for the vice presidency upon the resignation of Spiro Agnew, becomes the first nonelected president of the United States and is now in the wake of Watergate. The Pike–Church Hearings, the first full-court-press inquiry into the undertakings of the Central Intelligence Agency (CIA), are underway as well. Nonetheless, the Angolan matter is given priority consideration, and a process begins that will have an eerie replication exactly a decade later. Ambassador Nathaniel Davis (then assistant secretary of state for African Affairs), in a series of memos, attempts to persuade Secretary Henry Kissinger that a CIA action plan to assist FNLA and UNITA forces in Angola will not work. Davis's objections have their own foundation, however. He was most concerned that a political issue would arise—that there would be an inevitable disclosure of any covert undertaking resulting in a political price too high for Washington. In the face of anything but propitious circumstances he proposes, ipse dixit, the diplomatic option in Angola. In the patois of the diplomat, Ambassador Davis wrote that "it may be one of the highest tasks of statesmanship to thicken [the veneer of restrained international behavior] when that possibility exists."[4] Mr. Davis saw that possibility, incredibly, in Angola in the summer of 1975. Mr. Ford and Mr. Kissinger, unable for their parts to discern even the slightest "veneer of restrained international behavior" in this particular instance, approve the CIA action plan. In August stepped-up assistance to the FNLA (there had been modest political assistance earlier) begins arriving through Zaire. Likewise in August Pretoria orders lead elements of SADF into Angola. It is an auspicious moment from the South African standpoint—the beginnings of a joint undertaking with the United States. Again however, not unlike the Alvor Agreement and the Paris Peace Accords, it will be "an undertaking that was broken."[5] The affair leaves a bitter taste in the SADF officer corps, not to mention a residue of cynicism in the RSA Foreign Ministry. Most important, the minister of Defense, who will go on to become Prime Minister and State President, will not be able to erase the matter from his mind.

Bravo Group came out of Angola in the first months of 1976 "with their tails straight up."[6] This military miracle was the handiwork of Jan Breytenbach and a small cadre of brother officers and NCOs of SADF. A *Kommandant* of whom his Boer War precursors, Christiaan de Wet and Koos de la Rey, would have been proud, Breytenbach went into Angola in August 1975 with a daunting assignment. He was to gather up what remnants of the Chipenda faction of FNLA he could find scattered across the southern Angolan bush and forge them into a combat unit. Incredibly, by October Bravo Group was formed—albeit not yet forged—and placed in Task Force ZULU along with Alpha Group (an equally nondescript contingent of ex-Portuguese bushmen), under another singular SADF *Kommandant,* Delville Linford. After some difficult moments in which Alpha Group had to be brought around to the view that Bravo Group was not the enemy, this essentially Black, Portuguese-speaking force under Boer leader elements from the "racist South" (as Breytenbach describes them) launched *Operation Savannah.* Col. Koos van Heerden took Task Force ZULU under command and, although "surely a nightmare to any commander who treats war seriously,"[7] led his charges on a spectacular campaign northward. It was spectacular for rapidity of movement, averaging better than ninety kilometers a day, but even more spectacular for the training-under-fire achievements of Breytenbach and Linford. The forging process produced a Black/White combat unit that would become SADF's Three-Two Battalion, today ranking first among its infantry battalions.

By December, Task Force ZULU joined by Task Force FOXBAT (which had just formed up at Nova Lisboa—Huambo—with UNITA troops) was northwest of Santa Comba in front of Bridge 14 on the main access route to Luanda. Beyond the bridge lay Catofe and the Angolan capital heavily reinforced by Cubans. The South African contingent consisting of less than two thousand Permanent Force and Citizen Force troops "with a very meager ration of equipment,"[8] had inflicted sharp reverses on FAPLA/Cuban troops, culminating in a major thrashing of Cubans at Bridge 14. Nonetheless, it was clear that a critical decision point in the campaign had been reached, not in the bush but in Washington. With the vote of the U.S. Senate on December 19 to end involvement in Angola, the American connection is broken. Pretoria had no recourse but to retire below the Okavango and the Cunene and begin the process of building anew—a new strategy *and* a new military posture, unencumbered either by the commonwealth connections of the past or the prospect of alliances in the future. The fallback order of January 22, 1976, is a tiny metaphor of the grand decision to reopen the South Africa Question and, likewise, can be marked as the beginning point for a new SADF.

A New Appreciation

P W Botha marked the occasion of fifty years in public life in 1986. Having earned the credentials of the consummate politician in the course of that half century, he is basically of a managerial bent—a propensity reinforced by a long and admiring association with the South African Defense Force.[9] This factor would largely explain the approach he would take in the fortieth year (1976) in addressing the situation in which the Republic found itself following the fallback from Luanda. His tendency would be to think in terms of the management requirements—of rationalizing procedures—but it was clear that new structures and new systems could be put in place only on the basis of a new appreciation of the threat. As a result, at the direction of the still minister of Defense, an effort unparalleled in South African annals is launched in which a coterie of Botha associates begins to define *die aanslag teen Suid-Afrika*[10] and at the same time to develop a total national strategy in accordance with which the RSA will respond.

The Botha men confront nothing less than Africa in crisis: what they saw were failed experiments strewn as so much debris across a continent—monuments to Kwame Nkrumah's 1963 injunction, "seek ye first the political kingdom." Evidence was everywhere that the nascent African body politic (the state) was at the core of the burgeoning social, economic, and demographic catastrophe. For the politically attuned South Africans, *political instability* was the root cause of the African crisis.[11] In underscoring this factor they were projecting to the region an axiom basic to their thinking about the Republic itself: where political institutions are weak the sine qua non for nation building is absent. (Strengthened White political institutions, as we have seen, are, in their minds, the condition precedent for a "new dispensation" within the RSA—specifically the National Party!) Two decades after Mr. Nkrumah's clarion call, African states were not exploding with revolutionary fervor; they were imploding—collapsing in on themselves. Against a grim backdrop of somber statistics on caloric intake, nutrition, birthrates, life expectancy, technical skills, investment, balance of payments, and debt, the demise of political institutions had gone all but unnoticed except by Pretoria and Moscow. Yet the record of coups, assassinations, political corruption, and crime was nearly as graphic and in its strategic implications more portentous.[12] Precarious, fragile, tenuous, these states from their inception were impotent to deal with the manifold ramifications of the crisis of Africa. In a word they were vulnerable.

The ideological crisis attending the political instability on the continent did not escape the attention of the analysts in Pretoria. The tenets of African-Marxist socialism—upon which the kingdom was to be built—were being swept into the dustbins of history. The shortcomings of the "Soviet solution for Africa" (fashioned for the most part in the International Department of the Central Committee under Boris Ponomarev)[13] were now plain to the most dogmatic of frontline leaders if not to most Western observers. The South African assessment of this situation provided to the writer in 1983 was striking in contrast with that given during Mr. Botha's first year in power (1979). Senior intelligence officials did not attempt to veil their contempt for the Soviet record in Africa: they are failures, one was now being told; they have no solutions for Africa's problems and are reappraising their whole approach. "Soviet disenchantment with 'African socialism' is running deep," said one, "and they are responding in wholly predictable fashion—they are stockpiling arms throughout the continent!" The response was not simply instinctive; it was the genesis of a new approach.

The Botha analysts were in agreement that they faced a new situation insofar as Soviet purpose in Africa was concerned. Manifestly, the threat was no longer that of armed Soviet clients attempting to prosecute a war of national liberation against the Republic.[14] South Africa was not caught up in a classic colonial war: allusions to the "Algerian model" (by ill-informed outsiders) wherein the metropolitan power (ostensibly the RSA) was besieged by an insurgency—or even by something as evanescent as Mr. Julius Nyerere's "liberation movement in Africa"—were absurd on their face. In contradistinction to the Algerian case, insurgencies in southern Africa were external to the Republic, largely ineffectual, and were themselves linked to Africa's new metropolitan power (the Soviet Union). Soviet purpose in the eighties is not the arming of an ideology or an insurgency ("Moscow's illusions on that score have faded!"), but instead the arming of the one plausible institution left on the continent. Among those formulating the new appreciation, Intelligence people especially argued that Moscow, shaken by the collapse of political institutions, was turning to its "one, last bet in Africa"—the military institution.[15] It is not a matter of ideological alignment between the Soviets and these militaries, they hastened to explain; rather the point is that the latter will remember that it was the former who provided the wherewithal when the day for seizing state power from hapless politicians arrives. (An official interjected with words attributed to Kenneth Kaunda: ideology follows arms!) It is inevitable that Africa will undergo far-reaching political change, probably before the century is out. And should this occur at the impetus of externally backed African militaries, they warned, such seizures of state power will have repercussions carrying well beyond the *voortrekkerhoogte*.[16]

As they probed the chaos of newly independent states, the RSA analysts were drawn to the conclusion that they were engaged in a titanic struggle for the future of Africa itself in which insurgency was a rapidly diminishing element. What struck them with the greatest force was the "wholeness" of the emerging struggle. It ranged across the entire conflict spectrum: political-psychological, socioeconomic, military and terrorist. Utterly contemporary in its modalities, it was at once direct and indirect, sophisticated and brutish, conventional and unconventional. An unparalleled array of forces mounted from a variety of sources, East and West, now confronted the Republic.[17] They were compelled to describe it as *die aanslag teen Suid-Afrika!* South Africa was the center of gravity against which the main effort was directed; its fall, far from bringing down a colonial power, would lay open a continent to all that was alien and inimical. The fates (history if one prefers) had given to the new republic a role in determining the future of Africa itself, which it had not sought and could not reject. It was not mere coincidence that this should occur at that historical moment when P W Botha would reopen the South Africa Question. The two matters would move hand in hand toward their resolution.

A Total National Strategy

Viewing this chaotic landscape from the *voortrekkerhoogte*, the instinct of the Botha men was to think in terms of a sweeping alternative—a concept of their own for (southern) Africa. Utterly dismissed was the option of withdrawing into some mythical *laager*.[18] Paradoxically, perhaps, the very gravity of the African scene stretching before them generated a confidence among them that the crisis of Africa could be met with counterrevolution—that South Africa would have a seminal role in the destiny of the continent. The Republic after all was the regional metropole possessed of the continent's great conjunction of vital assets (capital, technology, industry, transport, telecommunications, electric power, entrepreneurial skills, etc.). The frontline states, on the other hand, were at a turning point suspended between failed experiments of the past and an undefined future, their leaders motivated by little more than an instinct to maintain control. In this volatile context would they not be prepared to take a pragmatic turn? Did not the desperate urgency among Africa's politicians to stave off disaster afford Pretoria an opportunity to outline an alternative? South African analysts were persuaded that nothing short of a total national strategy reflecting an entirely new appreciation of the crisis of Africa would suffice. They must deal with the immediate imperative of security, but at the same time they would also elaborate their own thinking with respect to the political, economic, and security future of Africa—that is to say, mount a counterrevolution.

The enterprise of strategy as it is practiced in South Africa today is at once classical and contemporary in its premises. Strategy consists of making choices, devising a schema, and selecting means to support policy. It is a process in which the practitioners are conscious of the requirements of objectivity. Policy in turn (following Clausewitz) represents interests translated into state objectives in which subjectivity may well play a part. Strategy is situation-specific; consequently it cannot be reduced to a *science*. In a word it is an *art*. (Reason is exemplified in art as well as in science!) The realm of the strategist is that of a goal-directed actor (or artist) functioning in or responding to an immediate, unique set of circumstances. Any contextual change establishes yet a new unique situation and *pari passu* new choices (i.e., strategic evolution). Just as it is the product of a new appreciation of the African scene "The Strategy" (as we shall refer to it hereafter) is the product of a mind-set—the mind-set of a coterie of men who will dominate security thinking in South Africa for the balance of the century.[19]

This mind-set (realist, pragmatic, *verlig,* and African) is informed to a remarkable degree by the thought of the late French strategist, Gen. André Beaufre.[20] Michael Howard, the distinguished British military historian, has written that for Beaufre

> the whole field of international relations constituted a battlefield in which the Communist powers, thwarted in the use of force by the nuclear stalemate, were attacking the West by indirect means. Strategy had progressed from "the operational" . . . through the "logistic" . . . to the "indirect." Political maneuvers should, therefore, be seen as strategic maneuvers . . . the trouble with this is that it is not simply a theory of strategy, but also a theory of international relations.[21]

The trouble that Howard finds in Beaufre's thought was precisely what the Botha men were searching for. It was this very point that strategy must consciously embody "a theory of international relations" (Beaufre's theory more specifically) that recommended the Frenchman's thinking to them. It takes account, as perhaps no other strategy construct in the world today does, of the wholeness of the Onslaught to which South Africa is subject. "Political maneuvers" are, indeed, to be understood as "strategic maneuvers," as are economic, military, and most especially psychological maneuvers. South Africans would have to devise their own.

The Strategy would evolve steadily under the guidance of P W Botha and Gen. Magnus M de M Malan (the coarchitects who would continue their partnership at the apex of the South African security system). It can be outlined in terms of its aims. The function of strategic aims is to provide direction and purpose to a broad spectrum of programmatic initiatives or, if you will, maneuvers. They are not ends in themselves; rather they point to the establishment of necessary conditions for the achievement of policy goals. They are focal points around which a variety of measures are to be concerted. Thus, in an early formulation, South Africa's strategic aims were set as *Stabilization, Normalization,* and *Rationalization.*

Stabilization, normalization, and rationalization are concepts encompassing clusters of diplomatic, economic, and psychological military initiatives aimed at achieving conditions, *external and internal,* indispensable to the realization of the supreme goals of the Republic. It is axiomatic in The Strategy that external and internal aims are reciprocal: success with the one depends on success with the other. The necessary condition of a cooperative regional environment is the reciprocal of a climate of peaceful evolutionary change within the Republic. Only out of such conditions can a new regional order ensue; only out of such conditions can a new dispensation within South Africa arise.

Stabilization is the first aim. (Once more it is "security first," externally and internally.) It encompasses that cluster of measures required to eliminate the threat of armed attack from the conventional military level to the basest level of the terrorist. Stabilization precedes *normalization:* it alone can make possible normal intercourse with other states, that is, the establishment of political networks in the region and an open (as opposed to a clandestine) commerce. Within the Republic stabilization is the precursor of welfare measures (housing, health, and education) and the development of infrastructure. Such programs of normalization cannot be put in place in a revolutionary-war setting. The eradication of revolutionary war is the essence of the stabilization aim within the Republic.[22] In a growing sense (highly visible in the eighties) stabilization and normalization are the twin pillars upon which a new order in the region and a new dispensation within the country rest. *Rationalization* suggests efficacious processes as well as new structures and new systems. It is perhaps too cold, too analytic, a term for encompassing the required new elements that must be brought into play (along with the discarding of old), but such is the mind-set. It is from this standpoint that General Malan speaks when he calls The Strategy "a plan for the management of South Africa's four power bases (the political, economic, social/psychological, and security) as an integrated whole."[23] While our focus will be on the security power base, the essence of rationalization is the effective integration of all four power bases through new systems and structures. The plan (The Strategy) will accommodate shifting priorities, external and internal, but its aims are fixed, as is the order of their realization.

Denigration of the Botha–Malan mode of thought, especially in the early eighties (abating somewhat in the late eighties as the West came to experience more directly "the modalities of contemporary warfare"), indicated a failure to grasp its contemporary nature. A proclivity for total war concepts in American circles was part of the problem. RSA analysts were not discoursing on the level of effort (along a vertical scale) directed against them, but rather on the multidimensionality— the comprehensiveness—of the effort (along a horizontal scale) directed against them. They were elaborating the nature of contemporary warfare and attempting to devise an equally comprehensive (and contemporary) counterstrategy. They were in the vanguard of strategic analysis—an advanced position still not attained by most Western nations. Mr. Botha began to outline The Strategy publicly before a National Party Congress in Durban, August 15, 1979,[24] where he spoke of "South Africa's determination to defend itself against outside intervention *in every practical way possible*" (italics mine). Reacting still to the Angolan debacle of 1975–76, the Prime Minister insisted that the RSA "give priority to its own interests" and went on to state that "as far as possible South Africa must follow a policy of neutrality." (Mr. Botha's understandable pique with Washington would rise and fall, but allusions to neutralism would fade during the course of the first Reagan administration. That new expectations relating to a Washington connection would, in turn, be dashed is a later part of our story.) Mr. Botha would state his aims with clarity and conviction from the beginning,[25] his personality permitting nothing else. Now his task was to set about achieving his aims or (more congenial to his own mind) "meeting the management requirements." We leave this to the next chapter.

Strategic Realities

As contemporary and varied in dimension as the Onslaught was coming to be understood, the "Botha Appreciation" would be rooted in enduring realities. The great geographic expanse of the continent and its ocean flanks remains the primary datum of threat assessment. South Africa's strategic horizons extend well beyond Limpopo and Zambezi,[26] with the region below the Zaire/Tanzania line (which for convenience we call southern Africa) retaining inevitable priority (see Map 1). In its preoccupation with defense of the realm, Pretoria, no more than any other government, can relegate to second place the "iron

Map 1. **Southern Africa**

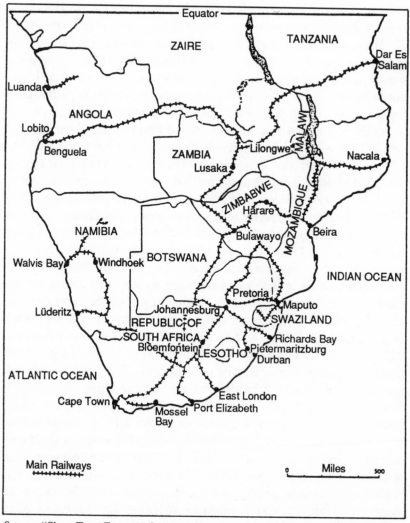

Source: "Short-Term Forecast: South and Southern Africa: Labour, Political and Security Developments," *Longreach Report* (Johannesburg: Longreach), June 18, 1988, p. 12.

law" of nonthreatening neighbors. "African armies simply" (the phrase is that of a SADF officer) do not pose an explicit threat to South Africa; however, a conventional military threat is posed in those instances where African armies, in addition to possessing externally supplied advanced weaponry, are braced throughout the order of battle by external command/advisory elements.[27] At the nub of the Republic's complex security problem is the concern that within the frontline states there is the potential for precisely this linkage: this is the baseline for all strategic planning for counterrevolution. Angola, among frontline states, has been the focus of such concern since 1976 (a concern that would peak ominously in 1987–88—see chapter 6). Over time it may not be the most critical case, but with the events of 1975–76 the Angolan Question and the Southwest Question had merged as one.

Union of South Africa forces marched into German Southwest Africa in 1915 with little difficulty. RSA forces have not found it easy to march out. In that vast expanse between the Cunene and the Orange rivers, rich with mineral deposits and richer still with economic potential, live barely a million people, of which but 10 percent are White. With the Portuguese barrier in the north down "Southwest" becomes an immense buffer between the Republic and Angola along the Atlantic coast. Here in 1965–66 South Africa experiences its first (and only) encounter with insurgency as small numbers of "SWAPO boys" infiltrate Ovamboland at the Angolan border by way of Zambia and the Caprivi Strip. They are members of the People's Liberation Army of Namibia (PLAN)—the armed wing of the Southwest Africa People's Organization (SWAPO). PLAN originated abroad in the early sixties following a SWAPO decision to commit itself to armed struggle. From training camps in Tanzania, Algeria, and points East, "elements" were sent back to Southwest Africa/Namibia by their Ovambo-émigré leader Sam Nujoma. (SWAPO itself had been formed in the fifties at the behest of Herman Tovio ja Tovio—at liberty after a second release from prison.) The initial spate of insurgency (1965–68) was dealt with handily by the South African Police.[28] It accomplished little more than to clarify for Pretoria that SWAPO, its name notwithstanding, was based on the Ovambo people, and that its success would depend on the manner in which it would undertake to enlist the support of other ethnic groups. Also clear was the fact that SWAPO/PLAN was sustained by external sources, some as close at hand as Zambia (the irrepressible Mr. Kaunda) and Tanzania (the irrepressible Mr. Nyerere), and some as distant as the Soviet Union.

The "bush war"—as the Southwest insurgency was coming to be known—was taken over by SADF in the early seventies prior to *Operation Savannah*. With the SADF withdrawal from Angola and with MPLA ensconced in Luanda, PLAN then had direct access routes into

Namibia and a new infrastructure that literally "hugged that of FAPLA." It would be impossible thereafter to sort out the Angolan Question and the Southwest Question. Moreover, inasmuch as President Neto was host to an increasing number of Cuban and East-bloc forces (a dividend of the 1976 Treaty of Cooperation and Friendship with Moscow), none of it could be sorted out from the East–West Question. Making the most of an ideal sanctuary in southern Angola, PLAN will step up its campaign among the Ovambo people with terrorist intimidation as the preferred mode of enlistment. In May 1978, SADF responds with its first cross-border operation since *Savannah*— the first in a series extending to January 1984 as the bush war reaches its peak.[29] The impact of SADF operations on PLAN's infrastructure and its command-control-communications (quite apart from casualties inflicted) is devastating, but with *Operation Protea* (1981) SADF encounters not only PLAN but FAPLA troops. Moreover, the minister of Defense, Gen. Magnus Malan, would tell the House of Assembly that "there were Russians everywhere" and that among other things they had built interlocking SWAPO and FAPLA defensive positions.[30]

A disturbing convergence of PLAN and FAPLA is among factors that lead Pretoria in late 1983 to suggest a suspension of operations in Angola in turn for a cessation of SWAPO infiltration into Namibia. SADF follows up with the final operation in the series (*Askari*),[31] which confirms that (1) PLAN is essentially finished as a military factor and (2) FAPLA-cum-Cubans is a rising conventional-military threat. The completion of *Askari* and its findings paves the way to Lusaka. The skills and intensity with which SADF conducted its cross-border operations between 1978 and 1984 attested to the determination of P W Botha to win the bush war. It was an absolute prerequisite to any negotiation of the Southwest Question: in short, stabilization must precede normalization. (In this same period cross-border operations directed against ANC sanctuaries, especially in Mozambique, were part and parcel of the same strategy.) Mr. Botha would tell Parliament in February 1983 that

> the Red flag in Windhoek can only bring untold misery to the people of South West Africa. (It) is the symbol of decay, of hunger and economic despair in Angola. It is also the symbol of decay, of starvation and of death in Mozambique and in Zimbabwe. . . . We do not wish that fate upon South West Africa.[32]

Yet at the same time pressures were building to move from a military phase in the bush war to a political phase. The new Reagan administration in Washington provided impetus for such a transition as it gave every indication that it wished to play a prominent role in southern Africa. Indeed, Washington indicated that it would take the Angola/ Namibia issue into its own hands, telling Pretoria that Soviet/Cuban withdrawal from Angola must precede settlement of the political future of both Angola and Namibia. Pretoria's reaction to Washington's preemption (as revealed to the writer by various RSA officials in the period 1979–85) was a mixture of pique, skepticism, and relief. As one of them put it, "we are not altogether privy to what is going on (between Washington–Luanda–Havana–Moscow)—but the matter is in your hands now!"[33]

Fears about the kind of regime that might sit in Windhoek following a "political settlement" (i.e., a SWAPO-dominated independent Namibia) lessened among Mr. Botha's men as the military situation improved and the proposals of Mr. Chester Crocker evolved. Throughout 1983–84 South Africans emphasized that the situation was not so undesirable that they could not be patient; on the other hand any step toward resolution of the matter was welcome. On February 16, 1984, in Lusaka an Agreement for the Disengagement of Forces "in the area in question" (south-central Angola) was reached. The disengagement process (specified in a document known as the "Mulungushi Minute") would stretch over a period of fourteen months and would be monitored by a Joint Monitoring Commission (JMC). By April 1985 the SADF withdrawal from Angola was begun and the JMC disbanded. PLAN activity on the Namibia side, it must be reported, did not abate but was easily contained.[34] The Lusaka Accord coupled with the N'komati Accord, which would follow a month later (March 1984), appeared to set the stage for a political phase in southern Africa and movement toward normalization. Neither accord, however, dealt with a matter of the highest priority for Mr. Botha and as a result "the promise of Lusaka and N'komati" would be short-lived.

To go back to the withdrawal from Angola in 1976, no sooner were Jan Breytenbach and his SADF associates back on the Rundu side of the Okavango than the "Long March" of Dr. Jonas Savimbi and his UNITA remnants began. Rejecting proffered advice from West and East, Savimbi retires deep into Ovimbunduland in the far southeast of Angola to reconstitute his force and appeal to the world.[35] Neither

John Vorster nor P W Botha had to be persuaded after *Operation Savannah* that a Leninist cadre in control in Angola was unacceptable. Unlike in Washington, the matter would not drop off the agenda in Pretoria even temporarily. Mr. Botha would continue the connection with Dr. Savimbi, maintain his viability, and make UNITA participation in any legitimate Angolan government ("the promise of Alvor") a basic plank in his regional policy.[36] It would only be after both Mr. Reagan and Mr. Gorbachev were on the southern African stage that the fate of a revived UNITA would again come to the fore. But in the dark decade for Dr. Savimbi (1975–85) Pretoria would keep the UNITA card on the table.

Portugal's withdrawal from Africa put the question of Angola/Namibia (and to a lesser degree that of Mozambique) in sharp relief, but it also served to obscure what has been historically the central strategic problem for South Africa. The problem was manifest at the turn of the century in the form of Imperial Germany's presence in central-east Africa. The discovery of gold, coal, diamonds, and copper on the high inland plateaus of southern Africa in the last quarter of the nineteenth century impelled northward Cecil Rhodes, hordes of *uitlanders,* and the British army, crushing any notion the *voortrekkers* carried with them of a pastoral republic on the *veldt.* In the aftermath of the Second Anglo-Boer War, Jan Smuts, a renegade Unionist, was impelled to look beyond the provincial horizons of his fellow Boers, conscious as he was of the strategic problem. Sir Halford Mackinder, in his *Democratic Ideals and Reality,* makes reference to General Smuts telling the Royal Geographic Society of "the German ambition to control the world" from Central Africa.[37] In the Age of Geography it was Mackinder who provided the intellectual underpinnings for the strategy Smuts held vital to the security of South Africa:

> The forests do not spread completely across to the Indian Ocean, but leave a belt of grassy upland which connects the grasslands of the Sudan with those of South Africa . . . immense, open ground, thus continuous from the Sudan to Cape veldt. . . .[38]

The threat posed by this reality (to continue in the idiom of Mackinder), a natural land avenue to the Cape along the Indian Ocean seaboard, does not arise from its exploitation by any present or, for that matter, foreseeable combination of indigenous (African) forces.

Rather, as in the case of Germany before World War I, the threat that so concerted the mind of Smuts is that of a *non-African major power* with lodgements most likely on the western littoral of the Indian Ocean standing astride the critical land/sea approach to South Africa. (The extension of the veldt to the Atlantic coast as far north as the Gulf of Guinea poses something less of a problem.) During the interwar years Smuts's concern for the strategic vulnerability of South Africa mounted. The salience of the "Eastern backbone" was a theme upon which he often expounded. As World War II approached, he told the Parliament in Cape Town:

> our borders are singularly indefensible. The Line of the Limpopo cannot be held. . . . If you want to defend this country you will have to proceed a great distance beyond it, and the question then arises how far beyond it. Those who know this continent know that the proper line of defense is in the highland of Kenya.[39]

The northern prospect of Jan Smuts differed appreciably from that of Cecil Rhodes and, if anything, was even more fanciful inasmuch as it turned on the assimilation of Rhodesia into the Union of South Africa! Smuts would contend with a strategic problem rooted in political, geographic, and historic realities through an Anglo–Boer Union— a new British Commonwealth that would extend to the Zambezi. (It was not yet time, however, for a bridging of the "Boer-Brit" fissure.) The Smuts concept was one of an economic bloc built around minerals and railroads and, to be sure, a White political bloc that would extend from the Cape to Katanga (Shaba). Not the least of the difficulties would be the Rhodesians themselves. As the 1922 referendum on incorporation into the Union approached, Smuts anticipated what result "ordinary Rhodesians" might produce at the polls:

> It would be a great thing to round off the South African state with borders far flung into the heart of the continent. But I fear that I am moving too fast, and patience will be necessary. . . .They (the Rhodesians) are afraid of our bilingualism, our nationalism. . . . In short they are little Jingoes and the sooner they are assimilated by the Union the better for them and for us.[40]

Hancock observes that the collapse of the Unionist solution "proved final, and of conspicuous historical significance in the long term."[41] Latter-day Nationalists would find, however, basic realities do not permit taking one's gaze from Rhodesia/Zimbabwe.

Looking out over southern Africa at the onset of 1976, John Vorster's beleaguered government saw that heavily armed, nonelected Leninist cadres holding sway in Angola and Mozambique did not constitute the whole of Lisbon's legacy. The Portuguese withdrawal (officially November 11, 1975) had impacted decisively on the Rhodesian War as well. "It is very clear to one," the Prime Minister told the House of Assembly (January 30, 1976), "that the communist strategy is to cause South Africa to fight simultaneously or as much as possible on three fronts, namely on the Mozambique, Rhodesian and Angolan fronts."[42] Inclined earlier to think of Rhodesia "as pretty much a British problem still," with the Portuguese withdrawal, Mr. Vorster changes his mind and launches upon a détente diplomacy aimed at a regionally fashioned political settlement for Rhodesia. Encouraged in his demarche by Kenneth Kaunda, the RSA Prime Minister meets with the energetic president of Zambia and a variety of Rhodesian leaders at the very moment he is ordering advance elements of SADF into Angola (August 1975). While the prize of a regional political settlement will escape him, Mr. Vorster was later able to tell the House of Assembly that "thanks to our African initiative we were able to prevent an escalation on the Rhodesian front."[43] This modest achievement would be crucial in any case for a now rapidly forming South African counterstrategy.

Against the spectacular backdrop of Victoria Falls, Mr. Vorster and Mr. Kaunda had come hard up against the new factor in the Rhodesian War—a reinvigorated and uncompromising Robert Mugabe.[44] Mr. Mugabe's Zimbabwe African National Union (ZANU), based on the dominant Mashona majority, was deploying a much enhanced Zimbabwe African National Liberation Army (ZANLA) from a base structure in Mozambique provided largely by the People's Republic of China (PRC). He would accept nothing short of unrestricted Black (Mashona) majoritarianism for the new Zimbabwe; no Pretoria–Lusaka–Salisbury–London formulas would be discussed. Mr. Kaunda succumbs to severe pressure from Moscow to provide sanctuary for Mr. Joshua Nkomo's Zimbabwe African People's Union (ZAPU) and its Zimbabwe People's Revolutionary Army (ZIPRA). Mr. Vorster again turns to Washington, the collapse of the Angolan venture notwithstanding. Détente diplomacy is at a dead end, but the alarm at this point, both in Washington and Pretoria, is sufficient to cause the two to undertake a joint diplomatic initiative. Misgivings in Pretoria that this initiative will fare no better than the Angolan undertaking will prove prescient.

An assiduous Vorster–Kissinger diplomacy throughout 1976 (from such venues as Lusaka, Pretoria, Bavaria, Geneva, New York, and Washington) attempts to salvage something from Rhodesia. However in a Lusaka speech (April 27, 1976), Secretary Kissinger, concurring in effect with new British initiatives, puts the United States behind a majority-rule solution. In November James Earl Carter is elected president of the United States, and the cadence of "one man–one vote" resonates throughout southern Africa with the vice president, Mr. Walter Mondale, and the U.S. ambassador to the United Nations, Mr. Andrew Young, leading the chorus.[45] Although the new administration in Washington had seized the moral ground, it would be the British who in the end would take the lead in the political-settlement phase. With the advent of the Thatcher government (March 1979), London convenes a Commonwealth Conference (again in Lusaka) with the queen presiding and logistical arrangements by South African Airways "as a courtesy to Mr. Kaunda." This, in turn, leads to Lancaster House (in London) where the British foreign secretary, Lord Carrington, presides over a five-month process longer than but not lacking in parallels with the Alvor Conference some five years earlier. A Carrington settlement of unabashed Westminster majoritarianism is imposed, locking in Mashona–Matabele tribal imbalance and shattering any last illusions Rhodesian Whites might have held about "being British after all." South African observers at Lancaster House saw the settlement as merely confirming Robert Mugabe's military dominance, which, however, needed London's *nihil obstat*.[46] The very British "unitary state" constitution (oblivious to African anomalies) issuing out of this revolutionary war was precisely the outcome they would be at pains to guard against in the revolutionary war in which they were now engaged.[47]

Self-proclaimed leader of the frontline states throughout the sixties and seventies (as well as of the Liberation Movement in Africa), Tanzania has failed to live up to its billing. For the ideologues of African socialism, Tanzania is the conspicuous failure of the postcolonial period. In the eighties putative leadership passes from "*Mwalimu*" (teacher), Julius Nyerere, to the hardly less ideological but more unpre-

dictable Robert Mugabe of Zimbabwe (surprise winner of the post–
Lancaster House elections). Disappointments with *ujamma* villages
and the great *uhuru* railroad aside, Tanzania possesses strategic significance for South Africa.[48] In the Pretorian calculus Tanzanian control
over its landlocked neighbors—by virtue of its Indian Ocean port of
Dar es Salaam and its placement at the top of the eastern land corridor
to the Cape—are factors that outlive transient political impacts such as
that of Nyerere.[49] A reality with which Mwalimu has had to come to
terms is the gravitational power of geographical propinquity, which
(intellectual affinity notwithstanding) draws both Mr. Kaunda and Mr.
Mugabe toward the Pretorian pole. Among the most powerful magnets
is South African Transport Services (SATS), the lusty, present-day
embodiment of the Cape Railway, which a century ago was itself
beginning to exert a strong gravitational pull southward.[50]

Zambia (along with Zaire) seeks the Atlantic at Lobito Bay over the
Benguela Railway and, alternatively, the Indian Ocean (although half
again as distant) at Dar es Salaam over the Tazara line. Problems
abound with both routes. Neither President Nyerere's showpiece railway (cut off from Chinese largess), with its limited capacity to handle
mineral traffic, nor the Benguela, following the better route but
plagued by the protracted Angola war, are competitive with the southern option. The Rhodesian/Zimbabwe rail system linked to SATS and
ports south of the Zambezi make realists out of otherwise ideological
presidents. Newly independent Zimbabwe finds its inherited Rhodesian Rail System a valuable legacy, but one that reinforces the pull of
Pretoria. Mr. Mugabe's dilemma is exemplified by his dual policy of
maintaining economic relations with the RSA while at the same time
severing political relations. A harsh rhetoric on all things South African is carefully calculated to enhance his frontline credentials without
at the same time impacting adversely on Zimbabwe/RSA bilateral
trade (the major trading partner for each).

Conducting a relationship with Harare at two levels is not without
its annoyances in Pretoria. For one thing it has permitted those in the
RSA who are so disposed (and they are legion) to remonstrate at length
against Mr. Botha's government as it sought to devise a contemporary
accommodation for a historically troubled relationship. The Botha regime, true to its African mind-set, was persuaded that Mr. Mugabe's
insistence on Mashona (ZANU) hegemony was, more or less, inevitable (it was all along implicit in the Lancaster House settlement) and the

only foreseeable option for stability in any case. Also potentially troublesome is an apparent payoff at the end of the eighties for dogged persistence on Moscow's part. A relationship spurned by Harare in the seventies showed steady improvement in the eighties. At the same time Mugabe is increasingly seen by Pretoria as the Castro of Africa just when Moscow may have had its fill of securing "loose cannon on deck." Still, the nub of the matter is whether there will be a Soviet buildup of Zimbabwe's armed forces. In addition there is Mr. Mugabe's own disposition to encourage the ANC and facilitate infiltration into the Republic. This entails pressure on "unfortunate Botswana" (a SADF viewpoint) as well as on Mozambique. Then there is his doctrinaire rejection of countersocialist currents in Zimbabwe; none of these factors bode well for stabilization of the country. In this connection London, ever a player where Zimbabwe is concerned, is expected by Pretoria to exert a quiet, steady influence in the upbringing of its Lancaster House offspring. In fact Mrs. Thatcher's stability across the whole southern Africa agenda may well prove a trump card on behalf of South Africa's regional objectives.

Lying in the strategic eastern corridor between Tanzania and the Republic, Mozambique may be the most significant of the contiguous states, inasmuch as it has potential as a buffer and, indeed, as an ally. Confronted with quite different situations in the two former Portuguese colonies, Pretoria (since 1975) has taken quite different stances with each. The Southwest Question did not permit the flexibility in the case of Angola that had been possible with Mozambique where bases of interdependence and mutual reinforcement have always existed. As in Angola, Pretoria observed the beginnings of insurgency in Mozambique, which in 1962 resulted in the formation of the Revolutionary Front for the Liberation of Mozambique (FRELIMO). It was of passing interest at the time that the very "western" Eduardo Mondlane assumed leadership and attracted attention, if not support, in the West. Notwithstanding this detail, FRELIMO quickly develops a jejune attachment to the People's Republic of China, facilitated in part through the good offices of Julius Nyerere. This explains (in part) an increasing radicalization of the Front and an ominous neglect of its own strong peasant–agriculture base. A still unexplained series of murders, including that of Mondlane, places the army commander, Samora Machel, at the head of the Front in 1969.[51]

PRC assistance to both Tanzania and Mozambique (i.e., FRELIMO) reaches its peak shortly thereafter but will then steadily decline in the seventies. By 1975, Machel is president of the Republic of Mozambique (*sans* election). Within a year the ZANU/ZANLA sanctuary in the north is established; while this facilitates PRC and Soviet support of Mugabe, the sanctuary, in turn, becomes a target of Rhodesian special forces. Maputo all but closes off the north to the rest of the world and joins in the sanctions against Rhodesia: the beginnings of an economic catastrophe are plain. Out of this setting the Mozambique National Resistance Movement (MNR or RENAMO) emerges and with the help of Rhodesia ("my enemy's enemy") launches attacks against the government of President Machel. The Soviet Union makes something of a grand entrance into East Africa at this point (1977) heralded by state visits on the part of USSR President Nikolai Podgorny. Buffeted by earlier ventures in West Africa, Moscow is nothing if not persistent in the face of perceived opportunities, especially when the PRC is leaving the field. Encouraged by the 1976 Angola success and undaunted by obvious discrepancies in "socialist conditions" in Tanzania and Mozambique (rather more African than Marxist–Leninist), the Soviets launch yet another assistance program predominantly military in nature. That the aid program should be military in character in the face of impending implosion in Mozambique did not escape the attention of Pretoria or for that matter most of the world. Unlike "most of the world" Pretoria would react but not precisely as expected in many quarters.

Mozambique opens on the vital Mozambique Channel and "the great island" Madagascar (the Malagasy Republic) through the Indian Ocean ports of Maputo, Beira, and Nacala. South Africa had occasion in the past (in the era of French and Portuguese colonialism) to be impressed with the strategic significance of this geography.[52] The new Botha government, with Portuguese and French barriers gone and a new "Imperial Power" entering Africa through Dar es Salaam and Maputo, was compelled to focus on the Mozambique front at the end of the seventies. The initial response, once Rhodesian forces were no longer active in Mozambique, was straightforward. In the period 1979–83 (the high-water mark of Soviet aid to Machel) South Africa supported "the enemy's enemy"—the MNR—encountering not only Soviet arms but Soviet personnel in the Mozambique bush. This effort was dilatory at best. It is yet another item in a mass of misinformation (if not disinformation) that SADF was bent on attaching itself to RENAMO and carrying it into Maputo on its shoulders! On the contrary it came easy to SADF (especially among Operations elements) to conjure up a Vietnam scenario of which they wanted no part.[53] SADF's undertakings from the outset were guided more by Intelligence considerations and the desire to have in-place assets. Charges of destabilizing Machel were greeted as a form of high humor! Instead, the precariousness of the regime (Soviet assistance was seen as compounding the ravages of drought, mismanagement, and corruption) and the absence of a viable alternative presented an opportunity to exploit a number of reinforcing factors.

The advent of FRELIMO in Mozambique did nothing to disturb the SATS connection with Maputo or the desire to restart Cabora-Bassa as an integral part of a southern Africa electricity grid controlled, to be sure, from Pretoria.[54] Nor did either side wish to disturb a longstanding pattern of Mozambique migrant labor in the Republic. (Not as visible was the émigré population in the Republic, adding significantly to the White contingent.) Early on in his tenure Mr. Botha had decided upon normalization with Maputo and was determined to launch a peace initiative. Privately encouraged by Washington (and others), P W Botha has his peace initiative under full power at the end of 1983. Throughout 1983, President Machel was under strong pressure from Western capitals (including Washington, which had just sent out Ambassador Peter de Vos) to respond to the Botha initiative. Discouraged by private talks in Moscow, Samora Machel decides to move toward "an agreement on nonaggression" with Pretoria. An intensive series of discussions is undertaken between Pretoria, Lisbon, and Maputo that will produce the Trilateral Agreement of Cape Town (May 2, 1984). The Cape Town agreement takes up the question of the Cabora-Bassa hydroelectric scheme and other matters on which the three governments will collaborate. Direct talks with the Machel regime, which begin in Swaziland in December and culminate in Maputo in February 1984, produce the N'komati Accord. It will be signed by Botha and Machel at the border town of Komatipoort on March 16, 1984.[55] (Those present for the occasion insist that the historic agreement was accompanied by a historic temperature reading, the SADF logistics effort barely achieving its objective of getting everyone, particularly Mrs. Elise Botha—wife of the State President—through the diplomatic ordeal!) The initial Swaziland talks had created four working groups: (1) Joint Security Working Group, (2) Joint Economic Working Group, (3) Cabora-Bassa Working Group, and (4) Joint Tourism Working Group. The N'komati Accord, in effect, converted the first of these into a Joint Security Commission with the charge to put the nonaggression agreement into practice. *Stabilization* measures would have to precede *normalization* measures.

The Joint Security Commission's immediate task was to clear away an irritant on each side: for South Africa this entailed elimination of the ANC sanctuary in Mozambique,[56] and for Mozambique elimination of RSA assistance to RENAMO. Up to this point in time—as much as its level of support and degree of enthusiasm would vary— Pretoria did little to disguise its playing of the RENAMO card. There were even suggestions that as N'komati approached "SADF—or someone—'loaded up' MNR."[57] Be that as it may, both sides were prepared to take the item off the agenda. Pretoria promised to talk with MNR leaders, assuming always that they could be reliably identified. In the Pretoria Declaration of October 3, 1984, the RSA formally accepted the role of mediator between Maputo and MNR. During the year Foreign Minister R F Botha undertook visits to "certain African governments" to advise them against providing further assistance to the resistance in Mozambique. It would not be long, however, before the euphoria of N'komati would dissipate as the enormity of the Mozambique crisis emerged. It was immediately evident that the economic dimensions outweighed the military and political. Again, from a South African official involved with the issue: "I have the feeling that the Soviets pulled out [of Mozambique], cutting their losses, with instructions to Machel to invite the South Africans in. . . . There is little in the way of basic infrastructure, next to no capital formation, nothing to attract South African business in terms of 'real demand'—Mozambique is a shambles!"[58] Against this assessment, however, Mr. Botha was moved by a longer term "vision" springing from factors of interdependence and mutual reinforcement. The realization of that vision would depend not only on the signatories to the N'komati Accord but on the outside world as well. As the summer of 1984 approached, a buoyant Mr. Botha, bolstered by the Lusaka and N'komati accords, flew off to Europe to engage the outside world in his vision. It would be his first direct engagement with that world as State President.

Notes

1. The political orientation of the former commander of Portuguese forces in Africa is the subject of debate. It is set forth to some extent in his own book

issued in the year of the coup: *Portugal and the Future* (Johannesburg: Perskor, 1974). See also A.J. Venter, *The Zambesi Salient: Conflict in Southern Africa* (London: Robert Hale, 1975); B.J. Oliver, *The Strategic Significance of Angola* (Pretoria: ISSUP 1984); and Howard J. Wiarda, *Transcending Corporatism? The Portuguese Corporative System and the Revolution of 1974* (Columbia: University of South Carolina Institute of International Studies, 1976). Venter quotes Spinola as calling for the development of an effective counterrevolution in the face of the revolution sweeping Africa. A conservative strategy that Spinola equates with Western thinking will not suffice; instead "an antireactionary counteroffensive is a necessity" (15). As we shall see South African strategists drawing upon a number of sources, arguably, will make Spinola's basic assessment their own.

2. For an unmatched study of the UNITA leader see Fred Bridgland, *Jonas Savimbi: A Key to Africa* (London: Coronet, 1987). Much utilized but early accounts of this phase of the Angolan conflict are John Marcum, *The Angolan Revolution*, vol. 2, *Exile Politics and Guerilla Warfare, 1962–76* (Cambridge: MIT Press, 1978); Colin Legum and Anthony Hodges, eds., *The War over Southern Africa* (New York: Africana, 1976); and Arthur J. Klinghoffer, *The Angolan War: A Study of Soviet Policy in the Third World* (Boulder: Westview, 1980). See also Gerard Chaliand, *The Struggle for Africa: Conflict of the Great Powers* (New York: St. Martin's Press, 1982); Stephen T. Hosmer and Thomas A. Wolfe, *Soviet Policy and Practice toward Third World Conflicts* (New York: D.C. Heath, 1983); and for clarification especially of the Portuguese role see the Public Broadcast System documentary *Angola* (Ottowa: Stornoway Productions, 1986). John Stockwell's contribution to this documentary is not entirely consistent with his *In Search of Enemies* (New York: W. W. Norton, 1978). However, see Theodore Shackley, *The Third Option: An American View of Counterinsurgency Operations* (New York: Reader's Digest, 1981). Finally, see two pieces by Alexander R. Alexiev: *UNITA and U.S. Policy in Angola* (Santa Monica: The Rand Corporation, 1987) and "The Soviet Stake in Angola: Origins, Evolution, Prospects," in *The Red Orchestra*, vol. 2, *The Case of Africa,* ed. Dennis L. Bark (Stanford: The Hoover Institution Press, 1988), 140–57. Alexiev indicates his reliance upon the PBS documentary *Angola* and its Canadian producer Kitson Vincent.

3. PBS, *Angola.* Like Mr. Alexiev the author met at length with "Kit" Vincent (producer of the *Angola* documentary) in 1987 especially concerning the latter's seminal interviews with Admiral Coutinho and Juan Benemelis of the Africa Section of the Cuban Foreign Ministry. Vincent's interviews provide what is undoubtedly the "hardest" information available. Vincent released to PBS in 1989 an updated edition of his documentary as well as a companion piece on Cuba. For an excellent recent summary of the Cuban role in Angola see W. Martin James III, "Cuban Involvement in the Angolan War: Implications for Lasting Peace in Southern Africa," *ISSUP Bulletin* (Pretoria) (April 1988).

4. Nathaniel Davis, "The Angolan Decision of 1975: A Personal Memoir," *Foreign Affairs* 57 (Fall 1987): 109–24. The personal memoir of Ambassador Davis is recommended to students as "must reading" inasmuch as it is a textbook exhibit of the "state syndrome"—in this instance where southern Africa is concerned. It will form again on the Angolan matter in 1985–86. Failing to carry the day, Mr. Davis resigns, but this does not result in a new viewpoint on the part of

his successor. See Neil Livingstone and Manfred von Nordheim, "The United States Congress and the Angolan Crisis," *Strategic Review* (Washington) 5 (April 1977): 34–43.

5. Feeling was still running high two years after the South African withdrawal from Angola. Speaking in Parliament on April 17, 1978, Mr. Botha reminded his colleagues, "They left us in the lurch. We are going to retell that story: the story must be told of how we, with their knowledge, went in there and operated in Angola with their knowledge, how they encouraged us to act and, when we had nearly reached the climax, we were ruthlessly left in the lurch by an undertaking that was broken." *Debates,* South Africa House of Assembly, col. 4852, quoted by M Hough and M van der Merve, eds., *Selected South African Strategic Perceptions* (Pretoria: ISSUP, 1988), 93 and 107. For stunning reinforcement of Mr. Botha's remarks see Fred Bridgland, "The Future of Angola," *South Africa International* 19 (July 1988): 28–37.

6. Jan Breytenbach, *Forged in Battle* (Cape Town: Saayman & Weber, 1986), 1. This is the personal account of the founder of SADF's premier Three-Two Battalion.

7. Ibid., 37.

8. Deon Fourie, "South Africa; The Evolving Experience," in *Defense Policy Formation, Towards Comparative Analysis,* ed. James M. Roherty (Durham: Carolina Academic Press, 1980), 104–5. On *Operation Savannah* see also Helmoed-Romer Heitman, *South African War Machine* (Johannesburg: CNA [Bison Books], 1985), 166–75; Hosmer and Wolfe, *Soviet Policy and Practice,* 79–88 and 224–25; and South African Defense Force Headquarters, *Nature and Extent of the SADF's Involvement in the Angolan Conflict* (February 3, 1977), Pretoria. The official history of *Operation Savannah* has been written but not yet released by SADF.

9. Professor Deon Geldenhuys of Rand Afrikaans University (Johannesburg) is perhaps South Africa's closest student of this particular matter. See especially Deon Geldenhuys and H Kotze, "P.W. Botha as Decision-Maker," in *Politikon* 12 (June 1985): 30–42, and D de Villiers and I de Villiers, *P.W.* (Cape Town: Tafelberg, 1984), 124–25.

10. This is the title of a lecture delivered by Gen. Magnus M de M Malan, newly appointed minister of Defense, before the Institute of Strategic Studies, University of Pretoria, September 3, 1980. It reflects the fact that the recently elected Botha government had been at work defining "the threat" well before taking power.

11. In an era characterized by unprecedented distortions of reality, perhaps most egregiously in the case of South Africa, a classic instance is the construct of Pretoria committed to the destabilization of neighboring (frontline) states. The contention today is all but immune to antidote, constantly repeated even by those in the highest quarters who know full well it is nonsense. Why those who are quite able to distinguish between cross-border operations aimed at the sanctuaries of the African National Congress and Southwest African People's Organization *and not at the host governments* fail to do so is one of many anomalies in the South African story. It is necessary to emphasize therefore that Pretoria's foremost foreign-policy goal is interaction with *stable,* nonthreatening neighbors! For a recent extended statement from Pretoria on this matter see Gen. Magnus M de

M Malan, "The Contemporary Strategic Situation in Southern Africa," lecture delivered at the University of Pretoria, November 2, 1988, reprinted in *Paratus* 39 (December 1988): 12–15 and 39.

12. *Africa Insight,* published by the Africa Institute of South Africa (Johannesburg), maintains a continuing compilation. A particularly unsettling coup occurred in Nigeria at the end of 1983. The just reelected President Shehu Shagari was overthrown in a military coup by Gen. Mohammed Buhari. While Buhari may well have eliminated a good deal of corruption (along with Shagari!), inevitably, to cite the laconic words of *The Economist* (London), "a new lot will be at the door, eager to be corrupted" (January 7–13, 1984, 12). South African analysts were not prepared to quarrel with this British assessment of a former colony. They were probably the first in the world (circa 1980) to discern the outlines of a looming crisis of Africa and to note the Soviets "bogging down in Africa." A sharp contraction in the volume of African trade at the beginning of the decade was among the signals of a broader crisis. The transition in the Soviet role in Africa coincides with this downturn in economic activity. It is upon more extended analysis that Pretoria finds the root cause in the African state.

13. See chapter 6 for further discussion on this point and the transition from the Brezhnev to the Gorbachev era insofar as Africa is concerned.

14. The South African analysts would contend that a 1983 Rand assessment that "[w]e may expect to see continued Soviet arms supply and training support for *guerrilla movements conducting so-called wars of national liberation* especially in Africa" (italics mine) was already overtaken by events. In the face of African reverses, the Soviets were shifting to new and more sophisticated modalities of warfare. See Hosmer and Wolfe, *Soviet Policy and Practice,* 169. For a discussion of the "ANC war," which Pretoria does not treat as an insurgency, see chapter 4.

15. Seth Singleton cites an impressive body of Soviet literature displaying a high degree of frustration in Moscow at the end of the Brezhnev era with African political and social structures. Soviet "Africanists," echoing much Western analysis, conclude that the military structure alone reflects society and, more important, is the only institution capable of seizing state power. See two papers: (1) "African Arms and the Gains of Socialism: Soviet Policy and Perspective," presented to the Inter-University Seminar on the Armed Forces and Society, Chicago, October 21–23, 1983, and (2) "The Future of Soviet Influence in Africa," report to the National Council for Soviet and East European Research, Washington, D.C. (September 1987).

16. Strictly construed, the term refers to the heights outside Pretoria where the *Voortrekker* monument and various defense facilities are located. We use it here to designate the regime as a whole.

17. One will encounter assertions in the literature such as the following: "Pretoria is flying blind in dealing with the *perceived Soviet onslaught*" (italics mine). See Helen Kitchen and Michael Clough, *The United States and South Africa: Realities and Red Herrings* (Washington, D.C.: CSIS, 1984), 28. If South Africans were clear on one point it was that *die aanslag* was far more than a Soviet undertaking. However, South Africans have never indulged themselves in the luxury of thinking their statements would be carefully analyzed, much less understood.

18. The strategic mind-set of South Africans is one of distant horizons. It is quite simply a mistake, in this context, to allude to a *laager* mentality. This is to confuse cultural defense of the *volk* with politico-military imperatives of state. This confusion of two altogether different matters is made not just in the Western press but among presumably more serious analysts. Just as mistaken is the variation on this theme that the thrust of the Botha regime was a "Fortress South Africa" rather than a regionalist thrust. The imagery of the Boers circling the wagons at every opportunity continues its spell, however, and stands as one of the interesting features of the South Africa story.

19. If one treads carefully, it is plausible to suggest that a contemporary school of strategic thought exists in South Africa today, the members of which are to be found in civilian and military life, inside and outside government. Certainly Prof. Michael H H Louw has had a considerable influence in this respect through his foundation work *National Security: A Modern Approach* (Pretoria: ISSUP, 1978), and perhaps more important, through those, directly or indirectly, who are in his intellectual debt. Outside of government, Michael Hough, Deon F S Fourie, H V du Toit, and others more concerned with political/psychological modalities of warfare are making an important contribution to our understanding of that contemporary phenomenon "revolutionary warfare." (See especially chapter 5.)

20. The two works most closely studied are *Introduction to Strategy* (London: Faber & Faber, 1965) and *Strategy of Action* (London: Faber & Faber, 1967). In the same vein and also influential is B.H. Liddell Hart, *Strategy* (New York: Praeger, 1968). Important mediators of Beaufreism at the Defense Staff College (*Voortrekkerhoogte*) in the past decade are Maj. Gen. D J Mortimer and Deon F S Fourie. General Beaufre came out to South Africa in 1974 at the behest of the South African defense attaché in Paris to lecture at the Defense Staff College. His discussion of indirect-strategy themes made a particular impact.

21. *Studies in War and Peace* (New York: Viking Press, 1970), 182. That strategic analysis is inextricably linked to the neorealist paradigm is accepted matter-of-factly within the SA contemporary school. See Colin Gray, *Strategic Studies and Public Policy* (Lexington: University of Kentucky Press, 1982), 188–89. Likewise, the inextricable connection of national policy and national strategy is a given. In his foreword to Harry G. Summers's *On Strategy: The Vietnam War in Context* (Carlisle Barracks, Pa.: The U.S. Army War College, 1981), Maj. Gen. Jack Merritt writes that "its central thesis is that a lack of appreciation of military theory and military strategy—especially the relationship between military strategy and national policy led to a faulty definition of the nature of that war" (vii). South Africans were at great pains to properly define the nature of the war in which they are now engaged and to understand the relationship of policy and strategy.

22. See chapter 4.

23. Malan, "The Contemporary Strategic Situation."

24. The *Rand Daily Mail* (Johannesburg), August 16, 1979, reported that Mr. Botha (in his first speech before a National Party Congress) "pulled together the broad outlines of his vision for the 1980s, but stopped short of spelling out the finer details of his plan for a *total national strategy*" (italics mine). The Prime Minister discussed "twelve broad principles," which would become a "twelve point plan." See *The Twelve Point Plan* (Johannesburg: National Party Information Service, 1981). Submitted to Parliament in March 1980, they can be found in

South Africa, *Hansard* (March 1980), col. 3222. The Twelve Points include the following:

1. The recognition and acceptance of the existence of multinationalism and of minorities in South Africa.
2. The acceptance of vertical differentiation with the built-in principle of self-determination on as many levels as possible.
3. The establishment of constitutional structures that provide for the full independence of the various Black nations in the Republic of South Africa, meaningful consolidation of the Black states and areas, and the acceptance of a socioeconomic program aimed at the development of such Black states and areas.
4. The division of power among White South Africans, the Coloureds, and the South African Indians within a system of consultation and joint responsibility where common interests are at issue.
5. The acceptance of the principle that each group should have its own schools and communities where possible, as fundamental to happy social circumstances.
6. The willingness to work together as equals and consult on issues of common concern while maintaining a healthy balance between the rights of the individual and those of the community, and the removal of unnecessary hurtful forms of discrimination.
7. The maintenance of effective decision making by the state, founded on a strong defense force and police force to ensure orderly government as well as a sound and efficient administration.
8. The maintenance of free enterprise as the basis of our economic policy.
9. The recognition of economic interdependence of the population groups of the Republic of South Africa as well as the acceptance of the properly planned utilization of manpower.
10. The goal of a peaceful constellation of Southern African states respecting one another's cultural heritage, traditions, and ideals.
11. As far as possible, South Africa must follow a policy of neutrality in the confrontation between the superpowers and give priority to her own interests.
12. South Africa's determination to defend itself against outside intervention in every practical way possible.

25. Mr. Botha would have nothing of "reform by stealth," it being suited neither to his temperament nor the exigencies of the South African scene. In September 1981, Prof. Samuel Huntington, having taken up "the politics of development," came out to South Africa to discuss strategies for transitioning to (as he put it) "a postapartheid system." (See his "Reform and Stability in South Africa," *International Security* 6 [Spring 1982]: 11.) Huntington recommended a broad body of literature and an even broader array of strategic and tactical suggestions to his audience. He went awry, however, when he insisted that "it is of the essence of the reformer that he must employ ambiguity, concealment, and deception concerning his goals." This would enable the reformer, inter alia, "to pacify conservatives by minimizing the significance of any one change and by implying that each proposed change . . . will be his last" (14–15). "The Professor," as a senior government official put it later, "did not listen very well to our presentation

of details of the local situation." Pacification of conservatives in the local setting was neither possible nor desired. The Strategy would be candid, clear, and unequivocal if inevitably slow in its progress. In a second visit to South Africa, Huntington would be less impressed with "reform by stealth" and more impressed with "reform by imposition from the top" in this unique setting. See his "Whatever Has Gone Wrong with Reform," *Die Suid-Afrikaan* (Winter 1986), Stellenbosch. Mr. Botha would follow neither path but instead a path prescribed by "political talent" for the local situation.

26. James M. Roherty, "Beyond Limpopo and Zambezi: South Africa's Strategic Horizons," *South Africa International* 14 (July 1983): 320–39, and *The Indian Ocean: Perspectives on a Strategic Arena,* ed. W.W. Dowdy and R.B. Trood (Durham, N.C.: Duke University Press, 1985), 267–81. Conventional demarcations of African regions and subregions may not be pertinent as RSA planners will not be constrained by such conventions.

27. Prof. William Gutteridge, among the ablest of scholars on South African security issues, writes that "the military danger lies not in the threat from indigenous black African states . . . (but in) a situation which would inextricably enmesh foreign forces or give them an excuse for activating an existing presence." See his "The Black African Military in the 1980's—Implications for South Africa," *Strategic Review* (Pretoria) (June 1981), 8. This differs from the SADF view, which does not contemplate the *direct deployment* of great power forces in southern Africa. If that were to occur, it would entail countervailing action from outside Africa and would quickly become transmuted into an East–West issue.

28. Perhaps the best study of South Africa Police to date is Max Morris, *Armed Conflict in Southern Africa* (Cape Town: Jeremy Spence, 1974). Morris underscores the historical function of SAP as border infantry—a role now largely supplanted by SADF. He notes, for example, that it was SAP infantry that was active in Rhodesia in the early seventies. For an account of SAP's intelligence activities in Namibia in the late seventies, *Operation Crowbar,* see Heitman, *South African War Machine,* 110–13. Gen. P J Coetzee (then commissioner of SAP), in a lecture on "Urban Terror and Counter-Measures" delivered to the Conference on Revolutionary Warfare and Counter-Insurgency at the University of Pretoria, June 28, 1983, stated that SAP "experience in Southwest Africa . . . proves the comparative success of the use of *specialized police tactics* and task forces in relation to more conventional, larger scale military operations . . . especially when dealing with un-uniformed gangs" (italics mine). On the question of SAP/SADF relations in dealing with revolutionary war within the Republic see chapter 5.

29. For a detailed and informed account of SADF's cross-border operations in this period see Heitman, *South African War Machine,* 134–65. There will be six major operations: *Reindeer* (1978); *Safron* (1979); *Sceptic* (1980); *Protea* and *Daisy* (1981); and *Askari* (1983–84). A number of minor operations and sweeps will be conducted in this period as well, some of the more specialized by Three-Two Battalion. For further discussion of these operations and the development of SADF as a premier counterinsurgency force, see chapter 4.

30. *Debates,* South Africa House of Assembly (September 21, 1981), cols. 4671–72. (Hough, *Selected Perceptions,* 78–81.)

31. The code name *Askari* is SADF's tribute to its "loyal Black soldiers," drawn from the "loyal Black soldiers" of Col. Paul von Lettow-Vorbeck, legend-

ary guerrilla commander of Imperial Germany in East Africa during World War I, from whom Jan Smuts and other South Africans learned much. See Edmund P. Hoyt, *Guerilla* (London: Macmillan, 1981). Hoyt has an excellent bibliography not only on Lettow-Vorbeck but on guerrilla warfare in Africa.

32. *Debates*, South Africa House of Assembly, cols. 132–33 (Hough, *Selected Perceptions*, 40). Throughout the early eighties researchers at the Institute for Strategic Studies (University of Pretoria) were developing studies on Namibia and Angola that would be reflected in government statements. See, for example, N. Marais, "The United Nations and Southwest Africa," and H.P. Potgieter, "The Southwest Africa People's Organization," both in the December 1981 number of ISSUP's *Strategic Review*.

33. Typical of the skepticism of the period was a report in the *Pretoria News* (May 18, 1985) that the RSA government "was enraged by a secret US plan for SWA/Namibia" that dropped total Cuban withdrawal. Officials were not prepared to believe that Mr. Crocker could leverage all of those involved from Luanda to Havana to Moscow, never mind Pretoria. As it developed, a fierce new military phase (1985–88) would be required over and above the most diligent diplomacy. (See chapter 6.)

34. For a summary of the situation at this point by Maj. Gen. George L Meiring, SADF (GOC in Southwest), see his "Current SWAPO Activity in South West Africa," in *Strategic Review* (Pretoria) (June 1985), 8–18.

35. The poignancy of that appeal (to Washington in the Carter years) is patent in *A Conversation with Ernest Mulato: The Political and Military Struggle in Angola* (Washington, D.C.: AEI, 1979).

36. Fred Bridgland excoriates Western liberals for their condescension and neglect of Angola—most pointedly with regard to the failure of Washington to demand free and open elections as specified in the Alvor Accord. His stinging question is, Why elections in Namibia and not in Angola? See "The Future of Angola," 28, and PBS, *Angola*.

37. (New York: W.W. Norton, 1962), 29. Also, William R. Lewis, *Great Britain and Germany's Lost Colonies, 1914–1919* (London: Oxford University Press, 1967). On the German movement during the interwar years to reclaim the African colonies, see Wolfe Schmokle, *Dream of Empire* (New Haven: Yale University Press, 1964).

38. Mackinder, *Democratic Ideals and Reality*, 81. Mackinder did note that "the Cape lay far removed from all overland threat throughout the nineteenth century; (adding) *practically South Africa was an island*" (italics mine) (135). The latter observation would be the basis for maritime-oriented strategies of twentieth-century South Africa.

39. *Debates*, South Africa Senate (1940–41), cols. 13–14 (September 12, 1940), quoted by Richard Dale, "South Africa: The Legacy of the Imperial-Commonwealth Connection," in *Defense Policy Formation*, ed. Roherty, 78–79. This was also a theme of the 1929 Rhodes Memorial Lectures delivered by Smuts at Oxford. See W.K. Hancock, *Smuts*, vol. 2, *The Fields of Force, 1919–1950* (Cambridge: London University Press, 1968), 221–29.

40. Ibid., 152. For a contemporary South African view see Colin Vale, "South Africa and Zimbabwe: Too Close for Comfort," *South Africa International* 12 (October 1981): 357–74, also n. 29.

41. Hancock, *Fields of Force*, 154.
42. Hough, *Selected Strategic Perceptions*, 47–48.
43. Ibid. For perhaps the best discussion of the theme of "the imperial factor lingering on in Rhodesia" and as a warning not to draw any parallels between the Rhodesian and South African situations, see Martin Chanock, *Unconsummated Union: Britain, Rhodesia, and South Africa, 1900–1945* (Manchester University Press, 1977).
44. The meeting—the first of two between Mr. Vorster and Mr. Kaunda—took place in a railway car "poised midway between Rhodesia and Zambia on a bridge high above the Zambezi gorge." See Robert Jaster, "The Rocky Road to Lancaster House: Lessons from the Rhodesian Conflict," in *South Africa International* 18 (October 1987): 112. This is a useful account of the political-settlement phase of the Rhodesian war but at the same time a premature estimate of the success of that process. For a fuller account of Mr. Vorster's diplomacy see Deon Geldenhuys, *The Diplomacy of Isolation: South African Foreign Policy Making* (New York: St. Martin's Press, 1984).
45. Mrs. Jeane Kirkpatrick, who would hold the UN post in the first Reagan term, has written that the Carter administration was notable for its "predilection for policies that violated the strategic and economic interests of the United States" and for its "moralism which rendered it especially vulnerable to charges of hypocrisy." Whatever else might be said of Mrs. Kirkpatrick's tenure at the UN, she avoided these particular pitfalls. See her *Dictatorship and Double Standards: Rationalism and Reason in Politics* (New York: Simon and Schuster, 1982).
46. The author interviewed Maj. Gen. Ian MacLean (commander of the Rhodesian Army) at his headquarters in King George VI Barracks, Salisbury, in August 1979 (Lt. Gen. Peter Walls, commander of Combined Operations, was already in London for the Lancaster House talks) and can offer the following corroboration for the South African judgment. "We are tired, very tired after ten years," General MacLean acknowledged. "We have no support from abroad"—cumulatively over a decade sanctions make themselves felt—"it is time to talk" was the gist of a weary commander's remarks over tea. "We are professional soldiers," he concluded, "we shall be prepared to support whatever government ensues." Today Sandy MacLean resides in South Africa. For an account of the Rhodesian War (going well beyond a regimental history) see Peter Stiff and Ron Reid Daly, *Selous Scouts: Top Secret War* (Alberton: Galago, 1987); J.K. Cilliers, *Counter-Insurgency in Rhodesia* (London: Croom Helm, 1985); Lewis Gann and T.H. Hendricksen, *The Struggle for Zimbabwe: Battle in the Bush* (New York: Praeger; 1981); and Paresh Pandya, "Foreign Support to ZANU and ZANLA during the Rhodesian War," *Strategic Review* (Pretoria) (November 1987): 1–31. For an intelligence-oriented account by the late director-general of Rhodesia's Central Intelligence Organization, see Ken Flower, *Serving Secretly: An Intelligence Chief on Record, Rhodesia into Zimbabwe, 1964 to 1981* (London: John Murray, 1987).
47. Lancaster House has been widely acclaimed in the West as a model for negotiating the end of a revolutionary war. See Henry Wiseman and Alastair Taylor, *From Rhodesia to Zimbabwe: The Politics of Transition* (New York: Pergamon, 1981), and Jeffrey Davidow, *A Peace in Southern Africa: The Lancaster House Conference on Rhodesia, 1979* (Boulder: Westview, 1984). The Botha

government, however, would draw its own lessons from the Rhodesian experience in conducting its counterrevolution not least from the settlement phase. For a lucid discussion of the latter, see N. Marais, *The Political Dimension of the Settlement Phase during a Revolutionary War* (Pretoria: ISSUP, 1982). Also in a cautionary vein are Richard Hodder-Williams, "Conflict in Zimbabwe: The Matabeleland Problem," *Conflict Studies* 151 (London, 1983), and David Willers, "Uneasy Neighbors: Zimbabwe and South Africa," *South Africa Foundation News* (December 1983), Johannesburg.

48. See Michael Sinclair, *The Strategic Significance of Tanzania* (Pretoria: ISSUP, 1979), and Richard Hall and Hugh Peyman, *The Great Uhuru Railway* (London: Victor Gallancz, 1977). One of the aspects of Mwalimu's architectonic socialism for Africa was a vast resettlement scheme of Tanzania's scattered population into *ujamma* villages. It ran contrary to deeper strains in the Tanzanian people. As for the Tanzania-Zambia Railway Authority (TAZARA), while it kept "the great *uhuru* railway" in better condition than the Benguela (in Angola), it has been far too short of locomotives and wagons to realize the port potential of Dar es Salaam. Finally, on the political legacy of Julius Nyerere, he leaves behind one constitutionally authorized party—*Chama Cha Mapinduzi* (CCM). In the presidential elections of October 27, 1985, Tanzania's nine million eligible voters had one name on the ballot for the sole party (CCM) on the ballot. Mr. Ali Hassan Mwinyi had no difficulty in winning. Such situations throughout Africa permit Mr. Roelf "Pik" Botha, minister of Foreign Affairs of the RSA, to ask Western reporters from time to time. "which African state is it that you would have us emulate?"

49. Sinclair, *Strategic Significance of Tanzania,* writes that "Tanzania is the most suitably located state in relation to the southern African region . . . the primary origin of (its) political influence is its *political strategic location on the African continent*" (italics mine) (74 and 79). There is a real military factor in the calculus, however. Apart from Dar es Salaam as a *point d'appui* for the Soviet Union, President Nyerere has put troops into Uganda and, more important, Mozambique. Today it is Mr. Mugabe's Zimbabwe National Army troops that guard railway corridors in Mozambique—a measure of repayment for FRELIMO assistance in the seventies!

50. Cecil Rhodes, "thinking of continents," pushed the Cape Railway through the Bechuanaland Corridor between German Southwest Africa and Boer republics. From Kimberley the line would go to Vryburg and Mafeking, through the eastern Kalahari to Bulawayo, and ultimately north to coal (Wankie) and the copperbelt. Rhodes insisted, likewise, on the most direct connection between Salisbury (Harare) and the sea over the Mozambique border (via Umtali), connecting with Portuguese trackage to the port of Beira. (This was the "direct" route to Europe by way of the Suez Canal!) The modern era was initiated in 1956 with four hundred miles of new track from Gwelo (on the Salisbury–Bulawayo line) to the port of Lourenço Marques (Maputo), staying north and east of the Limpopo. Finally, in 1974 the first direct connection with South Africa was established from a point on the recent Gwelo–Maputo line (Rutenga) to the SATS railhead at Beit Bridge on the Limpopo. Eighty years earlier Rhodes's strategy was to find a safe corridor between German and Boer "north to the hinterland." In the seventies the Rhodesians were compelled to reverse the strategy and seek a safe corridor south

between newly independent Botswana and Mozambique. The urgency with which the project was undertaken is attested by the fact that the 140-kilometer span between Rutenga and Beit Bridge was put down in ninety-three days! See John Hanford, *A Portrait of an Economy under Sanctions 1965–75* (Salisbury, Rhodesia: Mercury Press, 1976), 175. Hanford includes an indictment of economists along with much useful data! More readily available and more recent with much useful data as well is K.H. Butts and P.R. Thomas, *The Geopolitics of Southern Africa: South Africa as Regional Superpower* (Boulder: Westview, 1986).

51. See Thomas H. Hendricksen, "The People's Republic of Mozambique," in *The Red Orchestra*, 158–79.

52. In 1942, Smuts underscored the significance of Mozambique, the Channel, and Madagascar for South African security with his insistence to London that he occupy not just Diégo-Suarez but the entire island. Japanese naval activity in the Indian Ocean in the same year has since been assessed as inconsequential from the standpoint of affecting the war's outcome. South Africans, however, were impressed with the fact that they were not out of the reach of a major naval power. By 1971 Britain completes its withdrawal from "east of Suez" and abrogates the Simonstown Agreement in 1975. As for the continuing French presence in the Indian Ocean, a SADF officer remarked to the author that "it serves only French purposes." On the theme of the Soviet Union as the new imperial power in the field, see Colin Vale, "Boer War III: The Soviet Imperial Factor in South Africa," *South Africa International* 13 (January 1983): 172–88. Professor Vale's article is, inter alia, a commentary on Schreuder.

53. After the signing of the N'komati Accord (March 1984) when SADF was still being charged with assisting RENAMO, one somewhat exasperated officer offered the following: "What the hell, we can't even find half of them—and if we did we would have no good idea of who the leaders are!"

54. One of the earliest actions of the Botha regime was to sign a transportation agreement with Mozambique (February 1979). To help facilitate this agreement, construction of the largest rail-marshaling yard in the southern hemisphere began at Benoni in the Transvaal. Yet another at Bapsfontein was completed in 1982. For an account of economic relations at that point see Theodore Malan, "Mozambique and Zambia's Economic Relations with South Africa," in *Strategic Review* (Pretoria) (January 1981): 2–13, and for an early study of the Cabora-Bassa project see Keith Middlemas, *Cabora-Bassa: Engineering and Politics in Southern Africa* (London: Weidenfeld & Nicolson, 1975).

55. A case study of prepossessions tenaciously held, of suspension of belief, and ultimately, astonishment at the turn of events is offered in the coverage of Glenn Frankel of the *Washington Post* during the years 1983–86. For example, on February 5, 1984, he indicates astonishment at Machel's turnabout and the impending N'komati Accord but continues in disbelief that Botha seeks a *modus vivendi* with Mozambique! Mr. William Claiborne, subsequently dispatched to southern Africa for the *Post,* was prepared to view the complex scene through different eyes. Perhaps even more astonishing is the new thinking of the *New York Times* following the expulsion of its correspondent from South Africa. The *Times* is once again represented in southern Africa following frank discussions between the RSA ambassador to Washington (Dr. Piet Koornhof) and *NYT* editors in New York. One unfortunate result of the kind of coverage provided on south-

ern Africa by both the *Post* and the *Times,* until very recently, is that it tells us more about the respective newspapers than it does about the region. From a research standpoint this is a great pity. Finally, a curiosity of sorts must be noted, namely, the discrepancy between the editorial page of the *Wall Street Journal* and the columns of its correspondents in southern Africa. The two appear to have different agendas!

56. Bent as it was on achieving a nonaggression agreement with Machel, Pretoria would not refrain from cross-border operations aimed at the ANC sanctuary in Mozambique. SADF initiated such counter-ANC operations on January 30, 1981, hitting an ANC facility in the Maputo suburb of Matola. It "recrossed the Matola threshold" two months before start-up of the negotiations, hitting Maputo on October 17, 1983. In the interim it struck Maseru (Lesotho) on December 9, 1982. In each instance Pretoria was at pains to limit its strike to ANC targets but warning the host government at the same time that it could not tolerate such sanctuaries. Machel ordered the ANC out of Mozambique following N'komati for the most part into the arms of Kenneth Kaunda. ANC "External" took up headquarters at Kabwe just north of Lusaka. See Deon Geldenhuys, "Recrossing the Matola Threshold: The 'Terrorist' Factor in South Africa's Regional Relations," *South Africa International* 13 (January 1983): 152–71. We will discuss the counter-ANC war in chapters 3 and 5.

57. While wary of miring down in a Vietnam bog (through extended assistance to RENAMO), SADF was equally uncertain about the reliability or viability of FRELIMO. Prior to N'komati it cautioned that an agreement would be premature—that the Mozambique Question should be left wide open. They were overruled at the State Security Council (SSC) level and directed to be good soldiers. An ill-advised and abortive undertaking in the Seychelles (1981) contributed to a sober resolution of the RENAMO matter.

58. In contrast an indication of high expectations, if not euphoria, following N'komati would be found in the foreign ministry.

3 MEETING THE MANAGEMENT REQUIREMENTS

> The Defense of the RSA is not solely the responsibility of the Department of Defense. On the contrary, the maintenance of the sovereignty of the RSA is the combined responsibility of all government departments.
>
> —RSA Department of Defense, *White Paper on Defense, 1977*

The Afrikaner bureaucracy, unquestionably, is South Africa's foremost caste. Created by a populist, labor-oriented Afrikaner political elite, it was designed, as was indeed the apartheid system itself, to accommodate a steadily urbanizing White working class.[1] Throughout his public career P W Botha was a keen if sometimes impatient observer of this monolith. Possessed not only of strong convictions but of political insight, he appreciated the enormity of the obstacle in his path. A frontal attack on a critical component of the National Party political base would not do. Mr. Verwoerd's "edifice" could be (and would be) more readily dismantled! At a minimum, however, the bureaucracy would have to be circumvented if the Great Undertaking was to have any chance of success. Left to themselves, Mr. Botha was convinced, the executive line agencies would only become more lethargic. In the face of the Onslaught, what was required was imagination and innovation. The accepted pattern of the past was no longer acceptable. PW moved with alacrity to install a new driving force—a National Security Management System—whose beginnings he had been pushing[2] with John Vorster for some years. The NSMS would be a revolution in its own right, reflecting the management style of the new Prime Minister, and, more important, the urgency of reform in yet another aspect of Afrikanerdom.

The Battle for the Intelligence Brief

John Vorster's role in establishing the foundations of the present-day South African security system has been overshadowed by that of his successor. Yet it is important for what follows to review his tenure not only as Prime Minister but as minister of Justice. Mr. Vorster was at the center of a battle that has been key to the control of the security system: namely, "the battle for the intelligence brief." How he left the intelligence situation to his successor in 1978 is our entryway into the Botha management system.

South Africa did not have a "foreign intelligence capability" of its own in the years between World War II and the establishment of the Republic (May 31, 1961). Like other overseas dominions during this period, it relied upon London to furnish "appropriate information" (which in any case would not include intelligence concerning other British territories, such as the Rhodesias, Nyassaland, and the High Commission territories). It is only with departure from the Commonwealth—and the tumult following Sharpeville (March 21, 1960)—that a rudimentary (military) intelligence department of some twelve officers is established "to sift chaff from wheat."[3] Development is slow during the sixties as the fledgling intelligence section of the South African Defense Force (SADF) focuses its attention on the Portuguese colonies and on Southwest Africa. As we have seen, the People's Liberation Army of Namibia (PLAN), military wing of Southwest Africa People's Organization (SWAPO), makes its first forays into Ovamboland (Namibia) in 1965–66. (Chapter 2.) Initially this is treated as a police matter, and counter-PLAN operations are given over to the South African Police (SAP) and its organic intelligence unit (Security Police).[4] SADF begins to involve itself with the bush war in Southwest by 1971, but it is only in 1974 when the Portuguese barrier comes down that it "takes responsibility for the security of Southwest."[5] Security Police would continue to have an intelligence role in the operational area, however. This factor and, more important, the establishment of yet another intelligence service will create, inter alia, a coordination problem.

Security Police activity inside the Republic reaches a peak in the first five years (1961–66) that it will not again attain until the mid-eighties. It began with an effective, and widely noted, dispatch of subversive elements, the high point of which was *Operation May-*

ibuye[6] (July 1963). This undertaking gathered up a number of individuals already well known in South Africa, and who would become even better known over the course of time.[7] The major objects of inquiry at this point included the banned South Africa Communist Party (SACP)[8] as well as the banned African National Congress (ANC), the latter having seen fit to launch its military wing (*Umkonto we Sizwe* or "MK") on December 16, 1961 (the anniversary date of Dingaan's Day, commemorating the Battle of Blood River in 1838). Similarly, the Pan African Congress (PAC), the African Resistance Movement (ARM),[9] and the National Union of South African Students (NUSAS) came in for close scrutiny by Security Police. During this period SAP was located in the Ministry of Justice, while today it is in the Ministry of Law and Order. The then commissioners of police, J M Keevy and the popular "Jimmy" Kruger,[10] reported directly to the minister of Justice, then B J Vorster—but there is an anomaly. The minister of Justice and the chief of Security Police, one Brigadier Hendrik van den Bergh, were fellow internees during World War II and had formed a close friendship.[11] Out of this friendship a partnership emerged that would become a prominent feature of South African government during the sixties and seventies. The two men made the matter of internal security their own and rapidly came to appreciate the reciprocal character of intelligence and counterintelligence. Under "Lang Hendrik" Security Police took on a foreign-intelligence role underscored by SAP's deployment to Southwest Africa and later Rhodesia. Moreover, the war against ANC would go on both inside and outside the Republic, and Security Police would conduct that war in both theaters as, ultimately, would SADF.

Without gaining higher office Mr. Vorster could not act on the matter of how best to organize ("coordinate") an expanding intelligence enterprise. The opportunity to do so came suddenly: the assassination of Hendrik Verwoerd in September 1966 (not the first attempt)[12] vaulted the minister of Justice into the office of Prime Minister. Mr. Vorster asks Pieter Willem Botha, who had been named minister of Defense by Mr. Verwoerd shortly before his death, to continue in that portfolio. Mr. Botha will do so for the next twelve years and, frequently at odds with his Prime Minister, will become the dominant defense figure in the country. This dominance will not extend to intelligence, however—at least while the Vorster–van den Bergh partnership is in power. Vorster, as we have seen, had been persuaded (in large part by van den Bergh) that the Republic's intelligence needs were not being met by a small military intelligence section along with even the most effective Security Police. A new approach was required.

Mr. Vorster's first legislative step was to include a provision establishing a Bureau of State Security (BOSS) in the *Public Service Amendment Act, 1969*. The act, however, did not provide a full brief for the new intelligence agency; consequently, in the following year the Prime Minister convened a commission to inquire into "certain intelligence aspects of state security."[13] The findings of the Potgieter Commission are incorporated in the *Security Intelligence and State Security Council Act, No. 64, 1972*. Along with the *Defense Act* this seminal piece of legislation is a pillar of the South African security system. The 1972 act provides for a State Security Council (SSC)—the only cabinet committee with a statutory base—and an ample "brief" both for BOSS and Military Intelligence. The SSC has two mandates:

(1) *to advise* the government (at the request of the Prime Minister) regarding (a) the formulation of national-security policy and strategy, and the manner in which same shall be implemented, and (b) a policy to combat any particular threat to the security of the Republic; and

(2) *to determine intelligence priorities*.[14] (Italics mine.) It should be noted that while the SSC will advise the government on (national security) policy issues, it will determine intelligence priorities. Intelligence is placed at the apex of government—a position it retains to this day, albeit under changed auspices.

Under its brief, BOSS was to identify any threat or potential threat to the Republic and in pursuance thereof collect, evaluate, correlate, and interpret national-security intelligence. It was to submit "national intelligence estimates" (NIEs) to the government. (On this last point there is consensus that NIEs from BOSS went to John Vorster and then to elements of the government as he directed. This is not to imply that the minister of Defense did not see most of them.) Finally, BOSS was called upon to propose "*policy* relating to national security intelligence" (italics mine). Mr. Vorster wanted BOSS to have the widest possible brief and the new agency received just that. However, Military Intelligence received at the same time, in the same act, a wide brief as well, laying up problems for the future as if by design. Both would have a foreign-intelligence operations role; both would have a counterintelligence role; both would collect, correlate, and interpret;

and both would submit estimates to the government. Angola would soon provide a meeting point for two agencies on a collision course.

Military Intelligence focused on Angola with increasing intensity after the Lisbon coup (April 1974). When it was clear that promised elections would not be forthcoming and that the Soviet-backed Popular Movement for the Liberation of Angola (MPLA) was going to rule by dint of arms, the SADF section produced its own estimate of the security implications for South Africa. Mr. Botha delivered this estimate that pointed to both the National Front for the Liberation of Angola— FNLA—and the National Union for the Total Independence of Angola—UNITA—as viable opposition to the MPLA to the Prime Minister in June 1975. The estimate was instrumental in Mr. Vorster's decision to take up the Angola Question with Washington and, in conjunction with Washington, send forces into Angola. It has been suggested that Hendrik van den Bergh (now "Major General" as head of BOSS) was "uneasy about the venture from the start."[15] This is not the case: General van den Bergh fully appreciated the threatening Angolan situation and had been in touch early on with both FNLA and UNITA leaders, as had Military Intelligence. Moreover, he urged the Prime Minister to provide arms assistance to both groups but with the stipulation that BOSS serve as the conduit! Van den Bergh called for withdrawal only after it was clear to all that Washington was about to leave Pretoria in the lurch. With the military option in Angola no longer viable, he was quick to propose other options. If SADF had "a cynical view"[16] of van den Bergh's role in Angola (and throughout Africa for that matter), it stemmed from the growing operational character of BOSS, not to mention its direct line to the Prime Minister. The problem that was brewing was a turf problem, and not a break between hawks and doves.

In the aftermath of *Operation Savannah* Mr. Botha came under renewed pressure from his military people concerning the intelligence brief. While the argument for *one* intelligence service was beginning to be heard, the major appeal to the minister of Defense was put in terms of rationalizing the intelligence enterprise in behalf of an architectonic "total national strategy." The appeal, while lacking subtlety, was nicely tailored to the minister's well-known management and strategy propensities. The Strategy would be developed through a "national strategic planning process" contained within a "national security management system." All of this was now in the gestation process.

Intelligence must be at the heart of this process was the argument, indeed, at the heart of a sophisticated war effort that the Republic would have to mount in the years ahead.[17] Intelligence cannot be left to "a policeman"[18]; it must be placed at the center of the new system—an area the military even at this early point understood would be largely theirs. P W Botha was entirely disposed to entertain this line of argument, not just in terms of its "rationalization" theme but also because of what he had observed in his study of the Vorster–van den Bergh partnership. The minister of Defense was struck by the fact that the Prime Minister and the director of BOSS were alter egos. While the two were of one mind on the seriousness of Soviet efforts to penetrate the Republic, van den Bergh's most important role was that of personal emissary for Mr. Vorster. He traveled extensively throughout Africa developing networks that were essential to his Prime Minister's Outward Policy and, of course, to his own agency. BOSS emerged by the late seventies as a powerful dimension of the office of the Prime Minister, overshadowing in many respects not just the Ministry of Defense but the Ministry of Foreign Affairs as well.[19]

Mr. Botha would be aggressive in behalf of his strategy and management ideas, but as in the case of John Vorster, without acceding to higher office, there were limits to what he could accomplish. As in the case of Vorster, P W Botha's opportunity would materialize suddenly, if not quite so starkly, and the intelligence issue would be at the center of things. As the result of an "Inquiry" into the clandestine undertakings of the Department of Information, Mr. Vorster was compelled to resign in September 1978.[20] Following a difficult party caucus, Mr. Botha was named Prime Minister. In its findings the Erasmus Commission detailed the involvement of BOSS in the Information Scandal. General van den Bergh—always on the lookout for alternative courses of action—had been attracted by the intelligence possibilities within the Department of Information's brief.[21] The exposé confirmed once again for Mr. Botha the significance of the intelligence issue. One of his first actions as Prime Minister was to ask for the resignation of the BOSS chief. With Lang Hendrik retired to his farm, "the battle for the intelligence brief" was wide open.

While specific issues will linger on through the eighties—issues that would have to be addressed on a more or less continuing basis—the battle is essentially fought out in the two years following Mr. Botha's appointment as Prime Minister. The South African Defense Force, to no one's surprise, prevails: "The essentials have been turned over to us," a high-ranking SADF intelligence officer proclaimed in a 1983 interview.[22] Heavily involved in the turf battle, but now clearly in the ascendancy, this officer put stress on having captured what all along had been the primary objective, namely, the "strategic intelligence brief." What I am speaking of, he explained, resides in your Central Intelligence Agency (CIA), not in your Defense Intelligence Agency (DIA) or in the military intelligence branches. SADF had cast its argument for "an outstanding intelligence service"[23] in the idiom of strategy. As General Malan put it in a widely noted lecture following his appointment as minister of Defense (another victory), "Firstly, the intelligence machinery was set up to identify and define the different facets of the total offensive waged against the RSA, that is, to determine the total strategy of the enemy against the RSA."[24] From this point on SADF Intelligence (i.e., the Chief of Staff/Intelligence [CSI]) would be the principal source and formulator of strategic military intelligence in the national strategic-planning process. He would "write the strategic threat," but just as important, he would be instrumental in devising the counterstrategy.[25]

Intelligence roles and missions had to be reassessed in order to conform with "the essentials" passing to SADF. "These pretty much got sorted out in the early eighties," yet another senior intelligence official confirmed (1988). The major question from the beginning, he continued, has been "covert collection,"[26] that is, dividing this up in terms of geographical areas. SADF was emphatic, to say the least, that it must be the primary collector in southern Africa (NIS could have primacy elsewhere), inasmuch as this is the theater of direct military threat to the RSA. In this region, moreover, SADF will have primacy not just in military intelligence (order-of-battle, etc.), but in all collection categories. The CSI and his agency are authorized to make contact with groups such as Dr. Savimbi's UNITA and with other leaders in the region. General van der Westhuizen, for one, was not prepared to forgo all of General van den Bergh's practices, particularly in the political area. When the CSI is not personally engaged in the collection effort, it is likely to fall to SADF's counterpart of the British-style "Special Air Service" (SAS), the Reconnaissance Commando or "Recces." Heitman suggests in an unusual use of the term that the Recces can be described as "specialists in *strategic* intelligence" (italics mine).[27] Too valuable to be committed to combat, except on rare occasions, they will sometimes collect tactical intelligence, but their specialty is covert observation of a variety of enemy activities in rear areas. It was evident, for example, that elements of 4 Reconnaissance Commando from Langebaan in the Cape Province carried out the May 1985 undertaking in the Cabinda enclave in Angola.[28] The collection of long-range field intelligence is also a priority objective of SADF cross-border operations against ANC. These operations, in turn, assist the CSI in the discharge of his counterintelligence responsibilities both outside and inside the Republic. For all of the coordination problems that it entails, the Botha regime treated foreign intelligence and internal security as one and chose to involve three agencies. This follows from the basic conceptualization of the Onslaught and explains the elaborate machinery for integration and coordination at the national level. On internal security matters, as we shall see in chapter 5, the critical relationship is that between SADF and SAP. On the foreign-intelligence front, while SAP is not excluded, it is principally a matter between SADF and NIS.

Mr. Botha would not be content with simply dismissing the BOSS director and refurbishing the agency. Following an interim arrangement[29] ("while things were being sorted out"), a new National Intelligence Service (NIS) comes into being in June 1980. Dr. Lukas Barnard, a very junior Nat, was appointed director and continued in that office throughout the Botha term. If the Prime Minister's purpose was to achieve the sharpest possible contrast with Lang Hendrik, he succeeded brilliantly. Apart from putting a new face on things, Mr. Botha wished to meet certain political obligations in the Orange Free State and, for that matter, in the academic community.[30] In a 1983 interview with the author, Barnard granted that he was a political appointee—but the only one in NIS! What he was attempting to do, at least at the outset, was gather something of an academic coterie around him. This, in turn, had led to some early speculation that NIS had a severely restricted brief and would be little more than a think tank.[31] Manifestly, there was not the slightest possibility that NIS could take the expansive course followed by BOSS in the seventies. At the same time, the director made clear that part of his charge was to give definition to his agency and its mission beyond the bare statutory language. This was a delicate task: sensitive about his youthfulness and inexperience he sought not only to underscore his academic credentials (which included a Georgetown connection) and the assessment function of

NIS, but also to point out that he had special interests he would pursue.

It is standard practice among counterintelligence officers to note their paranoia levels and the consequent need for frequent vacations. Barnard was cast to type. If not ready for a vacation he was demonstrably anxious on the security question. The diverse activities of the Soviet Union—and other extracontinental powers—in Africa absorbed him. The flow of money and people in and among "front groups," sponsored perhaps rather more by the West than "the other side," was of special interest. These are the complex and sophisticated elements in the Onslaught who are in touch not only with certain governments in Africa but directly with our adversaries in the field: SWAPO/PLAN and ANC/MK. Front groups and their sponsors are mainstays of the psychological dimension of the Onslaught; they are literally engaged in psychological warfare against the RSA. All South African Intelligence officials expressed exasperation about the propaganda/counterpropaganda dimension, one of them conceding "we don't know quite what to do about it."[32] Barnard, however, was a man determined to devote his energies to the task. He singled out U.S. pressure on South Africa as poorly thought out and only likely to reinforce the innate Afrikaner tendency toward isolationism. To his mind, the purpose underlying monies flowing from official U.S. sources (e.g., Agency for International Development and U.S. Information Agency) and unofficial sources (e.g., AFL-CIO and church groups) to selected recipients in the RSA and in the region is errant and inexplicable.[33]

Still, none of this prevents comparing of notes ("professional-to-professional") with the United States and other services. Barnard stated that he had good U.S. contacts and wished to build on them, but on this subject there was a reticence that separated him from his military confreres.[34] He appeared eager to operate against hostile services, suggesting that NIS's counterintelligence function would be expanded. A qualification was added, however; NIS works in close collaboration with the Security Police, leaving the "hands-on stuff" to an organization eminently capable in such matters. In what could be construed as an allusion to the new order of things in South African intelligence, Barnard remarked that the British "pure intelligence" model might be the best one for him to follow. While too much should not be put upon this remark, it suggests that what he has in mind is a collection-oriented secret intelligence service, accompanied by a strong counterintelligence function that, in the South African setting, will be shared among three services. The observation takes account of the fact that the production of finished intelligence and the development of national-intelligence estimates (to the extent that this, too, has not been captured by CSI) have been lifted to the level of the State Security Council (SSC) and its Secretariat (SSCS).

Before turning to that matter, it is necessary to add that NIS has a foreign-intelligence-collection role that has grown with time. NIS operates particularly in Africa but overseas as well. There is evidence of RSA intelligence activity in South America and the Middle East in connection with arms export and countersanctions activities.[35] The international terrorist network is yet another focal point of interest. Perhaps more than most governments, Pretoria is concerned to know the thinking, even the private leanings, of major foreign leaders (both public and private) and appreciates how much of this intelligence can be obtained through nonconventional means. While Barnard does not wear the mantle of Lang Hendrik, he is steadily refining the brief of NIS and offering increasingly more input to the SSC and the State President.[36]

The National Security Management System (NSMS)

In the months preceding his appointment as Prime Minister, Mr. Botha steadily proclaimed the need for a total national strategy to fellow members of the House of Assembly.[37] He noted that the Department of Defense was diligently engaged in devising such a strategy but that other departments were reluctant to join in the effort. As he spoke, an ad hoc interdepartmental committee was at work on a requirement that had crystallized in the period following the *Security Intelligence and State Security Council Act, 1972.* It was patent that if the SSC was to function as intended at the apex of the nation's security system, it would require a support structure. If there was to be a total national strategy it must issue from a national strategic-planning process (not from a single department). Likewise, a national-security management system must be in place to put The Strategy into operation. None of this was provided for in the 1972 act. The interdepartmental committee, drawing on a 1975 study,[38] reported at the end of 1978. Throughout the following year the new Prime Minister officially adopted its recommendations. One is tempted to describe Mr. Botha's NSMS (on the basis of what is publicly known of it) as Byzantine, or as one wag has put it in local parlance, "Boer Baroque." No detailed delineation of the structure or workings of the NSMS has been promulgated by the South African government. Press conferences and press releases,[39] with partial if not always illuminating pieces of the whole, are of some value. "Principals" in the NSMS have on various occasions discussed with the author aspects of the system and on their candor we principally rely.

The rationalization of the security-management process, as Mr. Botha would have it, is undertaken within a wider, ongoing process of governmental and constitutional reform. While this undertaking predates his accession to the office of Prime Minister, it becomes, thereafter, one of "rationalizing the decision-making process to suit his own style of management."[40] No single fact explains the decision-making process in South Africa today, one of the principals confided to the author, so much as the obvious fact: "B J Vorster is no longer Prime Minister; P W Botha is!"[41] The new Prime Minister chose to begin at the top with the cabinet and the office of Prime Minister itself. It had been the style of Mr. Botha's predecessor, for example, to deal with major policy issues as discrete questions through ad hoc (cabinet) committees. Mr. Botha did not like ad hoc committees; he preferred first of all a smaller number of committees and he preferred them integrated in broad functional areas. At the same time, the new Prime Minister established a cabinet secretariat under a chief of Secretariat. This helped pave the way for reorganization of the office of Prime Minister, most notably the removal of planning branches from that office. In August 1981 the Security Planning Branch was transferred to the SSC Secretariat[42] and one year later the remaining planning branches (Economic, Social, Constitutional, Physical, and Scientific) were placed with the newly established Ministry of Constitutional Development and Planning. The rationalization process extended to the executive departments themselves, as Mr. Botha initially reduced them in number from thirty-nine to twenty-two. Rationalization appears to be synonymous not only with "functional consolidation" but with simple "reduction"—a notable achievement in government-reorganization schemes anywhere.

Constitutional reform had its inception in 1977 proposals from Mr. Vorster that were subsequently incorporated in a 1979 Draft Constitution Bill submitted to Parliament by Mr. Botha. It was this bill, passed in the spring of 1982 with modifications, that was approved by the

White electorate in the national referendum of November 1983. Certain features in the new constitution bear on the management of national security and require brief attention here. What Mr. Botha, in fact, had in mind concerning the office of Prime Minister was its elimination. A new office of State President replaces the previous offices of State President and Prime Minister. Today the State President is elected by an electoral college drawn on a proportional basis from the tri-cameral Parliament. The State President is not a member of Parliament, but his term of office (six years) corresponds with that of members. The State President forms and chairs a cabinet consisting of members of the three chambers and nonmembers as he chooses. Under the new constitution, the cabinet is the central policy-making body for "general affairs." To a greater degree than other extant examples of cabinet government, it is the instrument of the State President. For all of the attention that has been directed to the three-chamber legislature (with its incorporation of Coloured and Asian constituencies), the most dramatic feature of the new charter is its enhancement of executive power. The State President has the decisive responsibility (on occasion with the advice of the President's Council) of classifying policy issues either as "general" (for cabinet consideration) or as "own" (for Ministers' Councils on Own Affairs). Defense of the realm, the very first of "general affairs," proceeds from the cabinet to all three chambers of Parliament for majority approval.[43]

The SSC was State President Botha's principal executive device for formulating and implementing South Africa's counterrevolution. Three other cabinet committees[44] are part of the Great Undertaking as well, but the SSC is at the apex. To attempt to define the charter of the SSC in conventional terms, such as noting that foreign policy as well as defense policy falls within its purview, is hardly adequate. All elements required for a comprehensive strategy to construct a new order come under the aegis of the SSC. Its writ runs across the government and across the country. Alone among cabinet committees it is chaired by the State President. Just as important Mr. Botha is free to appoint ("co-opt") any government official—elected politician or career bureaucrat—that he chooses. Statutory members include (1) the senior cabinet minister;[45] (2) the minister of Defense; (3) the minister of Foreign Affairs; (4) the minister of Justice; (5) the minister of Law & Order; (6) the director of the National Intelligence Service; (7) the chief of the South African Defense Force; (8) the director-general of

Foreign Affairs; (9) the director-general of Justice; and (10) the commissioner of South African Police. No definitive membership list is published, but because of the discretion Mr. Botha has in co-opting members, the list will vary, consisting always of about fifteen people. What is certain is that whoever needs to be on the SSC at any given time will be there. This is the State President's strategy council, setting the guidelines and the framework within which line agencies (SADF as lead agency) will work toward regime objectives.[46] If there is any group, however, who understands the venerable maxim that "policy is 10 percent formulation and 90 percent execution," it is the Botha coterie. In recent years the burden has shifted to the policy-execution side of the system.

As indicated above, "the shortcomings of the state machinery for the combating of threats to the national security" were the subject of two committee reports, one in 1975 and the other in 1978.[47] Acting on these studies Mr. Botha moved quickly to provide the SSC with a formal support structure consisting of (1) a Work Committee; (2) a Secretariat; (3) Interdepartmental Committees; and (4) Joint Management Centers. The Work Committee is a subcabinet-level group (chaired by a deputy minister) that meets in advance of the council's regular fortnightly meetings for preliminary discussion of the agenda. In addition to having director-general-level membership from the agencies represented on the SSC, it will also include the chairmen of the other cabinet committee working groups (again attesting to the *primus inter pares* standing of the SSC). The Work Committee is not an agenda-setting group, but it will make recommendations to the council as to the advice it should provide the cabinet on agenda items. Without attempting to draw too close a parallel, the work of senior interdepartmental groups working within the framework of the National Security Council in the United States is an analogue. It is likely that the Work Committee enhances the role of career bureaucrats in the NSMS—an outcome the State President may wish to encourage in order to institutionalize his system.

More critical than the Work Committee, the Secretariat is the permanent, full-time staff organization supporting the SSC and its Work Committee. Staff personnel are drawn from government departments (some on a rotating or "secondment" basis), and at this level there is a significant defense presence.[48] The Secretariat does not provide advice; its task is to ensure that there is input from all participating departments and that their positions go forward to be heard. What is important to understand, however, is that the Secretariat is supporting a *joint* strategic-planning process. It is in this light that its handling of departmental input must be seen. It is in this context that its coordination and monitoring function is to be understood. In short, the task of the Secretariat is to facilitate the achievement of SSC established goals. In the course of this endeavor tensions will develop between the NSMS level and the line-agency level. To put the matter less felicitously, the NSMS (with the chief of the Secretariat as point man) is to "ride herd" on the line agencies. A director-general of one of these agencies told the author recently that "the NSMS is a lot of talk—we do the job out here. It is our budget, our people that are involved. We have the background and the experience—we'll get the job done."[49]

The Secretariat is the "switching center" of the input–output flow of the NSMS. Its central functions are executed through four branches: Strategy; National Intelligence Interpretation; Strategic Communications; and Administration. Here at the interstices of the NSMS one encounters *terra nullius;* almost no official documentation of the workings of the system exists. Only the most general inferential observations are possible. In the Strategy Branch, while the strategic-planning process is joint, there is reason to believe the process is dominated by secondments from SADF. At the same time there is also basis for the view that most line agencies are quite prepared to leave "that sort of thing" to SADF. As for Strategic Communications, General van Deventer (the first chief of Secretariat under Mr. Botha) has made plain his concern about combating the war of words, calling it "the vanguard of modern warfare," requiring specific attention. Until a policy decision has been made (and none has been to date) to launch a full-scale counterattack, this will remain a uniquely vulnerable area for a system designed to address all elements of the Onslaught. The Administration Branch, described as "purely administrative," may be innocuous enough except for possibly one detail, namely, the colocation of the NIS with the Secretariat "for administrative purposes." This permits us to return to the intelligence issue.

In his September 21, 1983, statement, General van Deventer said as much if not more about the National Intelligence Interpretation Branch (NIIB) of the Secretariat than any other element of the system. "No planning can be done without intelligence," he observed. "All decision makers require timely, unbiased, and objective intelligence." The interpretation of intelligence on a national level is done in the Secretariat (that is, in the NIIB) and not in the respective agencies. The NIIB "product" is a key element in strategy formulation. General van Deventer noted that the Secretariat does not collect intelligence; this is done by the intelligence services (among which he includes the Department of Foreign Affairs and Information). Each of the collecting agencies makes its own "first-cut" evaluation before passing along its product to the NIIB.[50] The branch, itself, is made up of "members of the intelligence community seconded from their respective departments." A senior member of the community, appointed on a rotating basis, chairs the branch. What then is the significance of the NIS being colocated in the Secretariat for administrative purposes? Geldenhuys and Kotze write that the entire Secretariat "resorts under" the NIS, ostensibly for logistical purposes, without being "professionally responsible" to the director of NIS.[51] While this may be of interest only to accountants and auditors, location can be a significant variable in a power equation! Again, under the heading of inferential conclusions, it is plausible to suggest that the NIS has grown in terms of its impact on national-level interpretation of intelligence and in terms of the role of the director and his access to the State President.

The 1978 ad hoc interdepartmental committee (IDC) called for formal establishment of IDCs "for each of the areas of common interest within the security field." Through this device executive agencies are organized or grouped on the basis of common concerns, but with the aim of addressing matters relating to national security in their specific fields. Fifteen were established at the outset where today an official list shows only twelve.[52] Each IDC is called upon not only to identify national-security problems among their common concerns but to suggest how each department in the grouping can most effectively participate in devising a solution. The departments are under the gun to get into the act (not to mix their metaphors!), explaining some of the restiveness of the aforementioned director-general. If Mr. Botha was determined about one thing, it was to spread the total effort across the government and not leave it with one department (although one department—Defense—may have to play a lead role for some time). The IDCs have a coordination function at the level of policy initiation, whereas the Secretariat's coordination function consists of processing these initiatives through the system and monitoring implementation. Rather than employ a rotating chairman, each IDC is chaired by the representative of the department "most concerned with the area."

The list of twelve interdepartmental committees released by the Secretariat may not be complete (see Figure 1). It does not include an IDC for Intelligence. Yet in an interview (uncommon for the willingness of the interviewee to speak on the record) Vice Adm. A P Putter, SAN, then serving as SADF/CSI, spoke openly of "the Intelligence Committee." He made it clear he was not speaking of the Secretariat's NIIB. "The committee consists of myself, Dr. Barnard, and the chief of Security Police"—no reference was made to Foreign Affairs. Admiral Putter was at pains to make the point that Dr. Barnard chaired the committee and that there was no rotation (a distinguishing feature of an IDC). In response to a question, Admiral Putter stated that the committee's function was "to develop intelligence policy with coordination of effort in mind." The committee was not a tasking body— "each of the line agencies does that." Turf issues had arisen but were largely sorted out early on: however, defining roles and missions was a continuing issue—a constant function—"one we work hard at." Exchange of intelligence and cooperation with other services is an objective, but "we don't have precisely the same interests or priorities as you people do. Opportunities do arise, for example, with respect to Soviet equipment we encounter up north and, of course, we're interested in what you can give us on ANC." While the CSI stated that "we are generally satisfied" with the profession-to-profession relationship, his remark lacked force.[53]

The specter of revolutionary war within the Republic has always been understood as potentially more disruptive of the Great Undertaking than any external threat. A NSMS, designed to combat the entire range of threats to the national security of the RSA, would not be complete without mechanisms to address the bases of unrest and to prosecute counterrevolutionary war. The Public Service Commission in its 1975 *Report on the National Security Situation* recognized that Joint Management Centers (JMCs) to coordinate security actions at regional and local levels would be essential and recommended their establishment. JMCs have become an increasingly prominent feature of the NSMS since the end of 1984. They are local-level committees having something of the character of roundtables of local leaders (of all races). Emphatically eschewing any executive authority, the JMCs convene in order to ascertain the current status of a wide variety of security issues in the sector; to bring out different viewpoints among,

Figure 1. **The National Management System: Organizational Structure**

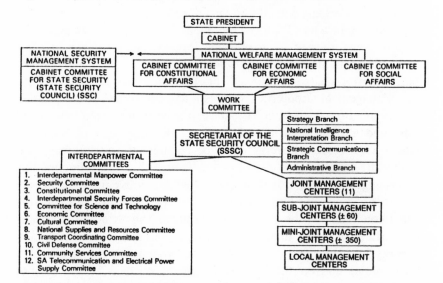

Source: Selected Official South African Strategic Perceptions, 1976–1987 (Pretoria: Institute for Strategic Studies), May 1988, p. 12.

again, a wide array of leaders; to suggest plans of action or initiatives; and to report back to the national level. The growing prominence of JMCs raises a delicate point: implementation of security plans is the responsibility of each executive agency involved, but "coordination and monitoring" (in this instance of critical internal-security measures) falls to the NSMS (and in this instance to the JMCs). In the words of a State Security Council secretary, "they are a marvelous device to keep me in touch with the grass-roots."[54] The SSC secretary clearly meant to imply that in having a direct line to the localities he was not dependent upon executive-agency channels for his picture of local circumstances. He meant to imply as well that it would be impossible to combat revolutionary war within the country without this chain of command.

While the 1975 commission report calls for a national-security staff organization, there is no stipulation concerning a national-level JMC. As late as 1983 General van Deventer (then SSC secretary) refers to JMCs only at regional and local levels. It is only with the emergence of "the Unrest" and the establishment of the State of Emergency (1986) that a National Joint Management Center (NJMC) is activated. Reporting directly to the SSC, it is to "regulate coordinated action at the grass-roots level and extend it to the upper levels."[55] For reasons not at all clear, Pretoria has displayed more than its customary reticence with regard to the group at the apex of the JMC system. However, officials associated with the NSMS with whom the author talked in the 1985–87 period were prepared to discuss what they then called the Joint Security Management Group (i.e., what is today designated as the NJMC). It is in this time frame that Mr. Adriaan Vlok is appointed minister of Law and Order (replacing Mr. Louis LeGrange) and is given the charge to oversee a government-wide response to revolutionary war within the country. He makes the NJMC his vehicle for directing this wide-ranging effort but is soon compelled to devolve upon the deputy minister of Law and Order (then Mr. Roelf Meyer and subsequently Mr. Leon Wessels) the chairmanship duties. The "Meyer Group," as one official referred to it at the time, is the forum in which both security initiatives and welfare initiatives from across the government (and coming up from the JMCs) are brought together. On the basis of these proposals the NJMC formulates its attack on the myriad internal security/welfare problems and takes it to the SSC for endorsement. The function of the NJMC appears to be twofold: it must elicit from the executive agencies a variety of initiatives and, secondly, once they are approved, monitor policy execution. One official was cryptic: "The task of the entire system, and this group in particular, is to keep the pressure on the directors-general in the agencies."[56]

In a later chapter we shall look at how Mr. Botha's government combats revolutionary war within the borders of the RSA (perhaps more successfully than any other present-day regime) and at some of the issues that arise in the functioning of the NSMS. Not the least of these issues are those posed by the "cheek by jowl" relationship of the security people and the civilian welfare agencies as they jointly prosecute counterrevolution. The prominence of SADF in this security–welfare effort is striking not so much at the highest level (the SSC after all is a civilian-dominated body), but at the working levels of the NSMS. Throughout the Botha years the secretary to the State Security Council and chief of the Secretariat—the man who may be said to drive the system on a day-to-day basis—has been a "three-star" general officer from the South African army.[57] This fact symbolizes the confidence the former minister of Defense, and now State President, reposes in SADF and why he has chosen to make it his lead agency in achieving a broad range of objectives both internally and externally. The NSMS, itself, could only have been institutionalized by a man confident of the capacities of SADF to carry out this assignment and confident of its subordination to his direction. Allegations that, on the contrary, this represents a militarization of the regime come from observers who have not had direct access to the NSMS. At best such observations constitute yet another example of "remote sensing" on the South Africa Question.[58]

Notes

1. South African civil service salaries may account for as much as one-half of government spending. See Ad D Wassenaar, *Squandered Assets* (Cape Town: Tafelberg, 1989), 73. The insightful impressions of an *Inspecteur General des Finances* in the French civil service, not only of the Afrikaner bureaucracy but of the challenges facing the South African government today, can be found in Pierre Mayer, "South Africa's Long Journey," *South Africa International* 17 (April 1987): 192–216.

2. Mr. Botha would concede that he might have made something of a nuisance of himself with his Prime Minister on the subject. The more important point is that he was moved not so much by shortcomings in the decision-making process, which surfaced in connection with the Angolan affair (1975–76), as a desire to be done with the "Vorster management system." The Defense minister was bent on achieving a comprehensive, coordinated management system that alone could be expected to implement a comprehensive strategy. This would be a system at his disposal, not that of the directors-general of the line agencies.

3. Deon F S Fourie, "South Africa: The Evolving Experience," in *Defense Policy Formation,* ed. Roherty, 102–3.

4. Security Police was established as a branch of the South African Police in 1947. Originally designated "Special Branch," this British nomenclature passed along with Commonwealth status in 1961. See also n. 28 in chapter 2.

5. South Africa, Department of Defense, *White Paper on Defense and Armaments Supply, 1986* (Cape Town, 1985), 1.

6. A contemporary account is H H W de Villiers, *Rivonia—Operation Mayibuye* (Johannesburg: Afrikaanse Pers-Boekhandel, 1964). *Mayibuye* is the Zulu term "come back," often used in the phrase "Africa, Come Back."

7. The most famous of the Rivonia trialists is of course Nelson Mandela, still detained although with amenities at this writing. Others are Walter Sisulu and Thabo Mbeki. Whites were caught up in the operation as well, including Dennis Goldberg, Lionel Bernstein, and Harold Wolpe, although not arraigned. The trial went forward under the new (1962) Sabotage Act, which Mr. Vorster had hastened to enact upon becoming minister of Justice.

8. Braam Fischer, onetime head of the SACP, served as legal counsel for the Rivonia trialists and would be jailed the following year under the Supression of Communism Act. Fischer had had ambitions of leading a guerrilla war within the

country, his lack of military credentials notwithstanding! Awarded the Lenin Peace Prize upon his incarceration, he was transferred from prison to hospital in 1975 and died shortly thereafter of cancer.

9. "Outside elements" associated with these organizations were by no means solely from the East bloc. ARM's explosives expert was a freewheeling former British army officer, Robert Watson, by way of Malaya!

10. A source in South African military intelligence made the observation to the author that "Jimmy Kruger was the best (at counterintelligence), if only we had him now!" (Kruger would become minister of Justice under Vorster.) It should be noted that this section is based on interviews with senior intelligence officials in South Africa over a period of years.

11. Gen. Jan Smuts, then Prime Minister, considered this action prudent. However, his rabidly anti-British Defense minister, Oswald Pirow, was not interned.

12. Only days after Sharpeville on April 9, 1960, Mr. Verwoerd was fired upon in Milner Park (Johannesburg) by "a deranged farmer," barely escaping death. The successful attempt, six years later, came in the halls of Parliament in Cape Town. Helen Suzman, a longtime member of the PFP, on announcing her retirement (May 1989) called it "the worst moment of her career."

13. Statement to the press by Lt. Gen. Andre J. van Deventer, SADF, chief of the Secretariat and secretary to the State Security Council of the Republic of South Africa (September 21, 1983), Pretoria, 1.

14. Article 5.

15. See Robin Hallet, "The South African Intervention in Angola, 1975–76," *African Affairs* 77 (July 1978): 347–86, especially 383–86. Professor Deon Geldenhuys rightly describes this account as "speculative." It has proven altogether premature and was based on unsubstantiated newspaper accounts of the day. Hallett's further suggestion that van den Bergh was in a dovish alliance with the Ministry of Foreign Affairs against the military can be laid aside as well. For an account that the author states must be largely inferential, but based on more substantial grounds than Hallett, see Geldenhuys, *The Diplomacy of Isolation,* especially 78–80 and 149. Professor Geldenhuys covers the Vorster period and the first three years of the Botha period with a concentration on foreign policy rather than the defense sector. Within these parameters it is the best account available. Geldenhuys, incidentally, notes that he was rebuffed in his effort to obtain an interview with General van den Bergh. There was nothing "dovish" about the boss of BOSS!

16. Geldenhuys, *Diplomacy of Isolation,* 80. The author shows that this view was not without basis. See also Flower, *Serving Secretly,* 128.

17. South Africa, Department of Defense, *White Paper on Defense and Armaments Supply, 1977* (Cape Town, 1976). The developing views of the Botha coterie would appear in a number of reports prior to PW becoming Prime Minister and then emerge full blown after 1979. See the section following on the NSMS.

18. Personalities as well as jurisdictional issues would be part of the intelligence-brief battle. Jimmy Kruger aside, "van den Bergh was simply a policeman" and "the police are dressed up in uniforms and call themselves generals" was part of the discourse. Again, the issue is one among three services not two. One senior military intelligence officer has made no secret of his view that only one intelli-

gence service is required; it is not the one that apparently Mr. Vorster and General van den Bergh had in mind!

19. It is important to point out that Mr. Botha did not conclude from his observations that he must have "a principal confidant" close at hand. He would have his own ideas about the role of intelligence and the principal instrumentality he would employ in behalf of his strategy. As for confidants, it is evident he has had many and from different sectors. See Geldenhuys, *Diplomacy of Isolation*, 95, for an early estimate of this situation, also n. 43 below.

20. Reference n. 11 in chapter 1.

21. The minister of Defense was particularly conscious of this inasmuch as General van den Bergh had gained access to a Defense Special Account to "canalize" funds to the Department of Information. At PW's insistence this practice was stopped and a Secret Services Account established upon which a number of agencies can draw. See Geldenhuys, *Diplomacy of Isolation*, 88.

22. I have cited this interview in my "Managing the Security Power Base in South Africa," *South Africa International* 15 (October 1984): 56–65. The analysis offered in that article must now be considered incomplete and for that matter unsatisfactory. What is now presented benefits from a considerably broader base of interviews with senior intelligence officials (1983–88).

23. As indicated above (n.17), South Africa's *White Paper on Defense, 1977* provides the tenor of the argument: "Since strategy is normally directed towards the enemy's actions, it cannot be determined purely on the basis of one's own actions, but the reaction of the enemy must also be determined; this in turn demands a counter-reaction. This characteristic of strategy calls for an outstanding intelligence service in order to forecast the action of the enemy" (5).

24. General Malan is clearly drawing on the 1977 *White Paper*. See his Lecture to the Institute for Strategic Studies, University of Pretoria, September 3, 1980.

25. It is in this critical respect that the mantle of Hendrik van den Bergh passes to CSI and not to the new National Intelligence Service. The mantle would be worn with ebullience by the first CSI in the eighties (Lt. Gen. Pieter van der Westhuizen) and with perhaps more restraint by the second (Vice Adm. A P Putter). Admiral Putter would be succeeded by Lt. Gen. Rudolph Badenhorst who, if reputation is any guide, can be expected to be more active.

26. This is the precise terminology used by the interviewee signifying clandestine collection of foreign intelligence. Foreign intelligence, in turn, will not include in some usages "operational intelligence," that is to say, intelligence collected on services operating against you. The latter is not synonymous with but closely associated with counterintelligence.

27. *South African War Machine*, 96.

28. This unit has special amphibious training and was lifted to and from the scene by submarine (based at Simonstown). For a full summary of the facts on the occasion of the recovery of Maj. Wynand du Toit some two years later, see the *Johannesburg Star*, September 7, 1987.

29. Reference is to the Department of National Security (DONS). The change of acronyms did not escape attention! In its brief existence it was placed under Mr. Alec van Wyk, a professional intelligence officer from BOSS. DONS was closely linked to the Ministry of Defense, a portfolio retained during this period by Mr. Botha.

30. Whether he succeeded with the academic community is problematical. As a faculty member at the University of the Orange Free State, Barnard was not without academic credentials in international relations. However, Professor Geldenhuys (a fellow Afrikaner academician) appears to express concern for the Republic when he writes that the NIS director's writings consist of "a peculiar compound of Machiavellianism and Calvinism." *Diplomacy of Isolation,* 149.

31. The NIS brief is essentially that contained in the *Security Intelligence Act, 1972* for the Bureau of State Security. While there is much scope here, the great difference will be new personnel—beginning with the Prime Minister and the NIS director.

32. General van Deventer highlights this dimension in his statement to the press on September 21, 1983.

33. For a later and fuller delineation of "the money flow," see Richard E. Sincere, Jr., *The Politics of Sentiment* (Washington, D.C.: Ethics and Public Policy Center, 1984), and Ansophie M. Joubert, "U.S. Involvement in South Africa—An Update," *American Review* 8 (2d Quarter, 1988): 2–13, Institute for American Studies: Rand Afrikaans University, Johannesburg. Joubert quotes Chief Buthelezi as follows: "There is something very wrong about the formula which directs American money into South Africa (aimed at making South Africa ungovernable in tandem with ANC's aims), whereas democratic forces such as *Inkatha* are denied political aid" (12). *Inkatha* is a Zulu-based extraparliamentary organization. See chapter 5.

34. One of the academic coterie, Dr. Daniel Opperman, sat in on the interview. Outgoing and affable, Opperman joked about his being the *quid pro quo* that had to depart Washington when Pretoria found "an unauthorized camera" in the U.S. ambassador's plane after a flight from Pretoria to Salisbury in 1979 and ejected the U.S. air attaché. Opperman was liaison with his old friends from Washington stationed in the RSA and was looking forward to a return visit.

35. The RSA connection in Santiago, Chile, is well known, as is RSA interest in Argentine affairs. The chairman of the Atomic Energy Corporation of South Africa (J W L de Villiers) remarked to the author (in 1983) that as far as the "bomb" is concerned, it is of more consequence to the RSA what Argentina does than what Libya does. Recently the question of long-range missiles and the Argentine "Condor II" project has come on to the RSA intelligence agenda. See chapter 4. As for Dr. Barnard, personally, he has participated in a number of the international meetings leading to the Tripartite Agreement on Southwestern Africa (December 1988).

36. In recent years Barnard's access to the State President has grown. Increasingly, Mr. Botha's speeches in Parliament reflect "strategic background" material provided by NIS on nonmilitary dimensions of the Onslaught. This material finds its way into public outlets in the Republic, such as the Institute for Strategic Studies (University of Pretoria) and the Institute for American Studies (Rand Afrikaans University). To this date, however, no attempt has been made to reestablish a major information program through the Bureau of Information or the Ministry of Foreign Affairs. See chapter 5.

37. *Debates,* South Africa House of Assembly (17 April 1978), col. 4860.

38. South Africa, Public Service Commission, *Report on the National Security Situation* (Pretoria, 1975).

39. The most extensive is that of General van Deventer, September 21, 1983. Also the "White Papers" (*Witskrif oor Verdediging en Krystuigvoorsiening*) issued in 1979 and 1982 are useful. See also Parliamentary *Debates* during these years for glimpses of the system, some of which are excerpted in Hough, *Selected Perceptions*.

40. Statement to the press, van Deventer.

41. By agreement almost all interviews are on a "no direct attribution" basis.

42. With the transfer of the Security Planning Branch from the office of the Prime Minister to the SSCS, General van Deventer is transferred to the SSCS and becomes the first SSC secretary in Mr. Botha's government.

43. In the event three-chamber majority approval is not forthcoming on a "general" matter, the President's Council has a legislative role to play: it will arbitrate between the conflicting chambers. There is no doubt that such arbitration will be consistent with the views of the president. The President's Council consists of thirty-five members elected proportionally from the three chambers (the majority of which can be expected to align politically with the president) and twenty-five members appointed from private life (fifteen by the president). The latter provision is of special relevance where P W Botha is concerned. His practice since becoming Prime Minister has been to draw heavily upon sources outside of government, particularly in the higher reaches of the corporate sector. Through the simple expedient of a telephone call (or other private channels) Mr. Botha seeks advice, or merely a sounding board, from trusted friends. The appointment provision in the President's Council can be seen as a device to formalize at least some of the earlier informal practices of the Prime Minister and to maintain the growing ties between the National Party government and business leaders.

44. The cabinet committees for Constitutional Affairs, Economic Affairs, and Social Affairs are grouped under a National Welfare Management System, which with the National Security Management System constitutes the overall National Management System. The welfare system is, however, subordinate to the security system in the strategic sense (i.e., "security first"). See chapter 5.

45. At the time of writing the senior minister was Mr. Chris Heunis, minister for Constitutional Planning and Development. It is on this basis that Mr. Heunis served as acting State President (January–March 1989) during the course of Mr. Botha's illness.

46. On the issue of the cabinet/SSC relationship the author has had something of a debate with Professor Geldenhuys. See his *Diplomacy and Isolation*, 91–96, and my "Managing the Security Power Base in South Africa." See also Lt. Gen. Andre J van Deventer, "State Security Council Not Sinister," *Paratus* 34 (November 1983): 9–11.

47. Reference n. 38 and accompanying discussion.

48. An estimate of less than fifty staff personnel in the early years of the NSMS should undoubtedly be revised upward. A more important consideration is the rank of personnel moving to the Secretariat from executive agencies.

49. The director-general was willing to concede that a NSMS was probably necessary and, yes, there were security aspects in what he was doing, but he did not need to be told too much about "his area" by committees "up on top."

50. However, two South African scholars contend that "it can justifiably be

asked whether these ... bodies (the intelligence services) readily convey their sometimes painfully gathered information to the SSCS." See Deon Geldenhuys and Hennie Kotze, "Aspects of Political Decision Making in South Africa," *Politikon* 10 (June/July 1983): 40.

51. Ibid.

52. In 1988 the SSC Secretariat released to the Institute for Strategic Studies, University of Pretoria, an outline of the National Security Management System. See Hough, *Selected Perceptions,* 3–27. Figure 1 is taken from this source. It also does not show the National Joint Management Center, which we discuss below.

53. Here the author must convey a personal impression. Admiral Putter displayed a kind of melancholy I have found, not infrequently, among senior SADF officers. I am convinced this mood derives, at least in part, from having to confront the fact of separation from the West—a fact made all the more difficult because of the existence of harmonious relationships at the working professional level with a number of foreign services. In this context, the fact of a great chasm at the political/strategic level is inexplicable to the SADF mind. Curiously, a kind of hopefulness persists but without optimism. There is corroboration for this "impression" in a 1982 paper by Admiral Putter (then chief of Naval Staff/Operations) on "South African Maritime Policy." The clearest and most succinct statement of South Africa's current naval predicament, it is at the same time a *cri de coeur.* See M. Hough, ed., *Contemporary Maritime Strategy* (Pretoria: ISSUP, August 1982), 40–47. See chapter 4 for discussion of the naval situation and chapter 6 for further discussion of the intelligence-sharing issue.

54. Not for direct attribution.

55. *Debates,* South Africa House of Assembly (15 September 1987), col. 5911. The minister of Defense, Gen. Magnus M A de M Malan.

56. Not for direct attribution.

57. Lt. Gen. Andre J van Deventer; Lt. Gen. Pieter van der Westhuizen; Lt. Gen. Charles Lloyd.

58. See literature discussion in the introduction.

4 FORGING THE SADF/ARMSCOR TEAM

> My years as Minister of Defense were among the happiest in the past fifty years. The growth of the Defense Force and the development of South Africa's armaments industry and the particular comradeship which I experienced in that organization, were sources of great joy to me.
>
> —Pieter Willem Botha, in an interview with the Afrikaans newspaper *Beeld*, April 30, 1986

Among the more notable characteristics of the "Boer-bashing school," the absence of historical perspective stands out. A case in point is the consternation in their ranks arising from the fact that South Africa should have recourse to arms (along with other instrumentalities of statecraft) in behalf of *national* interests. In fact the historical record on this point is quite remarkable. For most of this century "direct control over her own forces together with the experience of taking decisions in situations of wartime crises was abdicated"—depriving South Africa of a "tradition of reliance upon the military establishment." In the period between the Great Anglo-Boer War and *Operation Savannah*, rather than deploy the military to resolve disputes in which her own interests were directly involved, South Africa did little more than "provide the manpower for foreign field commanders and even governments to dispose over."[1] With *Savannah,* abdication of control is at an end, and the process of building SADF as a *national* force with a *national* tradition (earlier described as "PW's greatest achievement" and as the basis for many of his "happiest years") begins in earnest. Under the best of circumstances such a process requires time, although in this instance it will be accelerated by a more or less continuous deployment of troops in the field and by the emergence in tandem with SADF of Armaments Corporation of South Africa (ARMSCOR).

Much of the explanation for this achievement will consist in the exceptional flexibility and adaptability with which the Botha coterie will address impinging constraints. The technological constraint (exacerbated by an arms embargo especially after 1977) as well as the doctrinal and operational challenges of conducting contemporary warfare in all of its modalities will loom large. Still, the first and most stringent of constraints will be that of manpower. The nub of the matter for a new SADF, the manpower question is at the heart of the entire undertaking to dismantle apartheid, restructure the economy, and build the security forces. The skies cleared wonderfully following the retirement from Angola in 1976, illuminating the military situation for the Afrikaner mind with a clarity not previously experienced in the twentieth century. Now the Botha coterie is fully cognizant of the task confronting them and, for the first time, cognizant of the constraints that will weigh heavily on their efforts to respond. In an earlier chapter we saw how they defined the Onslaught and fashioned a "total national strategy" of counterrevolution. Now our discussion turns to the forging of the SADF/ARMSCOR team—those critical instrumentalities that have given to the Great Undertaking of P W Botha its prospect of success.[2]

Manning the Force

The Union Defense Force (UDF), established by the *Defense Act, 1912,* was renamed South African Defense Force in 1957 (*Defense Act, 1957*). SADF maintains the UDF tripartite structure of Permanent Force (PF), Citizen Force (CF), and Commandos (K), the latter two elements predating the UDF. Both the CF, derived from local rifle associations and British regiments established in the country prior to the South Africa Act, and the storied Boer Commando system were incorporated in 1913. In the same year, the PF was established as a new core entity. There are differences of view within the SADF officer corps about the optimal size of the regular cadre (the PF) but general agreement that a large professional force is neither feasible nor desirable. The Republic, in this view, is faced with significant military manpower demands, but these requirements must be met in accordance with South African norms and circumstances. SADF, consequently, remains the classic militia organization, adapting itself to the environment (physically, culturally, politically, and militarily) in which it operates. The Boer concept of the "citizen at arms" is the alpha and omega of all thinking about the manning of SADF. This is expressed in the philosophy that "responsibility for the defense of the RSA rests with all of its inhabitants" and in the aim "to involve all population groups in the country's defense."[3] Still, after twenty years of White conscription "the *Defense Act* does not make provision for National Service for Coloureds and Indians"[4] who by virtue of the 1983 Constitution are now eligible. This stands in conflict with the "all inhabitants" philosophy.

That the conscription issue is quintessentially political, not military, is appreciated within defense circles and, above all, by the State President. At the same time the institution that would be the crucible of a new tradition and a new nation cannot disguise its anxiety over continuing delay. A *verlig* officer corps sees National Service as the premier instrument not just for manning SADF, but for nation building, for citizenship development, and for counterrevolution. Added to these basic tenets of faith is a more immediate if no less compelling reason for extending National Service to all population groups. Annual "intakes" of eighteen-year-olds into military service are less disruptive of sustained economic growth than is frequent recourse to older, more skilled members of the Citizen Force and Commandos, most of whom are well established in the economy. Moreover, broadening National Service (to include at this point Coloureds and Indians) would directly meet an emerging requirement to enlarge the "continuous service" component of SADF. SADF's manning objective, which tends to shift with changing circumstances, is to achieve the most effective ratio of full-time to part-time service. Concerned that conventional reporting of SADF in terms of its tripartite structure (Permanent Force/Citizen Force/Commandos) was leading to "a widespread misconception"[5] of both posture and requirements, the RSA Department of Defense in recent years has issued new manning analyses. Today it emphasizes the distinction between the Full-time Force (FTF) and the Part-time Force (PTF). The distinction is drawn in terms of "type of service" rather than "type of personnel." Viewed in this way, the FTF constitutes approximately one-third of total SADF strength. More significantly, the FTF provides 87 percent of service "man-days." The salient point in this analysis is that the FTF, which "must supply troops on the ground," cannot be simply a volunteer force.

The core component remains the volunteer Permanent Force comprised of 12,500 White males and 5,500 Coloured, Indian, and Black males.[6] The PF, however, must be augmented by National Service Men (NSM), that is, the annual "intake" of White males who, having reached the age of eighteen, are fulfilling their initial, two-year "continuous service" obligation. They constitute approximately one-half of the FTF with more than 80 percent rendering service in the army. While the FTF spans all three arms of service (army/air force/navy) the "continuous service" component of the army at perhaps 75,000 is much the largest of the three. Difficulties in maintaining White conscription, much exaggerated by external sources, have abated in the late eighties with growing White consolidation. A larger matter is the continuing decision to forego conscription of Coloured and Indian males, especially in light of the need to increase the relative contribution of the full-time component. Not unrelated to this decision is the dramatic growth in the Botha years of enlistments ("attestings") from all population groups into the Permanent Force and other SADF elements. The PF first accepted volunteers from the Coloured population group in 1963. Their initial, two-year service period begins (today) in either "One" or "Two" Battalion of the army's South African Cape Corps (SACC) or in the SACC Maintenance Unit. For successful applicants, this leads to musterings in any one of the three arms of service. Those who do not meet mustering requirements may find an option in the Auxiliary Service. Coloureds have also volunteered directly into the Citizen Force and, since 1980, into the Commandos. Indians, almost without exception, have volunteered into the navy for, again, an initial two-year service period. Subject to available billets they may continue in the PF (navy); Citizen Force and Commandos are also options.

South African Blacks from the multiethnic townships first joined the Permanent Force in 1975. To train Black recruits the army added Two-One Battalion (now located at Lenz in the Transvaal) to its infantry training base.[7] Two-One Battalion offers both basic and advanced course training, fully recognizing that, because of varying educational levels in the country, Blacks will not advance as readily through courses as others. Recognizing as well that language differences are a barrier to promotion, the chief of SADF (Gen. J J Geldenhuys) has strongly recommended that White officers develop a fluency in at least one Bantu language. Because of the priority SADF attaches to "attestments" from Black ethnic groups, there has been a concerted effort to establish parity at all ranks including the matter of pay. Since 1984 Blacks have attained commissioned-officer status along with Coloureds and Indians. Two-One has served with distinction in the operational area, providing troops for such purposes as recently as 1988. Its primary function today, however, is to serve as the training base for regional battalions, the core units of the National or Independent Black states. While the first of these (Transkei, Bophuthatswana, and Ciskei) were in various stages of formation prior to the establishment of Two-One, it assisted with the now independent Venda Defense Force and has since formed units for the Swazi (111 Battalion New Amsterdam); the Shangaan (113 Battalion Letaba Ranch, Gazankulu); the N'debele (115 Battalion KwaNdebele); the Northern Sotho (116 Battalion Messina); and the Zulu (121 Battalion Josni, Natal). Whether these latter units move to a fully independent status or not, they are recognized as belonging to their respective chiefs and as making the maximum security contribution in their respective homeland areas.

The Part-time Force (PTF), made up of Citizen Force and Commandos, gives SADF its militia flavor. Citizen Force, the largest single component in the total-force structure, is perhaps the distinguishing feature of the entire organization. It consists for the most part of National Servicemen who, upon completion of their initial two-year continuous-service stint, assume a twelve-year obligation in the CF. In six two-year cycles, CF members must render 720 days of service. Thereupon they transition to the CF Reserve and until age fifty-five are liable for twelve days of service annually—an obligation that may be fulfilled in a Commando unit. The defense review of the early seventies gave to the CF responsibilities that have greatly tested the fundamental criterion that it is to be deployed "in extreme cases only, and then only for the shortest possible time"[8] Citizen Force was to be the principal element in conventional and semiconventional (counterinsurgency—COIN) warfare. As a result it is organized today by and large along two lines: first, into infantry battalions optimized for COIN operations with the army's Territorial Force and, second, into a variety of units to fill out the army's Conventional Force formations. The frequency of

CF deployments in these roles since 1975 has caused SADF to reexamine the Full-time/Part-time Force mix. The prospect of withdrawal from Southwest Africa provides some basis for the view that CF deployments ("service man-days") will decline in the near term. The internal-security mission within the framework of the Territorial Force remains and can be manpower intensive, but it is not expected that this requirement will exceed the capabilities of the Full-time Force in support of the South Africa Police. Pressures on the Commando Force, however, are not abating.

No element of SADF has been impacted as heavily or has undergone greater change as a consequence of South Africa's transformation than has the Commando Force. No longer is it possible to categorize the Commandos as Afrikaans-speaking (nor for that matter the Citizen Force as English-speaking).[9] Neither organization is any longer an exclusively White domain as we have seen. The Commandos still retain their territorial flavor: they are indigenous to the area in which they operate and their responsibilities are essentially local. However, the prototype, rural Commando is giving way to urban/semi-urban units among the approximately sixty in existence currently. (Today one is more likely to encounter a Commando Cessna pilot than he is a Commando horseman!) Commando units are organized in light-infantry formations for border and area security but increasingly into facilities-protection units, often with older, less fit personnel. Urbanization and demographic patterns compound an already difficult force-to-space ratio (as SADF is inclined to put it) in coping with internal security. The decades-long movement of the Boer to the cities has been accelerated in the eighties by drought and terrorist incidents, especially in the northern border areas. The Commandos are stretched thin there, making these areas less secure and more likely to be scenes of infiltration actions.

SADF is frank to concede that "persons in rural areas who will still be available for military service will probably be restricted to safeguarding hearth and home and *intelligence gathering*" (italics mine).[10] The need to increase the numbers of the Commando Force—from all population groups—has become one of SADF's highest priorities. A prime example of this problem is found in the Soutpansberg and Limpopo Valley at the Zimbabwe border. This is the Messina Sector of the Far Northern (*Verre-Noord*) Transvaal Command—a command that went "critical" following a nightmarish three months at the end of

1985 and the beginning of 1986.[11] The sector was the scene of classic terrorist incidents, part of a widespread ANC offensive throughout the Transvaal and Natal. In this period, eight land-mine explosions killing at least nine (including women and children) occurred along the Zimbabwe/Botswana border. The matter was now beyond the ken of the Soutpansberg Commando or any of the other Commandos in the region. Maj. Gen. George Meiring, coming off an assignment as GOC Southwest at the end of 1986, took over Far Northern Transvaal Command, relieving Maj. Gen. Charles Lloyd.[12] The command with headquarters at Pietersburg is one of two operational commands in the army's Territorial Force structure.[13] Air support is provided from the SAAF base at Louis Trichardt. In March 1986, Col. Lotus Swanepoel, sector commander at Messina, graciously received yet another visitor.[14] He outlined his situation with admirable clarity.

The sector extends from the intersection of the Zimbabwe and Mozambique borders with Kruger Park, 350 kilometers west/northwest along the Zimbabwe/RSA border (the Limpopo) to a point just west of the intersection of the Zimbabwe/RSA/Botswana border. The larger problem, the colonel explained, is the 30,000-square-kilometer area contiguous to this border for which he is responsible. Our task here (we paraphrase our hosts) is to implement a Border Stabilization Program. This entails first the protection of three major farming zones in the valley itself, and the widely dispersed farmers (perhaps no more than two hundred) in the arid Soutpansberg below.[15] In addition, however, the program seeks to retain, and add, farmers in the sector through a variety of government incentives, many of which are, perforce, designed "to protect hearth and home" and assist in intelligence gathering. Direct subsidies are provided to farmers (quite apart from building up Commando units) for fencing, mine-protected vehicles, and communications gear. Weapons and limited military training are provided to farm families as well, giving the whole thing all the appearances of a modern-day settlers and Indians scenario! This is precisely the situation in the Soutpansberg of the 1980s as it has been in Ovamboland (Namibia) for the past two decades.

The sector commander's "farm network" is his best intelligence warning and collection capability for coping with infiltration of a vast, largely empty area. The basic work of detection and reporting "illegals passing south" (usually in groups of two to four) lies with the farmers—the military for their part are pretty much confined to a reaction posture. While many of the infiltrators will prove to be "Zimbabwe Vendas" looking for work on Transvaal farms, SADF takes the straightforward view that "they are all ANC until otherwise established." It was matter-of-factly noted that this is sometimes established by turning them over to Venda troops in the 116 Northern Sotho Battalion (then in training and at the same time deployed in the sector as a reaction force) for interrogation. Occasionally ZIPRA elements from Matabeleland (Zimbabwe) will "get caught up with the ANC." Harshly handled by Mr. Mugabe's Mashona, they tend not to be hostile and consequently are sorted out from "the hostiles." This process of arrest and interrogation of illegals is a major factor in the vaunted SADF/SAP intelligence surveillance of ANC.

Surveillance of the Zimbabwe and Botswana borders, as well as the "depth" contiguous to those borders, can only be effective with the complete cooperation of bordering countries. The colonel was emphatic on this point as were, indeed, his superiors in Pretoria as 1985–86 had not been good years in this regard. (Twenty kilometers of electric fence and Gunite ditches running east along the Limpopo from Beitbridge seemed to be viewed by highly pragmatic SADF officers as "an interesting experiment." Up to this point the fence had collected various and sundry wildlife—examples of which were on display at Sector Headquarters—but nothing of the two-legged species. References to "our McNamara Line" were bandied about for the benefit of an American observer!) SADF has made it plain to Zimbabwe authorities that border stabilization encompasses a zone that extends twenty kilometers into Zimbabwe that in turn entails responsibilities on their part. Following the land-mine incidents, Harare hastened to assume responsibility for stabilization on its side of the border by deploying forces that included elements of the former Grey Scouts. (The Zimbabwe army is, of course, assisting with stabilization inside Mozambique.) Agreed-upon procedures call for the Messina sector commander and his Zimbabwe counterpart across the border to meet periodically for situation reviews. Colonel Swanepoel at this particular point in time was not entirely satisfied with the arrangement.[16] Similarly, efforts throughout this period to reach understandings with Botswana were anything but productive. Consequently, the worst was yet to come. The details take us into the ANC Question, which we will discuss in the next chapter. The Messina sector experience indicates, among other things, that Full-time Force units will increasingly be stationed throughout the country in a reaction posture to assist Commandos. The overlay of FTF and PTF units and regional Joint Management Centers thickened appreciably after 1985 as internal-security requirements rose.

Developing Doctrine

"We have a much better concept of ourselves today," proclaimed the OC of South Africa's Defense Staff College.[17] Echoing his colleague, Fourie, the brigadier reminded his visitor that before 1975 each of the "arms of service" fought independently as well as under foreign command: the army in north and east Africa, the air force in Britain and Korea, and (with feeling) "the navy off with the Brits fighting God knows what war for God knows what reason!" SADF in the 1980s is a different force—an integrated defense force—attuned to the exigencies, external and internal, of prosecuting counterrevolution. The 1975 Angola undertaking raised "republican concerns" within South Africa as to whether there was legal basis for the defense force to venture beyond the borders of the Republic or Southwest Africa. Certainly the old imperial notion of Jan Smuts of "anywhere in Africa" was no longer relevant. The issue was a sensitive one for both Mr. Vorster and Mr. Botha, and within weeks of the return of SADF units to the Rundu side of the Okavango there was legislative action. A provision in the *Defense Amendment Act, 1976* was a model of succinctness: a member of SADF may in time of war be required to perform service against any enemy *at any place.* (Italics mine.) The amendment removed any legal question as to whether SADF was confined in its operations to the Republic and Southwest. It also elicited a display of unity on the part of English-speakers and Afrikaans-speakers alike in Parliament that would build steadily in the years ahead. Members of the still intact Union Party were, not surprisingly, more emphatic than National Party members in their readiness to remove geographic restrictions. The debate did have portent for the Progressive Federal Party however. Mr. Harry H Schwarz, defense spokesman for the PFP, at first sought to confine SADF to adjacent areas but later voted for the amendment. Over the course of time Mr. Schwarz, breaking with many in his party, would support the new SADF concept and align himself with the defense leadership.[18]

Gen. J J "Jannie" Geldenhuys would be a leading formulator of the "new concept." In appraising the situation he confronted upon being appointed GOC Southwest (1977), he noted that while South Africa was in a *strategic defensive* posture this must be understood in *operational* terms as requiring aggressive, offensive operations. It would be folly, he informed his superiors in Pretoria, to rely on defensive operations (or a defensive mind-set) in what would certainly be a protracted conflict. It reduces very simply, Geldenhuys argued, to a matter of casualties. SADF cannot and must not sustain the casualties that would be an inevitable concomitant of manpower intensive, counterinsurgency and conventional warfare. By carrying the war to the enemy—by inflicting disproportionately heavy casualties—the task becomes manageable. SADF units will again have to be trained in "the way of war of their forebears." Once again, after three-quarters of a century, South Africans are fighting across the open spaces of that environment they call home. They can draw upon a taproot sunk deep in the veldt in the nineteenth century for sustinence; not yet a century removed from the Great Anglo-Boer War, its lessons are still part of the collective memory.

It was not mere coincidence that the Committee of Investigation into the Future Planning of the South African Defense Force and Related ARMSCOR Matters would be the Geldenhuys Committee.[19] Charged with conducting what amounted to the defense review for the eighties (there had been less systematic reviews at the beginning of the sixties and the seventies), the committee put particular emphasis upon those environmental factors that in its view "could affect the posture of SADF/ARMSCOR." There is noteworthy understatement here: the factors delineated in the report are the principal determinants of that posture—and of the manner in which SADF would fight on the battlefields of southern Africa! While a variety of "macro and micro" factors are assessed,[20] we focus here on "the influence of the space factor" because of its consummate importance for SADF operational doctrine. "Area is the only relatively stable factor as far as the RSA's environmental analysis is concerned," the committee noted, adding however that "the space between the RSA and its enemies has narrowed alarmingly." The operational impact of this relatively stable factor was underscored:

> The RSA is a vast country with extended borders and a long coastline that makes great demands on SADF. This means that *SADF has to*

operate in an area and not along a front. This requires special attention to logistics, strategic and tactical mobility, the need for blanket cover, decentralization of execution and a night-fighting capability.[21] (Italics mine.)

Operational doctrine is the meeting ground between the broad imperatives of strategy and the steady maxims of tactics, where if there is a "native genius" it will express itself. Intellectuals in South African military uniform—their numbers are not small—are today world leaders in the development of operational doctrine. "We in SADF have been, perhaps, too ready to take our strategic instruction from Beaufre and Liddell Hart," one of the principal mediators suggested to the author.[22] With operational doctrine it is otherwise; this rises straight up from the veld. When the problem is framed (as in fact it is framed for SADF) in terms of "how smaller forces defeat larger forces," it takes on a special cogency. What we are pointing to here is not a propensity for war but rather an acute understanding of how one wages war successfully in the native environment.

The new thinking about old ways of warfare of two men—Gen. Jannie Geldenhuys and Gen. Constand J Viljoen—is in place today at the army's Battle School (Northern Cape near Lohathla). Writing on "Mobile Warfare in Southern Africa," two officers from the school take the following from Thomas Pakenham's *The Boer War:* "There was one iron law of strategy imprinted on the minds of the Boers like a law of the wild—the answer to superior numbers is superior mobility."[23] Proceeding from assumptions that SADF will face a numerically superior force, an unfavorable air situation, and the unwillingness of the superpowers to tolerate a long-term conventional war lest they be drawn into it, the officers offer up a paean to the "dynamic element of warfare," namely, maneuver. The South African army, they aver, can win on any battlefield in southern Africa only "if it can move faster and fight more effectively" than its enemies.[24] The topography, the infrastructure, the obstacles, and the distances of southern Africa provide the requisite operational space for maneuver warfare. Consequently, all doctrine, training, tactics, and equipment must be optimized for this mode of warfare. It is in this critical respect—the capacity and opportunity for mobile warfare—that SADF strives to maximize its given advantage over potential enemies. Mobility and maneuverability are for naught, however, if it does not deliver the required fire at the required time and place; the objective, after all, is disproportionately heavy casualties inflicted upon the enemy. As another student of the South African military has put it, "The mechanized brigades are expected to conduct the maneuver battle with the aim of presenting the enemy to the armoured brigades for destruction at a suitable time and place."[25]

For all of the advantages conferred by the environment, SADF is, nonetheless, confronted with an unfavorable force-to-space ratio. This is compensated for in terms of unit design and by special attention to the logistics system. South African army formations consequently will possess strong reconnaissance elements and will be generally larger than counterparts in order to incorporate organic service and support elements. Gen. Constand J Viljoen (army chief, 1976–80, and chief of SADF, 1980–85), in the words of an admiring Citizen Force colonel, "the soldier's soldier, close to the men and close to the unit level, had a 'fetish' for keeping equipment at the unit level operational."[26] Viljoen saw his job as providing the wherewithal to make the operational doctrine work, much aware of the impinging constraints. "We have no illusions about strategic air mobility," the author was told. "We will not be able to haul a significant portion of the logistics load by air." It will be moved "overland by truck" using the road network that we have, and by using other vehicles off the road network with fuel only through Walvis Bay.[27] SADF is driven to maintain a stable and secure logistics system in order that "the young troopies have what they need to get the job done," but more fundamentally by insight into the requirements of successful mobile warfare in southern Africa. SADF officers are struck by the absence of vital logistic and command structures in the armies of neighboring states, which make offensive operations of any duration impossible. They are aware, however, that should "surrogates" enter southern Africa for the express purpose of remedying those deficiencies, the regional balance could be dramatically altered.[28] As we shall see (chapter 6) the events of 1987–88 in Angola came near to creating just such a crisis.

Fastidious attention is paid to the requisites for prompt mobilization and deployment of a trained, ready force. To this end, the army maintains in place a Corps Headquarters unit and headquarters units for both of its divisional formations (7th Infantry and 8th Armoured). In addition, a brigade of corps artillery, a parachute brigade, and other key elements are kept on operational status.[29] Each arm of service has a college for officer training and a staff college and draws upon the South African Military Academy (Saldanha Bay). At the top of the school system is the Defense Staff College on the *voortrekkerhoogte* outside of Pretoria. The service colleges accept "matrics" (secondary-school graduates) as officer candidates for the Permanent Force. Perhaps the most distinctive feature of SADF training is the army's Junior Leader Program. The Infantry School (Oudtshoorn), the Artillery School (Potchefstroom), the Intelligence School (Kimberley), and the Signals School (Heidelberg), for example, will train "junior leaders" (officers and NCOs together) for assignments to the national battalions and the Southwest Africa Territorial Force (*Suidwes-Afrika Gebieds-mag*). After "passing out" of their branch schools, they invariably move to the Battle School for critical maneuver-formation training, which incorporates lessons from the operational areas. A handful of junior leaders are retained in the Permanent Force, but the great majority become an essential component of the Citizen Force or in some instances the Commandos.

The manpower constraint joins with the space factor as codetermin-ant of how SADF will fight on the battlefields of southern Africa. In fact Heitman contends that "the manpower base situation *mandates* that ... SADF adopt a policy of pre-empting any serious threat that cannot be deterred" (italics mine).[30] Reflecting the thinking of senior SADF officers, he stresses that "with the bulk of the Army available only upon mobilization it is essential that SADF not be surprised by any major attack. An attacker with the advantage of surprise could hope to inflict *a defeat in detail* by forcing SADF to accept combat *piecemeal* ... it simply would not be feasible to allow an enemy to roam unhindered while (SADF) mobilizes and groups for battle" (ital-ics mine).[31] In spite of the political problems that preemption poses, it is the indispensable complement to deterrence in the form of a large, ready reserve force that can be mobilized quickly (but not always quickly enough). Deterrence with the threat of preemption is a policy imposed by circumstances (by environmental factors) and dictates a "short, sharp war" scenario. If intelligence dictates the need for pre-emption (e.g., a cross-border operation), it is expected that this can be carried out by Permanent Force elements of the army and air force, although even here reliance on other full-time components (or even elements of the Citizen Force) may be necessary. The preemptive strike may be sufficient in and of itself to relieve the crisis; it will in any event buy time for required mobilization. Posed in this scenario is the role of the air force—that arm of service that SADF today strives mightily to prevent becoming a diminishing asset.

In his opening remarks to the Conference on Contemporary Air Strategy at the University of Pretoria, Gen. Constand J Viljoen, then chief of SADF, expressed his concern that "the conventional military threat to the Republic lies mainly in *a sudden reversal* of the military balance in southern Africa *by the Soviet Union and its surrogates*" (italics mine).[32] Should "a disparity in the strength of air power on the conventional side in favor of the Republic's hostile neighbors" emerge, he continued, the RSA's freedom of action could be constrained. The series of operations in Angola culminating with *Askari* (January 1984), successful in all dimensions (including air), did nonetheless raise questions within SADF of the capacity over time of the South African Air Force (SAAF) to play its vital role in preemption-cum-deterrence. "We don't have a major counter-air problem," Mortimer remarked during our May 1985 discussion. "The looming problem is that of providing close air support within the ground/air team concept of operations." However, Angolan operations at the end of 1985 and the culminating series (*Modular-Hooper-Packer*) in 1987–88 would cast a harsher light on the issue. In a much delayed meeting with the press in Windhoek (February 1989), Col. Deon Ferreira,[33] SADF field commander for *Modular-Hooper-Packer,* stated that "the enemy's Soviet MiG–23s were the single most serious threat to our operations. We were constantly harassed by them, but fortunately UNITA had *Stingers* which kept them at a high altitude."[34] Then came the epilogue at Calueque.

There had long been an understanding between Luanda and Pretoria that the Ruacana Scheme built by South Africa on the Cunene River, just inside Angola, to provide electric power and water to Ovamboland was off-limits in the ongoing fighting—that (Angolan) Military Region Five was not part of "the area in question." This understanding (quite possibly against the objections of President dos Santos) was broken abruptly on the morning of June 27, 1988. A Cuban/FAPLA force in three columns moving from Techipa toward Calueque was intercepted at the halfway point by a SADF force. In a fierce firefight the Cuban/FAPLA columns were routed with losses of some three-hundred troops (one SADF officer was killed). The South Africans had been prepared for this foray after Cuban forces had earlier moved south from their defensive line (the "Line of the Benguela," or roughly the sixteenth parallel approximately three hundred kilometers north of the Namibian border). What they were not prepared for was what happened during the afternoon of the twenty-seventh. Twelve MiG-23 ("Flogger") fighter/attack aircraft, flying from Angola's major military air field at Lubango, passed over Techipa and dropped to "a very low altitude" (perhaps less than two hundred feet), below radar detection, and hit the Calueque dam ("barrage") wall and pumps. Three of some twelve to eighteen 500-pound bombs damaged the wall, temporarily cutting off water and electrical power to Ovamboland. One bomb overshot the wall by 600 meters, hitting a camouflaged "static position" of SADF troops and killing eleven.[35]

The incidents of June 27, 1988, underscored two points—if, indeed, any further underscoring was needed. Serious troop losses can be incurred even when those troops are "standing down" (far more than in the firefight hours earlier) and—more far-reaching—there was now a new dimension to the air situation. The afternoon air strike was not the result of pique following the thrashing on the ground in the morning. In fact, Cuban pilots had been extensively trained and rehearsed for just such a mission. Their approach was not detected, in part, because the densest air-defense network in the world (apart from the approaches to Moscow) made SAAF reconnaissance a dicey thing. The South African Air Force is known worldwide for its "world-class" contingent of pilots and a superb ground-support system. The crisis inheres in the aircraft inventory. Throughout an extended dinner discussion following the Calueque episode Lt. Gen. Dennis Earp, SAAF, was somber.[36] "The issue for us is not control of the airspace over Angola," he emphasized, "we are not interested in rolling around in the Angolan skies dogfighting with MiGs—even the most favorable kill-ratios would not be that helpful." The South African air chief had a larger concern: the finite number of air frames (especially tactical-fighter aircraft) available to SAAF. These would have to be husbanded with the greatest care and committed only in the most critical instances. While not wishing to be explicit on this point, Earp left little doubt that the priority allocations would be air cover and air support for deployed ground forces, and then for sovereignty in South African airspace—in that order. In reply to the question "What will you do if the aircraft inventory becomes critical," the general concluded with the following: "If worst comes to worst we shall do what we have to do."[37]

Inability to replace the Avro MR-3 ("Shackelton") squadron, either through foreign purchase or domestic production, has significantly altered the maritime air role of SAAF (not to mention the role of the navy itself). While the loss of long-range maritime-reconnaissance capability is not as freighted with implications as "block obsolescence" of the tactical-fighter force (or even the air-transport component), it has had international impact. The Joint Maritime/Air Surveillance Center at Silvermine (under Constanzia Ridge near Simonstown), once a key component in the Western ocean surveillance/intelligence network, is a wasting—if not already wasted—asset. Headquarters for both SAAF's Southern Command and SAN's Naval Command/West,[38] there is all but no antisubmarine warfare (ASW) function today and only "close-in" coastal reconnaissance with *Albatross* (Piaggio P-166S) aircraft. Strike aircraft (MB-326 *Impalas*), should they be needed, are available to Southern Air Command. As something of an indicator of South African frustration with the West (NATO) on the question of Silvermine, restriction to the administrative level was waived in the present case and admission to all three tiers of the bunker granted.[39] A full Silvermine tour is to step back into a 1950s "time quark"—into a museum of vintage technologies: Siemens, AEG Telefunken, Omega, and Racal among others. (Capacities that are now "desk-top" were occupying rooms!) With the "Shackletons" laid up and with a diminishing number of surface platforms and sensors, the data feed into the center is a trickle. In the language of Command/Control/Communications and Intelligence (C³I), Silvermine does not have real-time capability; it can display twelve-hour situation estimates on shipping along the South African sea frontier. Likewise, it can control single service and SADF joint operations in the two command areas. Designed to withstand nuclear attack, Silvermine is also designed to be part of an alliance system that has yet to come to fruition. The trauma for the South African Navy (SAN), if not for SADF as a whole, has been acute.

On a bright morning of May[40] when we reached the overlook point, where our escort was kind enough to stop before descending to the South African Navy's (SAN) Simonstown Station, one could see a *Daphne* submarine "standing out" on the dappled waters of False Bay. A second was in two-year lay-up (undergoing a full-scale upgrade) in the dockyard below, and the third, and last, of the SAN underwater flotilla "was not about."[41] The diminished circumstances of a nation splendidly endowed with Mahan's "maritime assets"—with immense potential as a regional maritime power—would be painfully laid bare this day, all the more sharply etched in a spectacular setting on Drake's "fairest of all capes." Banter over coffee at "Admiral's House" (a handsome imperial artifact) began with "Is SAN a full-fledged member of SADF today, and not out looking for 'some bloody war of its own?' " "You have been talking to Mortimer alright," came the genial reply of ComNavCape. The commodore and his associates were prepared to turn to realities poignant as they might be. One such was tied up only a few hundred yards away. "You know Grimbeek[42]—he has the *Pretorius* now." Our attention was directed to the *President Pretorius,* sole remaining frigate (last of four UK Type 12 "Rothesays") in SAN.[43] It seemed an artifact, itself, belying substantial capabilities as the single major platform in the surface force. The frigates have given way to the FACs (Fast-Attack Craft) as the centerpiece of South African sea force. These are the *Minister*-class missile boats carrying the *Skerpioen* surface-to-surface missile (an ARMSCOR evolution of the Israeli *Gabriel* system). The FACs are not a satisfactory centerpiece, however. "It is too small a platform." ("It is a young man's platform," interjected an evidently knowledgeable source!) "It does not have the range, and we cannot put the surface-to-surface and surface-to-air systems on it of which we are capable."[44]

It was a wholly incongruous situation that was being outlined—in a controlled, matter-of-fact manner that attracted attention but did little to conceal underlying currents. This was not a "Third World navy,"[45] but rather a "First World navy"—without ships! SAN was gradually losing contact with the Royal Navy and the United States Navy, becoming less and less familiar with RN and USN ship types, procedures, and tactics. "We have to write our own manuals to deal with this vintage stuff," remarked the dockyard OC. "We've had to become quite ingenious to continue to do repair and maintenance. If we can't find parts, we manufacture them here in the dockyard."[46] The message was plain: it would take years to "come back on line" not only in terms of underway procedures but in the more critical shore-support functions, even if there were the slightest signs of naval *rapprochement* from the West. South Africa's separation from the Western maritime community—the fact that today it is not a participating partner in Western maritime strategy—"is not a situation which arose from South Africa's own making," General Viljoen told an academic audience in

1982.[47] SAN's retrenchment in the 1980s, its shrinking force structure, and its decision not to undertake, unassisted and isolated, a "blue water" role, stems from "the abandonment of the Western navies of *their joint responsibilities* in defending the Cape Sea Route" and "from the arms embargo imposed on South Africa" (italics mine).[48] There was no one at Simonstown that day who would disagree with Viljoen.

South Africa has not foresworn its maritime patrimony. It neither contemplates a diminished maritime role nor does it intend to restrict its maritime strategic thinking. This said, it is also the case that South Africa has not articulated a "national maritime policy" that takes account of immense assets—the full Mahanian spectrum of seapower—at a national or even alliance level. As a result, the naval element of sea power, rather than developing in directions drawn from a national maritime policy, has developed along lines (using the plaintive words of Admiral Putter) "prompted by the steady dissolution of South Africa's military relationships with the major Western nations."[49] SAN is today what many in the Republic—far from all—feel it must be, namely, the maritime component of SADF with its role and missions defined within SADF parameters. Putter does not altogether absolve South Africans from responsibility for this situation. Many were beguiled, he suggests, by "the spurious shelter" that the Simonstown Agreement appeared to offer and, after 1975, by the continuing belief that they were "part of the Western alliance." For all of the advantages it conferred, according to another South African scholar, the Simonstown Agreement "was also a curse." "It removed the necessity for SAN and, far worse, the South African government to think about naval strategy . . . responsibility for naval strategy was *abdicated to London*" (italics mine).[50]

SADF's maritime aims to which SAN addresses itself today are, first, to protect the Republic's maritime assets along an extended sea frontier (the ports, harbors, yards, docks, and their supporting infrastructure). This mission also entails maintaining the integrity of sea communications along that frontier. Second, SAN must defend the country against seaborne or sea-supported aggression. The posture is the strategic defensive but again with a view to offensive operations. At best a limited "sea-denial" mission is possible, what with a surface force (the *Pretorius* aside) consisting of a dozen Fast-Attack Craft, four seaward-defense boats (UK *Ford* class), and harbor-defense craft (thirty *Namacurra*, lightly armed boats). SAN has a counterinsurgency mission (as an integral element of SADF), namely, "the logistical support of reconnaissance units engaged in landward operations in contiguous areas."[51] (That third submarine again!) Within these parameters, SAN has found it impossible to develop a "force concept" that would justify appreciably higher expenditures. Thus, in response to those who would call for "a navy air arm," Admiral Putter has had to respond that "the navy's requirement for an indigenous air capability (is) simply too small to make this a cost-effective proposition."[52] Similarly, while Durban shipyards can build platforms larger than the *Drakensberg*—and leaving investment priorities aside—the requirement does not exist at this point. (That is not to say that something larger than a *Minister*-class boat might not emerge!) In the face of all this, senior naval officers tell themselves (and those who will listen) that lines of communication will be kept open to Western navies for that ultimate day when they reconsider broader maritime strategic realities. For its part, SAN is prepared to again take up the task of supporting Western interests in the southern ocean ("a thankless task from which it derives precious little") when the West is again prepared to have a "blue water navy" at the Cape.

ARMSCOR: Providing the Means—with Gaps

Armaments Corporation of South Africa is said to have had its inception (the source denied that the story is apocryphal) in the notorious inability of the Afrikaner bureaucracy to accomplish anything in a timely fashion. So exasperated had Prime Minister Hendrik Verwoerd become with civil-service efforts to develop a new rifle that after ten years he had had enough. Verwoerd circulated a memo among relevant government offices suggesting the separation of arms production from the civil service. Encountering, to his surprise, little resistance, he forthwith appointed the Steyn Committee (1962) to develop legislative proposals. The *Armaments Act, 1964* was the first of a series that in 1976 produced the present ARMSCOR.[53] The legislation is informed by two themes that go far to explain South Africa's approach to the development and manufacture of military equipment and weapons. First, an indigenous armaments industry is established in which nine state subsidiaries[54] form the nucleus of a vast, private (70 percent) network of manufacturers and contractors. Second, this public sector/private sector mix is publicly controlled by ARMSCOR's board of directors (itself consisting of public and private members)[55] and its management team. The function of the board is to broadly oversee management in terms of budget and production goals and in terms of key strategic imperatives (viz., technology). The managers, under an executive general manager (*uitvoerende hoofbestuurder*),[56] run not only headquarters but the state subsidiaries and the hundreds of affiliates through an elaborate series of boards and committees. "You must keep in mind, however," a Ministry of Defense spokesman noted, "that ARMSCOR is the other leg of the Ministry of Defense responsible to the minister." The unique conjunction of SADF and ARMSCOR—of defense force and defense industry—under one leadership has produced unexpected dividends for a country under embargo for two decades.

Long ensconced in Pretoria's *Visagie Straat* in the *Sinodale Sentrum* of the *Nederduits Gereformeerde Kerk* (NGK) (alongside the Atomic Energy Corporation no less), ARMSCOR collects all of its managers on the seventh floor. "There are some ten of us—it's very convenient in terms of running the operation."[57] Scheduled to move into Erasmus Castle (complete with a reputation of being haunted) in a new headquarters complex in suburban Pretoria, it remains to be seen how efficiency will be impacted by a more mundane setting! Linkage to SADF is principally through the Defense Planning Committee (DPC), which in its present form dates from 1976. Established to "ensure the participation of all members of the defense family in the planning process," the DPC consists of the chief of SADF as chairman, the chiefs of each arm of service, the chiefs of (SADF) staff for operations, logistics, and finance, the chairman of the board of ARMSCOR, the executive general manager, and a representative from private industry. Its key function is to make procurement recommendations to the minister of Defense on all components of force structure. The DPC meets at least quarterly to make "go or no-go decisions" on systems developed to user specifications (i.e., SADF). "We in ARMSCOR do not drive weapons decisions—that is for SADF." The "seventh floor" does have something to say about technology-base matters—about what is plausible and what is not. But ARMSCOR is in business to meet its customers' needs. Today the customer list goes well beyond SADF and SAP to include defense forces around the world. (We shall come back to this point.)

ARMSCOR's stature and fame derive, more than anything else,

from its accomplishments in support of an army in the field. It has developed infantry, armor, artillery, signal, transport, and logistic equipment optimized for the conditions in which the *Suid-Afrikaanse Leer* fights. In addition, it provides timely solutions to field problems as they arise. The conversion, adaptation, and upgrading of systems are coupled with startling new systems created out of the exigencies of southern African battlefields. Many of these systems are well known today, ARMSCOR having gone, more or less, "public" at the beginning of the eighties in connection with its marketing efforts.[58] The Military Vehicle Division (known since 1982 as SAMIL) exemplifies the interface between SADF and ARMSCOR perhaps as well as any element. SAMIL has designed, developed, tested, and deployed to the field an astonishing array of vehicles, all from three basic truck-chassis types (SAMIL 20, 50, and 100). *Eland* armored cars (originally derived from French *Panhard* licenses and components) and *Ratel* infantry fighting vehicles have given wheeled vehicles a new standing among those dedicated to armored and mechanized infantry tactics. In October 1988 ARMSCOR unveiled the *Rooikat,* a classic, indigenous achievement.[59] Its rapid-fire, computer-assisted 76-mm gun, low profile, and high speed make it the best wheeled armored vehicle in the world and ideal for the *veld. SA Leer,* while not considering the "main battle tank" (MBT) optimal for southern Africa, chooses to keep the option open in the face of significant numbers of Soviet tanks in the frontline states. In the absence of adequate antitank capabilities, the standard view that "the way to deal with a tank is with a tank" holds. The conversion of some 250 British *Centurions* into *Olifants,* complete with new engines, gearboxes, and 105-mm guns with "enhanced" ammunition and laser range finders gave SADF a capability that proved timely in Angola in 1987–88.

Lessons driven home by Angolan operations include no stronger imperatives than that of "range and reach" for field systems. Early on came the discovery that 5.5 (140-mm) guns were falling short (an upgrade of the system followed). This was demonstrated by Soviet BM-21, 122-mm rocket launchers ("Stalin Organs"), or in SADF terms, multiple-artillery rocket launchers (MARL systems). ARMSCOR did not have captured "Stalin Organs" in hand long before they tired of reverse engineering and decided they could do better on their own.[60] Drawing on its air-to-air missile technology (its V-3 *Kukri* program), Kentron had prototypes of the *Valkiri* MARL system in the field in time for *Operation Protea* in 1981. Today a much improved *Valkiri-5* has a 127-mm double base, solid-propellant rocket motor, twelve launch tubes (down from twenty-four), range in excess of twenty kilometers, and is drawn by a SAMIL-50 truck. Built in conjunction with Somchem, it is a worthy companion to the showpiece of SADF/ARMSCOR, the supreme achievement of a traditional art in South Africa, the G-5 and G-6 155-mm field guns. The G-5 towed by a SAMIL-100 tractor and the self-propelled (wheeled) G-6 are the best operational 155-mm guns in the world today. Featuring South African gun-barrel metallurgy and innovations with "basebleed" ammunition, these guns have the longest reach and sharpest accuracy of any in their category. They, too, appeared between the Lomba and Cuanavale rivers in 1987–88.

In interviews with ARMSCOR officials over the period 1979–88, invariably one theme quickly came to the surface: the worsening relationship with the United States insofar as import restrictions are concerned. This constantly occurred in connection with discussions of "the greatest problem facing us today"—the limited combat-aircraft inventory. A UN arms embargo is hardly the problem, one was informed: "The *United States* is driving this problem, contesting every 'nut and screw'." In the eye of the storm is Atlas Aircraft's *Cheetah* program— a complete rework and refit of the Mirage III (and ultimately F-1) tactical fighters. "There is only a finite number of air frames we can work with, and then I don't know what we'll do" (although later—see below—there would be a discussion of options). "Some of *your people*," this official went on, "can't believe we are redoing the air frames—they seem to think we are getting them from Argentina or somewhere. We don't have the *Lavi* (Israeli Advanced Fighter Project, canceled in 1988 under U.S. pressure)—we have some people from the project, not just from Israel but other countries as well" (italics mine).[61] South African technologies that will make the *Cheetah* a formidable multirole fighter/attack aircraft include the V-3C *Darter* "all-aspect" air-to-air missile "slaved" to the pilot's helmet sight. It has evolved out of Kentron's decade-old *Kukri* system. Antipersonnel, cluster-bomb munition packages developed by ARMSCOR will be part of the total system as well. Indoctrination and familiarization of SAAF pilots (in two-seater versions of the *Cheetah*) takes place at 89 Combat Flying School in Pietersburg. In addition to its rework capacity, Atlas can mount a limited production run of one aircraft type. In

1982 it closed down production of the *Impala* strike aircraft and since has been developing a light attack helicopter (the perhaps over-publicized *Alpha* XH-1, which is somewhat short of "state-of-the-art") and an improved *Puma* XPT-1 troop-carrying helicopter. Production decisions on both have to be weighed against the possibility of other indigenous options. The great achievement of Atlas in any case (overlooked in some quarters) is to capitalize on local private-sector capacity to manufacture components and, through system-integration techniques, to incorporate these components in weapon systems. Life-extension programs on the "Shackletons" and "Canberras" are cases in point.

More than one ARMSCOR official, however, has pointed to a broader challenge: "It's no secret," said one, "our highest priority at this time is the development of a full family of missile systems." In addition to the air-to-air system this would include air-to-ground missiles, surface-to-air missiles, and, significantly, multipurpose, surface-to-surface (ballistic) missiles. A senior SADF officer was almost ebullient on the subject: "We have a proud tradition of ordnance and munitions to draw on (going back to the Ammunition Section of the South African Mint and the old Boer gunsmiths)—we can do it, we must!" ARMSCOR Board Chairman Piet Marais has corroborated this at least to the extent of saying that "long-range (ballistic) missiles are very much within our capability."[62] The R&D work is underway in the Kentron and Somchem subsidiaries and, while particularly directed to find "stand-ins" for strike aircraft, it addresses the emerging requirements of all arms of service. ARMSCOR has made the *Cactus/Crotale* low-altitude, surface-to-air (SAM) system available to SADF through French licenses and imported components. At the same time, SADF is the only defense force to come back from a campaign with an intact Soviet SAM-8 system in tow! (This point is related to intelligence sharing with the United States.) Whether ARMSCOR will spend time on reverse engineering of the SAM-8 (as it did with the Soviet BM-21 MARL system) remains to be seen. The option of concentrating on its own high-altitude system seems more likely.

The concluding campaigns in Angola drove the SAM project just as they drove the air-to-ground project and, above all, the medium-range surface-to-surface missile (SSM) requirement. Hostile, high-performance aircraft on well-protected fields in neighboring countries must be "covered." Overland operations and air strikes, while not ruled out as potential means of coverage, are likely to encounter increasing levels of resistance. There now seems little question that the major offset option for a looming SAAF aircraft shortfall is a SSM system in the five-hundred-kilometer range, if not a second system at the one-thousand-kilometer range, so compelling is the distance factor. The medium-range SSM project faces challenges in terms of propellants, guidance, and warhead technology—all within ARMSCOR capabilities, however. It is likely as well that South Africa has some access to Israeli *Jericho* SSM technology and what appears to be the joint Israeli-Argentine *Condor* project. Vast, open expanses of territory with low-population densities define most of the theaters in question. Such parameters suggest to some, inevitably, the utility of a nuclear warhead. It is impossible to elicit any such thinking from SADF/ARMSCOR sources, but the author has encountered reluctance on the part of individuals in uniform to support a nuclear requirement. Something of a composite view is that "this is a budget-buster for one thing and sends us down a road to the unknown. The nuclear matter is for politicians. Besides, we have excellent conventional warheads."[63] Medium-range SSM systems should make their appearance in southern Africa soon.

Such a development is likely to have only marginal benefits for the South African Navy (SAN). "The navy is number three after the army and air force on the ARMSCOR list, I'm afraid," was the taciturn observation of one of the management. The replenishment ships *Tafelberg* and *Drakensberg* have been refitted as command ("mother") ships for the Fast-Attack Craft—one for each ocean. Conceivably, they offer platforms for SSMs and, conceivably, shore-based, medium-range SSMs could support the coastal-defense mission, but these do not rank with landward priorities. "We are conscious of what Argentine pilots accomplished with *Exocet* (a short-range French SSM or, in this instance, employed in the air-to-surface mode from French *Super Etendard* naval strike aircraft) in the Falklands war." The episodes in Prince George Sound dramatized the fact that the SAN surface force is without adequate SAM (anti-air) capability as much as they demonstrated the hitting power of *Exocet*. Again, the issue is whether SAN will have frigate-sized platforms, and this will be controlled by broader imperatives than naval force structure design. Beyond extensive modernization of the twenty-year-old *Daphne* submarines, there is no commitment to new construction. There are some possible applications of the *Skerpioen* here, and discussion of "heavy torpedoes" with nuclear warheads for *"Daphne* diesels" is heard in South Africa as elsewhere.[64] Those are not decisions for ARMSCOR or, for that matter, the Defense Planning Committee.

ARMSCOR went international at the beginning of the decade during the term of John Maree as executive general manager (1979–82). The export-minded Barlow Rand manager "seconded" to ARMSCOR to take on problems of rapid growth in budget and personnel (i.e., "contain costs") quickly pointed to export markets as a time-honored device to preserve critical skills, to keep production lines open, and to keep unit costs competitive. Under his successors (Fred Bell and Johan van Vuuren) ARMSCOR has become the RSA's leading exporter of manufactured goods (exceeding Mr. Maree's Barlow Rand) with buyers in more than thirty countries (none of whom Pretoria chooses to officially identify). This represents some 60 percent of South African production.[65] ARMSCOR managers are frank to admit that the export side provides a stiff challenge to them to stay competitive in weapons and other military systems. They cannot hope to compete in the international arms market without providing state-of-the-art systems. In turn this requires them to offer a select shopping list in which they are at the forefront, a requirement that in no way alters the fact that SADF drives weapon-system choices. The prominence of South Africa in the eighties as an arms exporter has had its effect on the RSA/Israeli relationship where there are now some ragged edges. "When we were simply on the take, only a buyer," it was explained, "and they (Israel) were the seller, things were fine. Now that we are very active as an exporter there is a rivalry in the relationship that has produced instances of being at loggerheads with each other. There is only a limited number of the right kind of customers out there for both of us." Once importing 70 percent of its military requirements, South Africa today, in the face of frantic efforts to maintain the arms embargo, imports 5 percent of its requirements. ARMSCOR not only has a manager in charge of exports but one in charge of imports or, it was noted, "smuggling if you like." Mr. Fred Bell, who came to ARMSCOR with a background in munitions, worked hard on both ends of the trade balance. So successful was he that upon his departure in 1985, he was given a special portfolio in the "sanctions-busting enterprise." [66]

In an interview at the highest level of the SADF/ARMSCOR team, the author was told that "only by living under an embargo could one understand how it feels." (Those feelings, incidentally, were close to the surface!) The source then related the gist of a very unsatisfactory discussion he had had with two visiting British M.P.'s. The visitors put two questions to their host:

(1) If you could secure equipment from abroad today, which items would you want, and

(2) In the past SADF officers have been in staff course in the U.K.—were these valuable—would you choose today to resume them?

"My response to those questions," my source stated, "was simply this: 'Can you say at all to me that there is any possibility whatsoever that any sort of equipment can be secured at this time, or that staff courses can be arranged?' Their reply was in the negative, and so I said that, of course, it was wholly pointless for me to answer their questions."

Our discussion then turned to the RSA/U.S. relationship and what might fall within the realm of the possible. "However much the 'regional climate' in southern Africa might improve, or however much progress we might make toward 'a new dispensation,' it is difficult for us in the RSA to imagine the *UN* rescinding its embargo resolutions." (This general view was expressed in a 1986 interview.) "What we really need to know is whether in any respect it is within the realm of the possible—should there be political progress—for *USG* (U.S. government) to unilaterally make specific, selected exceptions to the embargo. Unless and until there is a complete airing on this point it is useless to talk about specific end items: it is pointless to alert the International Monitoring Mechanism over a case of 'smuggling.' Broader talks are required." The case of Silvermine and the whole issue of Cape surveillance was referred to as a case where your own interests are more engaged than ours, but where various new capabilities are required if there is to be full utilization of this resource. The interview ended on an amicable note: earlier feelings having subsided, my source was joking about how Americans are much easier to discuss these matters with than are other foreigners. "You Americans have a capability of putting me at ease." This bit of hospitality notwithstanding, this officer would not be at ease until a new era had dawned, and he did not believe that the realization of that day was entirely the responsibility of the Republic of South Africa.

After some early and anything but unique difficulties in developing its unique (surprisingly bureaucracy-free) SADF/ARMSCOR team, the

RSA is a world leader in meshing weapons requirements with weapons development and production—the arms embargo no doubt having played its vital role as spur. Ian V. Hogg, editor of *Jane's Defense Weekly*, as close an observer of ARMSCOR as it is possible for any non–South African to be, has explained this achievement in the following terms: "The South Africans have not only caught up with but have, in many areas, surpassed the rest of the world in armaments development . . . *and they have succeeded in their aim because they have kept that aim limited*" (italics mine).[67] The "limited aim" philosophy has allowed SADF/ARMSCOR to carefully select focus areas upon which to concentrate their efforts and, indeed, the Geldenhuys Committee has reaffirmed this aim.[68] The results for the South African army have been little short of spectacular, making it, no doubt, the best equipped "light army" in the world. Results for SAAF and SAN have not kept pace in spite of some surprising achievements. Inexorably, a debit side to the limited aim philosophy has come into view in recent years. (The choice of this approach, after all, was dictated more by iron circumstances than by, let us say, rationalization.) "We know something about sanctions and how to deal with them," a former ARMSCOR general manager confided, "but over the longer term sanctions will deprive us of vanguard technology and we cannot afford that." No amount of ingenuity can make up for the fact that the RSA does not live and share in the world of leading-edge science and technology. In the final analysis, if South Africa is to have a frontline air force, however modest in size, and a navy that will again be part of the Western Maritime Community, this will occur as the result of political breakthroughs and not just the heroics of ARMSCOR. This is one of a number of factors that make the SADF officer corps *verlig* and outward oriented. The frustration, which in some respects is strongest in the army, will be seen in a different dimension in the following chapter.

Notes

1. Deon F S Fourie, "South Africa: The Evolving Experience," in *Defense Policy Formation*, ed. Roherty, 87–88. Fourie argues that the government of Louis Botha would not have moved into German Southwest Africa except at the behest of London. This is underscored by the rebellion that broke out among Afrikaners (including such founding fathers of the new Union Defense Force as C F Beyers and S G "Mannie" Maritz), which Botha had to put down before pro-

ceeding. The story of South African forces abroad through the first half of the
twentieth century is all but synonymous with the life and career of Jan Smuts.

2. The fundamental task of SADF as it is described by Mr. Botha himself in
the preface to the *White Paper on Defense and Armament Production, 1973* is to
ensure that "the Government will have the time and the freedom of action needed
to develop its internal and foreign policies." What Mr. Botha may not have
anticipated in 1973 is that he would ultimately call upon SADF to take part in the
development and implementation of those policies as well.

3. South Africa, *White Paper on Defense, 1986*, 17.

4. Ibid., 19. The Progressive Federal Party, rather than include Coloureds
and Indians in National Service, in November 1984 called for the abandonment
altogether of conscription and an "enlarged professional army." Its subsequent
demise cannot necessarily be traced to this one factor!

5. Ibid., 4. Manpower issues as they affect both the military and the economy at large are formally considered by the Defense Manpower Liaison Committee. This committee, which supplanted the short-lived Defense Advisory Council
in 1982, is made up of Ministry of Defense and corporate-sector members receiv-
ing somewhat more publicity than does the similarly constituted board of directors of ARMSCOR. The criticality of the manpower issue was immediately
evident to the new minister of Defense in 1980. See General Malan's remarks to
the Annual Meeting of the Volkskas Bank (Pretoria) as reported in the *Financial
Mail* (Johannesburg), August 15, 1980.

6. Precise manning data is not available from SADF. Such numbers as are
used here can be found in such sources as *Journal of Defense and Diplomacy,
International Defense Review, Jane's Defense Weekly,* and the International Institute of Strategic Studies annual *Military Balance.* Some of the international "defense press," as distinguished from the press generally, has established excellent
rapport with SADF/ARMSCOR. SADF includes in the full-time component, in
addition to Permanent Force personnel, National Servicemen, Service Volunteers
(White females and Coloured and Indian males who render one year's "continuous service"), the Auxiliary Service, and civilian members of the Department of
Defense.

7. In 1988 Xhosa-speakers from the Cape (Crossroads and Khayelitsha) were
attested into the Permanent Force. They are trained at Wingfield by the Group
Forty Training Detachment and then assigned to the Cape Regiment. It is expected that they will be effective in securing the townships around Cape Town.
For a now-dated account of Two-One Battalion, complete with editorial peregri-
nations, see Kenneth Grundy, *Soldiers without Politics: Blacks in the South African Armed Forces* (Berkeley: University of California Press, 1983), especially
chapter 9.

8. South Africa, *White Paper, 1986*, 5.

9. It is evident to even the most casual observer that SADF has not cast off
all of the *accoutrement* of its British lineage. In fact in 1949 the Commandos took
on British order.

10. *White Paper, 1986*, 6.

11. While the Unrest began with the events of September 1984 (chapter 5), it
achieves one of its peaks at this juncture. Durban is racked by bombings; the
Pondo-Zulu clashes occur in Natal; there are incidents at Moutse in the Northeast

Transvaal including the slaying of a community leader, Chief Ampie Mayisa, just before he is to meet with U.S. Assistant Secretary of State Chester Crocker; twenty-five die in one week at Queenstown and Mamelodi, and there is a rocket attack on the SASOL facilities. Some six thousand are arrested at this time (five thousand subsequently released); SADF under "emergency provisions" obtains police-arrest powers; and the war against ANC escalates.

12. After a brief retirement General Lloyd would succeed Gen. Pieter van der Westhuizen as secretary to the State Security Council in September 1987.

13. The Territorial Force of the army is distributed through ten commands in the Republic and the Walvis Bay Military District. The Eastern Transvaal Command is the second command with special operational responsibilities by virtue of its location.

14. The author visited Messina Sector Headquarters on March 6, 1986, for discussions with Colonel Swanepoel and his staff.

15. Many of the farms are "game ranches," owned by absentee owners including the minister of Defense, General Malan.

16. Informed that Colonel Swanepoel was encountering a problem with the agreed upon arrangements, a senior official was visibly perturbed. The latter, known for his readiness to act, simply stated that "he would look into it." See chapter 2, n. 11.

17. Interview with Maj. Gen. (then Brigadier) D J Mortimer, Commandant SADF Defense Staff College, *Voortrekkerhoogte* (Pretoria), May 18, 1985.

18. Interview with Mr. Harry Schwarz, Progressive Federal Party, Cape Town, August 1979.

19. The committee was established by the minister of Defense (Gen. Magnus Malan) in March 1984 with then chief of the South African army (Lt. Gen. J J Geldenhuys) as chairman. Upon completion of its work, the committee chairman was appointed chief of South African Defense Force (November 1985), succeeding Gen. Constand J Viljoen. For a summary of the Committee Report see chapter 1 of *White Paper on Defense, 1986*.

20. They can be summarized as follows: irrespective of diplomatic breakthroughs that may occur, conventional-warfare capabilities in neighboring countries are on the increase; accelerating urbanization of the country is making rural South Africa less secure; an increasingly stringent manpower picture confronts SADF, which, however, must be balanced against manpower policies that will not militate against an expanding economy; and continued attempts to import arms must be made in the face of an unrelenting embargo—at the same time SADF must choose weapons systems for development from the indigenous technology base with greater selectivity.

21. *White Paper on Defense, 1986*, 3. The area of the RSA is 1,100,000 square kilometers!

22. The initial enthusiasms for new ideas among Staff College students, this source continued, was such that some would come back with "off the wall" variations of principles they had been taught! In due course the essential environmental factors made themselves felt as a result of frequent deployments in the field.

23. Col. R de Vries and Lt. Gen. I McCaig, SADF, "Mobile Warfare in Southern Africa," *Strategic Review* (Pretoria) (August 1987): 12. The authors go on to observe that "the instinct for guerilla warfare is inherent in the nature of the

South African. Recent external operations by RSA forces support this view. This ability, *which is a legacy from our forefathers,* must be permitted and encouraged to gain momentum and develop to full maturity" (italics mine) (19).

24. Ibid., 11.

25. Helmoed-Romer Heitman, *South African War Machine* (Greenwich: Bison Books, 1985), 43.

26. Interview not for direct attribution.

27. Interview with General Mortimer. Mortimer became chief of the army's Logistic Command after serving for more than a decade as OC of the Defense Staff College.

28. See for example Col. W G Lombard, SADF, "Armoured Warfare: Evolution and Tendencies," *Strategic Review* (Pretoria) (December 1984): 6–13, and n. 32.

29. A compelling example of readiness for large-scale operations is South Africa Medical Service (SAMS). The surgeon general (Lt. Gen. Neil Knoble), who reports directly to the chief of SADF, heads a service of some eight thousand. SAMS trains "operational medical orderlies" for service with field units and maintains an extensive field and base hospital system tied into Africa's premier medical system. It is appropriate here as well to mention the Chaplain's Service (Maj. Gen. Chris Naude, Chaplain General), which plays a larger role in the daily lives of SADF service men and women than most such services.

30. *South Africa War Machine,* 24.

31. Ibid. A senior SADF officer provided corroboration to the author: "We do not have the luxury of making mistakes—as you do—perhaps we overreact at times, but if we err we err on the side of safety!"

32. M Hough and van der Merwe, eds. *Contemporary Air Strategy* (Pretoria: ISSUP, April 1986), 3.

33. Colonel Ferreira is one of the more colorful figures in SADF Permanent Force in the mold of Jan Breytenbach and Dellville Lindford—in fact a successor to Breytenbach as OC of Three-Two Battalion. The author had the pleasant experience of his hospitality in Sector 20 (Rundu, Namibia) in May 1985. See chapter 6.

34. *Paratus* 40 (March 1989): 14.

35. The *Cape Times* (Cape Town, RSA) for June 29 and June 30, 1988, carry somewhat detailed accounts.

36. The author was in South Africa in June 1988 but met with General Earp the following month (July 28, 1988) at the Mayflower Hotel in Washington, D.C. Earp had just retired as chief of SAAF (July 1, 1988), relieved by Lt. Gen. Jan van Loggerenberg, and was on a private visit to the United States. A member of SAAF's distinguished Two Squadron (the *Cheetahs*) on deployment to Korea, he is well known to the U.S. Air Force.

37. Discussion of this "pregnant phrase" is reserved for the section on ARMSCOR at the end of this chapter. General Viljoen, clearly worried about the air situation at his retirement, saw in the exploitation of technology a possible way out of the crisis. See Hough, *Contemporary Air Strategy,* 4–5, and J T Ackerman, "Air Superiority in Southern Africa with Specific Reference to the RSA and Angola," *Strategic Review* (Pretoria) 10 (November 1988): 39–57.

38. Naval Operations Command Cape was divided in 1985 into Naval Com-

mand West with jurisdiction up to the Cuenene River and Naval Command East (Durban) with jurisdiction to the Mozambique border.

39. Visit to Silvermine for tour of facilities and interviews, March 11, 1986.

40. Visit to Simonstown for tour of facilities and interviews, May 28, 1985.

41. See chapter 3, n. 28, for what this submarine "was about" at this time. All three *Daphnes* (*Maria van Riebeeck, Emily Hobhouse,* and *Johanna van der Merwe*) will be transformed, although the visitor was mercifully spared classical allusions to nymphs turning into laurel trees!

42. Commodore H J Grimbeek, SAN, was Naval Officer Commanding at Walvis Bay and host for our visit on August 9, 1979.

43. Two had been laid up and the third, the *President Kruger,* was lost at sea (April 1982) in a collision with the replenishment ship *Tafelberg.* The *Tafelberg,* a converted Danish tanker, "was in" on this day sporting a new helicopter deck. It would soon be joined by a South African–built sister ship, the *Drakensberg.*

44. Not for direct attribution; however, n. 37 is applicable here.

45. The assessment of a U.S. Arms Control and Disarmament Agency (ACDA) official whose task, inter alia, it appeared was to bring about just such an outcome!

46. The then Dockyard OC (Commodore Stolzen) and the then ComNavCape, immediately preceding the Command division (n. 38), Commodore Beddy, could be said to embody the South African naval ethos.

47. See M Hough, ed., *Contemporary Maritime Strategy* (Pretoria: ISSUP, August 1982), 5.

48. Ibid.

49. See his "South African Maritime Policy," in *Contemporary Maritime Strategy,* ed. Hough, 43. Prof. Deon Fourie (himself an army Citizen Force colonel), commenting on Admiral Putter's paper, calls this the single most important sentence in the paper "that needs to be understood outside the country" (58). For a more recent statement of the reluctance of SAN officers to accept the "small navy" role, see Capt. E P Groenewald, SAN, "The Requirements of Small Navies with Specific Reference to the RSA," *Strategic Review for Southern Africa* 11 (May 1989): 51–80.

50. R K Campbell, *Sea Power and South Africa* (Pretoria: ISSUP, April 1984), 9.

51. A du Plessis, *South Africa and the South Atlantic Ocean: Maritime-Strategic Analysis* (Pretoria: ISSUP, June 1987), 63. An excellent overall analysis if somewhat optimistic in tone.

52. Campbell, *Sea Power and South Africa,* 41. A forceful if sometimes querulous account in contrast with du Plessis.

53. Prior to 1976 a munitions or "Armaments Board" was separate from the production corporation. In that year the Armaments Board and the Armaments Development and Production Corporation dating from 1968 were merged to form ARMSCOR.

54. The ARMSCOR subsidiaries are Atlas Aircraft/Telcast (Kempton Park), Infoplan (Pretoria), Kentron/Eloptro (Pretoria and Kempton Park), Lyttelton Engineering Works (Verwoerdburg), Musgrave (Bloemfontein), Naschem (Lenz and Potchefstroom), Pretoria Metal Pressing (Pretoria West and Elandsfontein), Somchem (Somerset West and Wellington), and Swartklip (Cape Flats).

55. Only the chief of SADF, because of his legislative responsibilities for armaments supply, is an ex officio member. All other members including the chairman are appointed by the State President. In its present form (since 1976) "Kommandant" Piet G Marais has been the sole chairman. While the other members' names are not officially published, ARMSCOR will publish a photograph of the board revealing, inter alia, that the minister of Defense and the chairman of the Atomic Energy Corporation are included!

56. Since 1979 ARMSCOR has had three *hoofbestuurders,* John Maree (1979–82), Fred Bell (1982–85), and Johan van Vuuren (1985), not to be confused with the *Voorsitter,* P G Marais.

57. This section is based largely on a series of interviews with individuals associated with or closely connected to ARMSCOR, including but not confined to John Maree, S C van Rooyen, Theo Vorster, and Johan Adler. Interviews are not for direct attribution and in many instances are paraphrased.

58. There is considerable "open literature" on ARMSCOR today. This section draws, for example, on various numbers of *Jane's Defense Review, Jane's Military Review, Jane's Defense Weekly,* and *International Defense Review.* Again, Heitman, *South African War Machine* (chapter 8) and *Leadership* are helpful.

59. See "South Africa Unveils War Machine for Sale Abroad," in the *Washington Post* (October 23, 1988); also "Die Rooikat," *Paratus* 39 (November 1988): 42–43.

60. Michael Gething and Anthony Preston, "Mother of Invention," *Leadership* 7 (1988): 148, quote one South African manufacturer as saying "it is easier to throw away old Soviet kit and start again from scratch." An ARMSCOR source provided an account of an overseas customer attempting to do some reverse engineering on the G-5 barrel, only to have it blow up in their faces. "They did not have some of the basic knowledge in hand!"

61. This has been an especially sensitive item in "the worsening relationship." What was not mentioned was that South Africans who had been in Israel in connection with both Lavi and Kfir programs were now back at Atlas. Atlas association with Taiwan's Indigenous Defense Fighter (IDF) project was another subject not discussed. Taiwan has been shopping for technology at least since 1982, developing its own components, and learning systems-integration techniques in much the same fashion as South Africa (although in closer association with the United States). South African contact with Taiwan's CIST (Changshan Institute of Science and Technology) has been a matter of press speculation for years. See the *Wall Street Journal,* December 12, 1988.

62. Quoted by Helmoed-Romer Heitman, "Arsenal," *Leadership* 7 (1988): 141. See also "Industry Review—Commandant Piet Marais, Chairman of South Africa's Armscor," *International Defense Review* 10 (1984), Geneva.

63. See chapter 3, n. 35, re interview with J W L de Villiers, chairman of South Africa's Atomic Energy Corporation. Also consult the work of Prof. Jack Spence (University of Leicester, UK) for a balanced assessment of the South African nuclear program. His "South Africa—The Nuclear Option," in *Defense Policy Formation,* ed. Roherty, 107–25, has not been superseded.

64. See, for example, Eric H. Arnett, "Nuclear Torpedoes for New Nuclear Powers," *Proceedings* 115 (June 1989): 98–101, United States Naval Institute.

65. So successful was ARMSCOR's foray into the international arms market

that as early as 1984 the Security Council of the United Nations had to call upon its members not to buy South African exports. In keeping with ACDA's emphasis on controlling critical components, the Security Council, on the "import side," was targeting aircraft parts and maintenance assistance—not altogether successfully. See Michael Hough, "The UN Arms Embargo against South Africa: An Assessment," *Strategic Review* (Pretoria) 10 (November 1988): 22–38.

66. An ARMSCOR official was pleased to pass along the following. When Fred Bell was *hoofbestuurder,* he was visited by a representative from the U.S. Embassy who told him that, whatever sympathies the Reagan administration might have for the RSA, "it would observe the arms embargo." Mr. Bell's response was one of great relief. He remarked that in the past "when we have gotten into bed with you in these matters, the results have been calamitous—you simply pull up stakes and leave us high and dry. Now we know what we must do on our own and that is a great help." No account of the response was given.

67. "Something New from Africa," *Jane's Military Review* (1983–84), 140.

68. See n. 20.

5 COMBATING REVOLUTIONARY WAR, 1985–1989

> There is nothing more difficult to take in hand, more perilous to conduct, or more uncertain in its success, than to take the lead in the introduction of a new order of things.
> —Niccolo Machiavelli, *The Prince,* VI

> I think that if the Afrikaner, who has no other fatherland, really wants to fulfill his task in this country . . . (h)e must do it as a community which wants to practice leadership . . . which wants to let other people share in the freedom which he won for himself.
> —P W Botha, interview with *Beeld,* April 30, 1986

The "Current Unrest" in the Republic of South Africa had its inception in the Vaal triangle "following upon the occurrences of 3 September 1984 and thereafter."[1] With this, pari passu, the second phase of the regime of now State President P W Botha begins. A year that began with an improving regional climate (the completion of *Operation Askari* and the conclusion of the Lusaka and N'komati agreements) and a new constitution becomes, with the disturbances of September/October, a year of transition. Now the center of gravity (following Clausewitz again: that point at which the primary effort of the enemy is directed) lies within the borders of the Republic, not outside.[2] South African analysts begin to trace a metamorphosis in the Onslaught in which its latent revolutionary character is manifest. Their assessment of the new situation, starting as it does with the pathologies in the townships, will be productive. Explicit recognition is given to the fact that "unfortunately current socioeconomic conditions lend themselves to exploitation by revolutionary elements" and to the fact, moreover, that "any (latent) revolutionary situation is the result of a complexity of factors."[3] The challenge presented by the Unrest, at least implicitly, is counterrevolutionary in its essentials: the complexity of factors, if skillfully sorted out, allows for the crafting of effective counterrevolutionary measures. Extant conditions, to be sure, have given rise to legitimate grievances that require immediate, urgent attention, yet in this analysis the Unrest, in and of itself, is not seen as constituting (in the South African context) a revolutionary situation. Prevention of this dread metastasis is not beyond the province of a regime committed to a new dispensation, provided it is prepared to act decisively.

There was consensus in the Botha regime on the identity of the metastatic agent and an implacable determination to eliminate it. The African National Congress, self-styled vanguard of the Onslaught, had long since declared its war on the Republic when in June 1985 from its "headquarters-in-exile" (Kabwe, Zambia) it announced the launching of "armed mass insurrection" within the RSA.[4] The ANC Executive Committee in effect joins with Pretoria's analysts in their estimation of the significance of what is taking place in the townships. The moment had come for "cadre" and "masses" to link up in a "people's war." In the ensuing four years (1985–88), across a broad spectrum of violence encompassing terrorism, sabotage, boycotts, and strikes, the ANC will attempt to render the Republic ungovernable. It is one of the signal accomplishments of Mr. Botha's government that it will smash the "armed mass insurrection" campaign. The South African Defense Force in a collaborative effort with the South Africa Police (marked by superb intelligence and decisive action) will savage *Umkhonto we Sizwe* (MK), foreclosing insurrection and revolution as pathways to a new dispensation. Strains will develop between the security forces and civilian agencies as they confront the "new faces of war," particularly in the townships. There will be strains along the central axis itself—between Mr. Botha and his generals—as the State President places SADF in the vanguard of the new phase. On this anvil the South African civil-military relationship will be tested and its soundness confirmed.

Cross-Border Operations against the ANC

The military phase of ANC's declared war against the RSA did not begin in the mideighties but at the outset of the decade.[5] In the midst of SADF's 1978–1983/84 series of operations against SWAPO/PLAN

(*Reindeer* through *Askari*), it became plain that ANC had opened up a second front within the Republic's boundaries from sanctuaries in Mozambique and Lesotho. In the years immediately preceding N'komati (and Gorbachev), *Umkhonto we Sizwe* carried out its first systematic campaign of terror, sabotage, and (by no means least) propaganda inside the RSA. Described by Pretoria as an example, par excellence, of orchestration,[6] the campaign was designed to show common cause with SWAPO/PLAN but also to isolate the Republic internationally and portray SADF as the destabilizing agent in southern Africa. Unconcerned with subtleties at this point, SADF cracked back sharply, hitting ANC facilities first in the Maputo suburb of Metola on January 30, 1981, next at Maseru (Lesotho) on December 9, 1982,[7] and then returning to Maputo on October 17, 1983.[8] The Prime Minister did not conceal his ire at the turn of events. He told Parliament that he had offered neighboring states nonaggression agreements "in which we state that we will not allow our territories to be used against one another ... evidently these offers are falling on deaf ears. If those gentlemen want to do that and want their territories to become the gathering places of ANC and SWAPO terrorists, I say here today: We shall remove those nests for you." Mr. Botha then underlined the policy of the Republic: "Every country which offers shelter to anti–South African terrorists will have to deal with the security forces of South Africa *as far as those terrorists are concerned*" (italics mine).[9]

Prior to the signing of the N'komati Accord (March 1984), perhaps nine of ten ANC entries into South Africa were via the "main channel" from Mozambique. Pursuant to that agreement, however, Maputo closes down the ANC base structure in the country—Pretoria taking considerable time to satisfy itself on the point. Denied a highly valuable contiguous location, Kabwe relocates the bulk of its eastern-front assets to Zambia and Angola, which are not contiguous to the RSA. Indisputably, Botswana, erstwhile friend and neighbor of the Republic, now comes under enormous pressure from the ANC. Willingly or unwillingly (or both) the former Bechuanaland Protectorate will be the new "main channel" for infiltrating MK and underground operatives into the target country for "armed mass insurrection." Not all of the traffic will originate from third countries (Zambia, Angola, and still Tanzania) as Botswana itself will become an "ANC nest." To try to preclude this development Pretoria presses the government of President Quett Masire to enter into a bilateral defense arrangement going well beyond a nonaggression pact. A flurry of private talks takes place between foreign office and defense officials from both sides. SADF, for its part, seeks to establish direct ties with the fledgling Botswana Defense Force (BDF), founded only in 1977. While some responsive chords are struck at this level, they are muted by Masire. Sensitive to geographical propinquity with the RSA, the Botswana president is not prepared to depart from "ideological solidarity" with frontline states. There would be no agreement insofar as security matters were concerned, only protestations from Gaborone that it would continue to adhere to its policy of not allowing its territory to be used as a base for operations against the RSA![10]

In the ten months preceding June 1985, South African Intelligence identifies thirty-six acts of terror and violence on the part of the ANC "which were planned and executed from Botswana." In mid-June SADF strikes across that border for the first time, hitting ANC targets in Gaborone, killing twelve. Repeated entreaties with the Botswana government to the effect that its "no bases" policy was utterly fanciful went unheeded. The "dash through the Kopfontein Gate" (into Gaborone) came less than a month after a raid into the Cabinda enclave in northern Angola. In the week of May 19, elements of Four Reconnaissance Commando disembarked from a *Daphne* to join up with UNITA elements in what Pretoria adamantly asserts was a mission directed against one of the ANC relocation sites in Angola. The "Recce" unit was surprised by FAPLA forces, losing two killed and one captured (Maj., then Capt., Wynand du Toit);[11] the remainder of the unit departed the area in the manner of their arrival. The writer was at SADF headquarters in Pretoria when the reconnaissance into Angola was announced. SADF leaders displayed all of the chagrin that goes with the venting of a covert operation. This was exacerbated by the seeming failure of Washington to accept General Malan's statement that the undertaking was directed against the ANC and lay quite outside the purview of the "Mulungushi Minute" provisions of the 1984 Lusaka Accord. (In fact SADF was at that very point, completing the withdrawal of its forces from Angola.) The suggestion from abroad that the reconnaissance was aimed at Cabinda Gulf Oil Company (CABGOC), unaccompanied as it was by any particulars, was especially resented. The acrimony over cross-border operations would intensify from this point onward.[12]

In May 1986 (within two days of discovering the largest arms cache yet—in a Krugersdorp suburb) SADF struck again. "Small elements of the army" hit a terrorist transfer center just outside of Gaborone and an ANC operational center and a terrorist transfer center in Harare.[13] Simultaneously, South Africa Air Force bombs ANC facilities at Makeni Plots near Lusaka. (SADF will enter Zambia again in April 1987—presumably from the Caprivi Strip—to look at ANC lines into Botswana and Zimbabwe.) The foray into the three Commonwealth states came at a time when the Eminent Persons Group (EPG), a product of the 1985 Nassau Commonwealth Ministers Conference, was in South Africa pursuing its peace initiative. This was not the sort of irony that would deter Mr. Botha from such undertakings, nor was the outrage that issued on schedule from the usual sources. In the House of Assembly the following day the State President was pleased to "take full responsibility for the actions of our security forces. I congratulate them and assure the country we will do it again when the occasion demands." Not disdaining irony altogether, Mr. Botha quoted remarks of Ronald Reagan following the U.S. Libyan raid to the effect that self-defense was not only America's right but its duty and that the mission was wholly consistent with Article 51 of the UN Charter. "Like the United States of America and every other civilized government," he continued, "we reject internationally organized terrorism. We likewise will not tolerate terrorists hiding in other countries with the intent to perpetrate crime against people in our country who prefer to work and live in peace."[14]

The tempo and bitterness of the ANC campaign to render the RSA ungovernable will go largely unnoticed in the West, preoccupied as it is with antiapartheid agendas, but the cross-border operations will not go unnoticed. Nothing will demonstrate Western hypocrisy to South Africans quite so much as the constantly repeated charge that Pretoria seeks to destabilize neighboring states. The force of the dictum concerning the constantly repeated lie will be brought home as well. Time and again South African officials will tellingly lay bare the patent absurdity of charges that a nation desperate to turn to its internal problems would seek anything but regional stability. Time and again these officials will delineate the obvious distinction between striking at sanctuaries of the Republic's enemies in host states, and striking at those states themselves. It did not take long for Pretoria to conclude that international law, precedent, practice—the record itself—have no bearing on the matter whatsoever: an altogether different imperative was at work and would stay in place. South Africa would have to act in behalf of its interests without benefit of reasoned response from abroad, much less approval.[15]

Huge arms caches uncovered at Broderstroom (May 1988) and in the Western Cape (July 1988) indicated what the balance of the year held for SADF and SAP. Arrests in connection with these discoveries turn up White MK operatives and confirm earlier evidence of a Libyan line to the ANC. SADF is again back in the environs of Gaborone (March and June of 1988), killing, inter alia, the MK resident commander Solomon Molefi. Botswana is not alone, however, in carrying heavy ANC traffic. Developments in Swaziland, hard on the Mozambique border, vindicate Pretoria's concern that the N'komati process will be slow in closing down ANC eastern-front operations. The South African Police, who will play a larger role than SADF in demonstrating to the ANC Executive Committee the folly of their choosing the "armed mass insurrection" option, concentrate their intelligence efforts on Swaziland with ample dividends. A senior ANC official, Ismail Ebrahim, is "apprehended" in Swaziland at the end of 1986 and put on trial in the RSA. In the following year two other ranking ANC personages "are killed while traveling by car" in Swaziland. After SAP kills nine infiltrators at the Swazi border (June 1988), one close observer of the ANC notes (with restraint) that "a succession of arrests of incoming cadres at well-timed roadblocks manned by Security Police seem to confirm that police are reasonably well informed about the ANC's regional lines of communication."[16] SAP estimates that perhaps 90 percent of infiltrators over the Swazi border are netted. It makes no claims as to actions inside Swaziland.[17]

The cross-border operations of SADF and SAP in the ANC war notwithstanding, the central theater of operations throughout 1986–88 lay within the Republic.[18] It is in this theater, following establishment of the National State of Emergency (NSE) in June 1986 (renewed each year thereafter through 1989) and the putting in place of a new Law and Order team,[19] that ANC will take punishing losses largely at the hands of SAP. The impact on ANC morale and discipline is heavy, producing major political bouts within the Executive Committee and a reconsideration of basic strategy. An ongoing debate as to whether MK should focus on "hard" or "soft" targets has been difficult to chart in view of the difficulty of correlating the presumptively prevailing view within the Executive Committee with what, in fact, was taking place in the field.[20] Much the more serious issue dividing the committee, however, is the wisdom of the main thrust itself and the formulation of its position. Recognizably vague in many critical areas and clearly implausible as the basis for any future negotiating position, the foundation principles of the ANC contained in the Freedom Charter[21] come under review. Taking account of the chagrin of South African businessmen in the wake of the 1985 Kabwe meeting,[22] as well as signals emanating from Moscow on the virtues of mixed economies, the Executive Committee decides upon a clarification of the charter. In 1988 it issues "basic guidelines for the foundations of government in post-apartheid South Africa." The ANC *Constitutional Guidelines for a Democratic South Africa* are accommodationist in terms of the capitalist aspirations of RSA businessmen and in terms of constitutional democracy only on the basis of a tortuous interpretation.[23] By this action, however, ANC initiates the process of positioning itself for the political-settlement phase, a phase about which (as we have seen from the Rhodesian experience) Pretoria has much reason to be skeptical. In adopting a posture of willingness to negotiate, ANC reserves judgment on a "people's war," pending an assessment of results at the year's end.

A bruising twelve months, running beyond the October elections to the end of 1988, provides the answer on "people's war." Responding to defeat on the battlefield, the impending loss of Angolan bases,[24] and under pressure from all quarters about "a worsening image," the ANC Executive Committee turns to old wine in new bottles. The decision is taken to pursue a nonrevolutionary struggle in which violence, while not eschewed (a concession to MK leadership—but no longer graced with the appellation "insurrection"), is made secondary to the potentialities of "mass democracy." Underlying this seminal transition in strategy is the emergence of Thabo Mbeki (promoted from publicity chief to director of the Department of International Relations) and the decline of Chris Hani, chief of staff of MK. Mbeki, then heir apparent to Oliver Tambo, must be credited with the new strategy, markedly political and markedly international. Its essence is familiar: the order of the day is to take part in and direct Popular Front movements ("open organizations" such as the United Democratic Front founded in 1983) and reach out to Black trade unions (i.e., the Congress of South African Trade Unions—COSATU—and to the extent possible, the National Union of Mine Workers—NUM). The strategy, somewhat in evidence prior to 1988, also entails an international quest for legitimacy.[25] Finally, it requires at least temporary accommodation (setting aside of differences) with both the South Africa Communist Party (SACP) and a reviving Pan-African Congress (PAC).

The Pan-African Congress and its military wing, the Azanian People's Liberation Army (APLA),[26] have reasserted themselves on the southern African scene. Created in 1959, in a fall out between "Charterists" and "Africanists" in the ranks of ANC, PAC for more than two decades was a minor player in the revolutionary struggle. Today, ensconced in the frontline states (particularly Zimbabwe), it gives every evidence of a strong Libyan connection and an equally strong aversion to moderation messages from Moscow. The likelihood of ANC gaining the concurrence of PAC/APLA in the strategems of nonrevolutionary struggle (even on the basis of expediency) appears slight. The little noticed release of aging PAC president Zeph Mothopeng, who had been serving a fifteen-year sentence under the Terrorism Act, did not stay the hand of APLA. Maintaining the alliance with SACP, however, is another matter. It is not lost upon South Africans (especially Afrikaners) that ANC and SACP chose Dingaan's Day (December 16) to form their alliance in 1961. This pact is seen as a declaration of war that continues to this day.[27] Mr. Joe Slovo, once the leading White Chief of ANC but no longer officially a member of the Executive Committee, is currently secretary general of SACP.[28] He has taken on major responsibilities on the labor front and for recruiting additional White members to the alliance. His outreach campaign to open organizations, seen as a promising tack early on, has not achieved expected goals. The adroitness of Pretoria (minister of Law and Order Adriaan Vlok) in banning even for brief periods those open organizations that seemed most vulnerable to Mr. Slovo reaches its peak in the months leading up to October 1988.

Defense and police officials in South Africa have gained an acute understanding of the dynamics of promoting and maintaining a revolutionary climate—of what is effective and what is ineffective. The mass organizations (invariably coalitions of only loosely concerted interests), operating at the boundaries of the legally permissible, present a complex problem that in the final analysis must be resolved by political means. Far easier to contain and neutralize are the hard-core, ideologically driven cadres (i.e., ANC, SACP, PAC, and SWAPO) and their military wings (MK, APLA, and PLAN). In its final year in office the Botha regime succeeded in removing the question of a new dispensation from the jurisdiction of military wings. Whatever future role ANC adherents may play in the governance of South Africa (and this applies to SWAPO as well in Namibia) it will not be by dint of armed struggle. What the ramifications of this "missing element" will be in a postrevolutionary phase provides an intriguing question for theorists but most especially for the unsuccessful warriors. The larger question, no doubt, is whether mass, open organizations will now become the metastatic agents of national democratic revolution, or whether they can be contained as instruments of political evolution. The question lies outside the purview of this study, except to the extent that it is part and parcel of the "security-cum-welfare" programs of the Botha government in the townships. The armed-struggle aspects will be present in these venues and will be given due priority, but it is in the townships that Pretoria demonstrates its perspicacity in coping with unrest by taking counterrevolution to its next stages. SADF will not be permitted to stand down from this task.

In the Townships

It was not the minister of Defense's purpose to revamp, revise, or otherwise alter the basic elements of the "total national strategy" as he stood in the House of Assembly in September 1987 to review the unrest situation. Instead, General Malan elaborated for his colleagues a six-point program that the government (with all diligence) was implementing in the townships. "The national security of South Africa is currently being threatened," he said, "by a *revolutionary onslaught* which primarily desires, at the moment, *the forcible overthrow of this dispensation*" (italics mine).[29] Malan had not risen to discuss the merits of "this dispensation" but to again emphasize "security first and foremost, *so that we can differ politically in a peaceful situation*" (italics mine). Yet his six points would be couched in terms of a counterrevolutionary program directed at the new center of gravity (Soweto, Alexandria, Mamelodi, Uitenhage, Langa, Guguletu, etc.). The new situation, in short, requires an adaptation of The Strategy. Always first and absolutely at one with Afrikaner mentality, "security" is now cast in terms of "stabilization" (i.e., the restoration of order). This is done with the notation that the Black man respects the security effort, if not welcoming it, and that earning this respect is essential to evolutionary change. "Welfare" entails a systematic effort to meet basic needs first, specifically to develop and refurbish the infrastructure of the townships. A new order of housing, health, education, and training is put forward as the underpinnings of economic reform, in itself a powerful stabilizing force. Security and welfare—no longer understood as sequential in a linear-progression model—are interlocked in the townships. They become the twin pillars of the crowning endeavor, namely, the negotiation of power sharing (a new dispensation).

Six requirements must be met, Malan contended, if the Unrest is to be alleviated and that climate established that alone offers the prospect of successful negotiations:

1. Law, order, and stability must prevail. ("That is the *main reason* why the security forces are being utilized internally" [italics mine].)

2. Third-level structures (town councils) must function effectively. "Alternative" structures will be eliminated.

3. There must be prompt satisfaction of the need for urban housing and land ownership.

4. Creation of job opportunities is essential. The "First World" of South Africa must reach out to the "Third World" of South Africa.

5. Education and training for all population groups must be advanced. ("This country cannot afford 'a People's Education.' ")

6. A joint (private sector/public sector) plan must be put in place to prevent the country from being undermined by strikes.

National State of Emergency (NSE) measures were in their second year of operation as the minister of Defense spoke and were clearly serving to make the task of meeting the six requirements a manageable one. By the end of 1987 the security forces (SAP supported by SADF) had all but succeeded in achieving the one goal that transcended all others—the elimination of *intimidation*. To achieve this objective, if nothing else, the State President had put NSE measures into effect, having learned from bitter experience that "wherever there was rioting, there was intimidation."[30] Intimidation was the tool of revolutionary mobilization; no effort toward its eradication could be spared. The question of who controlled the townships was the very essence of the matter. In the twelve months leading up to NSE (June 1986) some 900 Blacks had been killed in the townships with more than 150 killed in the last month (May 1986). In May 1987 there would be 8 such deaths. Nearly forty town and community councils collapsed in 1985–86 under pressure from the popular resistance. Only five were dissolved in 1987.[31]

Strategic hamlets and *regroupements* are conventional means of coping with intimidation in rural areas, but in urban areas, where community resettlement is not plausible, the intimidators must be taken out of the community. Moreover, steps to identify and remove them must be taken quickly so that a significant police/military presence does not become an issue in itself.[32] The complexity of factors (to which reference has already been made) now asserts itself. The criminal element, invariably, will make its appearance; mere anarchists will range the streets; and then there will be "the vanguard" (the "comrades" often, but not always, appearing under the aegis of white bandanas and AK-47s). This "hard core" is perhaps 3 percent swimming in the 97 percent: coercion and intimidation will be discovered in "the presence of real grievances." The pressures on the community—on Black town councilors and Black policemen in particular—are enormous. The houses of officials are razed; car bombings and "necklacing" are worked all in public view to underscore a pervasive private litany of threats. The immediate objective is to dissolve existing institutions and establish alternative structures in their place, structures such as revolutionary councils and people's committees to install a "people's education" in the schools. The "comrades" must be disengaged from "the people" before a tacit sympathy generated by the ostensible clarity of ANC/PAC goals is made over into revolution. Police intelligence before and during the Unrest is effective: some six thousand are swept up during the peak period. Approximately five thousand of these will be peeled away and released revealing the core one thousand who will be detained indefinitely.[33]

Deploying on two occasions in late 1984 "without firing a shot" (including the massive Sebokeng deployment of seven thousand troops), SADF initially takes the view that "we will deploy to assist the Police when we must—but the salient dimensions of 'the unrest situation' are outside our ken."[34] The position expressed to the author in 1985 was that, while we (SADF) must consider the contingency of Black insurgency (historically the Eastern Cape has been a sensitive area: "the Xhosa can be troublesome"), there is no greater misrepresentation of things than to suggest that insurrection is likely. There will be no insurrection. A host of new measures is necessary, however, as the bungling of the Uitenhage disturbance (March 1985) demonstrates.[35] The proposal to increase SAP from forty-eight thousand to seventy-five thousand is a good one. (It would grow only about ten thousand in strength by the end of the decade.) The police/population ratio in this country is a joke—"for a so-called police state!" The need for development of appropriate police tactics and crowd-handling procedures—the need to understand the dynamics of the situation you are dealing with—is critical. This argument wherein SADF (*SA Leer*) would confine itself to a supporting presence on the periphery of a police problem would not carry. At the behest of the State President, SADF steadily enlarges its role in the townships. The military involvement grows throughout 1986 and will culminate in the appointment of the deputy minister of Defense as minister of Law and Order.

Adriaan Vlok, member for Verwoerdburg in the House of Assembly, is of the new political generation. It would not be altogether fair, however, to style him a "New Nationalist" inasmuch as he had been about the business of reform well before the *arrivistes* made their appearance. He is, in any case, precisely the person to whom John Maree would pass the baton: "You will find him absolutely tops!"[36] An ingratiating, unassuming lawyer, the new minister of Law and Order had already established himself as politically skilled. As Machiavelli reminds us, there is probably no more challenging dynamic than sociopolitical reform in a besieged polity, and as the Florentine would undoubtedly have agreed, there was probably no one more suited for the pivotal role in such a dynamic (in the South African setting) than Adriaan Vlok. His transfer from Defense to Law and Order represented a twofold "move" by the State President. First, Mr. Botha meant to convey his determination that the two ministries should jointly take the lead in dealing with the Unrest situation and, second, he meant to make his own mark on the advent of a new generation of National Party leaders. In the late 1980s (not unlike the situation with Justice in the mid-sixties) Law and Order is a major vantage point from which to bring about bureaucratic change (i.e., to enlist, or commandeer, the bureaucracy in the counterrevolutionary program). Lacking such bureaucratic transformation a new generation of political leaders will count for little. The new minister was handed a herculean task.

Vlok exuded confidence.[37] His confidence had risen, he noted, almost in concert with the implementation of NSE measures "and with the realization that we would have to do the job in the townships ourselves, that there would not be any outside help—only hindrance." (It was evident that this minister reflected the thinking of his president!) Vlok was more bemused than irate about then current press reports of his "detention of children." ("You should see some of the so-called children!") What has happened is that "we have taken the hard-core types out of the townships for the most part; their attempt to build alternative structures and intimidate people so that they would not rely upon established structures had to stop—and we have stopped it." The NSE provisions (which he would call "negatives") "have worked almost dramatically—the de-escalation of incidents must now be seized upon." The next step—a step about which he was obviously excited—was to alleviate the most pressing needs: repair utilities, fix potholes, reopen clinics and schools. "It is astonishing how much talk there is of *these measures* and how little of *political dispensations*. We have missed opportunities in this regard which we cannot afford to do again."[38] This theme, frequently heard from a number of sources and invariably in the context of commentary on the performance of government agencies in the townships, was the crux of his problem. Again, extraordinary confidence—even enthusiasm—asserted itself. "We are attacking this issue on a broad front. A total security/welfare effort is being welded together and we are succeeding." Could his visitor accompany him the next day to Mamelodi and see for himself? (Regrettably this opportunity could not be seized upon.)

To ensure that opportunities would not be missed again, the State President had made his new minister of Law and Order chairman of a newly established Joint Security Management Group (JSMG).[39] Vlok was now, effectively, the government-wide manager of the all-out attack on the unrest situation. He confirmed that it is in this forum that "we have to lean upon middle-level officials on both the security and welfare sides"—his charge after all was to expedite the security–welfare effort *and* shake up the bureaucracy. (Because of the press of other duties—internal security—chairmanship of the JSMG would soon devolve upon his young deputy, Roelf Meyer.)[40] From the now "activated"[41] National Joint Management Center (NJMC) in Byron Place (Pretoria), the "Meyer group" sets out to refurbish the townships. Mamelodi and Alexandria will be pointed to as successes that hopefully can serve as models. Electrification is brought to Alexandria in a joint SADF/ESCOM undertaking, "which would have taken ten years under ordinary circumstances." A SADF colonel, fresh from combat in Angola, is informed that he is going to be a city manager, the details of his resume notwithstanding. Today on another assignment this colonel confesses to astonishment at how much could be accomplished once the orders were given. Accustomed to "civic action"[42] in outlying areas of the Republic and Namibia, SADF becomes a powerful presence in the Joint Group but more so in the streets of the townships. Senior officers in many instances would find the long-term ramifications more worrying than would some of their subordinates. Before turning to those concerns, we must deal with yet another critical element of counterrevolution in the townships.

Although the Botha strategists had all along recognized "Information" as one of the new faces of the war in which they were engaged, they had not been able to take appropriate weapons off the shelf. Since the scandal of 1978, the nettlesome "Information Question" had been pretty much allowed to lie in repose in the Ministry of Foreign Affairs—with occasional scant attention from a deputy minister. In 1986 the State President, as part of his NSE and as part of his all-out effort to smash armed mass insurrection, sends "information" to war. An independent Bureau for Information (split off from Foreign Affairs) is established and quite literally placed on the front line. Mr. David Steward is seconded from Foreign Affairs to head the Bureau for Information (and report directly to the State President).[43] Since its inception it has been a key participant in the counterrevolutionary effort and no small factor in its success. In his reappraisal of the role of "information" Mr. Botha also raises the issue to the presidential level. The deputy minister of Information is taken out of Foreign Affairs and put in the office of the State President. In March 1988, Dr. Stoffel van der Merwe will be elevated to minister of Information and Culture (still in the office of the State President) and given sweeping jurisdiction over the film industry and South African Broadcasting Corporation (SABC) as well as the print press.

David Steward, like Adriaan Vlok and Roelf Meyer, exemplifies the new Nationalist leadership. Affable and urbane all, what is at the same time unmistakable in each of them is a toughness best seen in their commitment to the counterrevolutionary program of "security-cum-welfare." Each sees a new dispensation in the offing but only when the twin pillars are firmly in place. While he must, of course, see to it that Defense and Law and Order "put their best foot forward" in media relations ("the Police are under a punishing spotlight in a very difficult situation"), Steward sees his bureau as having a far more important role to play. Embodying a view that he declares stems from hard experience in recent years, Steward spoke of a weapon in his hands of which he will make maximal use in the ongoing struggle.

> This government has learned a great deal the hard way about itself, about communicating with others, about what it wants to say, and how it wants to say things. For example, we know now that you cannot have a policy of "reporting reform" so as to show the world how well you are progressing; it creates an insatiable appetite—no one is ever satisfied.

He then outlined the new approach of his government:

> What we are determined upon is to keep emphasizing that the terrorists are not going to win, that the process which we have articulated will go forward. This is a process which serves the interests of South Africans; it does not make an attempt to satisfy international demands. We tried that and found it a losing business!

There was clearly no apology for the new information policy; there was the conviction of having made an important discovery about information handling within a reform dynamic if not a revolutionary dynamic.

Steward was frank in stating that "throwing out the TV people"[44] was a small factor in explaining the de-escalation of incidents in the townships. Quick to attribute the de-escalation to his brethren in the security forces, he did allow that "it was eminently helpful not to be reporting on the security measures!" There was no disposition to underestimate the power of the media in his remarks. On the contrary, the new policy is testimony to its effect on a worldwide audience and an attempt to utilize that power in behalf of policy. In the mind of the head of the Bureau for Information the critical element in "the kind of war we are fighting" is psychological. He could not disguise his awe at "the power of symbols manipulated by organized groups," nor did he disguise his determination not to be defeated on this front. Steward was ready with an example of the power of television "to manipulate symbols overcoming all rationality." "Take the case of Western embassies in the RSA," he pointed out. "The embassy people are especially difficult to deal with. They will tell you they understand this and they understand that, but of course there is nothing we can do about 'liberation'!"

Continuing on this theme Steward advised that the national television network (SABC) will not convert "news" into "entertainment" "as is the case in the USA." The purpose of reading the news is not to mesmerize the audience, consequently in South Africa news will retain its essential dullness. Mr. Riaan Ecksteen, director-general of SABC, would suggest nothing to contradict the Steward philosophy, although there would be indications later of some disagreement.[45] The value of disconnecting the periphery from the local crisis through restrictions on the media (television in particular) was demonstrable throughout 1987 and 1988. Almost by this means alone "manipulative groups" in the West, which had come to play a disturbing part in the revolutionary onslaught, were taken out of the war. There was the suggestion that Western nations, had they been in South Africa's place, might not have had either the insight or the courage to adopt such measures. The United States, it was noted, sustained a psychological defeat in Vietnam, however successful it may have been on the battlefield. This would not be an aspect of the war in southern Africa: "We have learned something from the Vietnam war whether you have or not."[46] For those officials who had appreciably advanced their country's quest for internal stability by "disconnecting the periphery," there was little inclination to think about reopening a program closed down for a decade. Returning to a major international information program would have to await developments. "We have only now learned that what the rest of the world thinks about a future South Africa is not as important as our own commitment to our own future. Today, following our own path we are making progress," Steward concluded.

Military and Civilians

The distinguished French commentator on southern African affairs, Gerard Chaliand, was among the first (if not the first) to note the innovative role of the SADF officer corps. This was due to the fact, he wrote, that "their *vision* springs from a *global* analysis and not purely *local* considerations."[47] Chaliand did not suggest, as have less knowledgeable observers, that this implied any usurpation of civilian roles— only a propensity for a "total assessment" of the new situation. This

propensity, far from providing the basis for a coup, will underlie growing concerns in the eighties (peaking during the Unrest) about SADF
roles and missions. The Defense Staff College OC can be styled without hesitation an intellectual in military uniform. Having thought seriously for many years about the institution of which he was a member,
he appeared collected on a broad range of issues—save one: "I must
confess to being ill at ease with revolutionary war."[48] In the closing
quarter of the twentieth century his institution was strongly disposed to
develop proficiency for conventional war in southern Africa—it being
quite out of the question for the region to escape from East–West
rivalries. To be called upon to take part in and for that matter play a
vanguard role in a complex counterrevolutionary program was, one
gathered in listening to the OC, unanticipated. This was not just
understandable distaste on the part of the military professional in
having to confront that most opprobrious of legitimate missions,
namely, "to come to the aid of the civil." The reality of a responsibility for internal security explained his discomfiture only in part.
The larger concern was that new doctrine and new forces, precluding preoccupation with the external sphere, must now be part of the
total assessment. (It was also understood that these were the issues
with which the British army had been wrestling for years—and
which they had not satisfactorily resolved.) Vision and innovation
would be required to ease civil-military strains in a difficult adjustment to revolutionary war.[49]

In the decade 1975–84 SADF directed its energies, intellectual and
otherwise, to the region with notable acumen, as Chaliand has pointed
out. By the mid-eighties, however, the Onslaught had taken on added
dimensions compelling the officer corps to clarify for its own purposes
(as well as those of the political leadership) an expanded counterrevolutionary role. A choice between two roles—one conservative and the
other more creative—appeared initially to have plausibility. In the conservative role SADF would stand as the ultimate guarantor of the processes of internal evolution that the political leadership had defined, set
in motion, and that they meant to control. This option is little more
than the conventional "aid to the civil" mission with the recognition, to
be sure, that more than the usual amount of "aid" may be required. The
task is one of ensuring orderly dynamics within the Republic (or, as
put earlier, "no insurrection"), but allowing for a necessary preoccupation with the external sphere. A more creative role, on the other hand,

would place SADF in the ongoing process of evolution as "a catalytic agency" along with other leadership cadres. Given the fact that the military, inevitably, will occupy a pivotal position in a nation under attack, and given the prestige SADF had garnered from successes in the field, any notion of choice at this point proves illusory.[50] The State President had made the choice for a creative role.

"You must remember that John Vorster was under great pressure from the Right to clamp down on SADF—and he did; they (the Right) understood even then that SADF was *verlig* (enlightened, reform-ist)."[51] P W Botha, on the basis of his long association with the officer corps understood this most keenly of all. He knew their capabilities for leadership on and off the battlefield. It was precisely this mind-set and this range of capabilities that he was determined to have in the fore-front of the reform movement during its most trying period. "Is it any wonder that we are now cast in the leadership role of the regime's reform effort?" The purely rhetorical question was put to the author by a rising SADF general officer.[52]

> The *primal* function of SADF is to defend the national state from for-
> eign enemies! But now we are caught up in something else. The great
> transformation through which the RSA is proceeding poses a broad
> array of security issues. There is, *first,* the regional question, but then
> there is also the "unrest which accompanies reform"—upon which the
> ANC and other outside elements play. We must deal with it all. Today
> the security question is in so very many respects the reform question
> and we can not disengage the two.

This friend of many years was frustrated. Throughout numerous conversations he was the embodiment of the *verlig* officer, displaying professional concern about a growing involvement in the reform pro-cess. There were two specific concerns. First, how long will it take "Pieter" (Lt. Gen. Pieter van der Westhuizen, then secretary to the State Security Council) "to educate the civilian agencies." How long before they will become full members of a process that ultimately must have them at the helm, "releasing SADF for its priority missions." Second, there is the civil-military problem. The general's disdain for those who had been misrepresenting the problem was patent. "We have one all right, but it is the very opposite of the traditional military takeover. We are being encouraged by civilian agencies who now tell us how indispensable we are (to the reform process), who tell us that the real issues are security issues, that we have the tools for the job, that we have the backing of the State President, etc., etc."

Returning to the prior matter this general was direct if nothing else (as the species is wont to be):

> Westhuizen is now recognized by others in the system as having been the conceptualizer—and now the driving spirit—of the reform program. However, at the SSC level and in the Joint Security Management Group he has an enormous problem where he is confronted with civilian agencies which have neither a well-defined concept of the multidimensional problem, nor any scheme of attack. Pieter is in the awkward position of having to spell out to *civilian* bureaucracies the various *welfare* aspects of the "security-cum-welfare" strategy and goad them into action.

(This officer had observed in an earlier conversation that "Magnus—at least in his own mind—has a concept of total strategy to deal with total onslaught, but we're not sure anyone else does!" Evidently it had fallen to "Pieter" to translate for the civilian agencies, and perhaps some of his brethren, just what the minister of Defense was attempting to convey to them.) Concluding on an equally unequivocal note, the military man made the political point that nothing was so much needed to advance the reform movement as a favorable outcome at the polls. By "a favorable outcome" he meant not just success for the National Party in the parliamentary elections two months hence (May 1987) but a continuing and broadening mandate to push the reform process in accordance with Nationalist Principles. This was the real weapon that was needed in the assault on the Afrikaner bureaucracy.

Lt. Gen. Pieter van der Westhuizen has played a central role in the regime of P W Botha.[53] After the intelligence restructuring at the beginning of the eighties he was appointed chief of staff for Intelligence (CSI) in SADF. During his tenure it was the key Intelligence post in South Africa. "In coming to the State Security Council (in 1985) I have brought a number of my CSI functions with me," the youthful general observed in one of our conversations. This would not be the only consideration in explaining the prominence of the SSC secretary position during Westhuizen's tour. Energetic, almost driven, widely traveled, widely read, *verlig,* he was the ideal choice for a military figure in the highest echelon of the "security-cum-welfare" program of counterrevolution. His intense belief in the undertaking and his talent are one side of the coin; the other side is his anxiety to move beyond the internal dimensions and again focus on the external realm. He is emphatic that the *raison d'être* of SADF and his own first concern are one and the same, namely, the threat posed to the Republic from beyond its borders and the conventional-war-fighting capability needed to cope with that threat. Nothing must be done to compromise the professionalism and effectiveness of the force. Yet SADF is always at the disposal of the State President. At this moment (in the decade of the eighties)— a moment of crisis for the Republic—the State President requires an agency not only to coordinate, but more important, to move the pieces of the program forward. Somewhat jokingly General van der Westhuizen had remarked to the author in 1983 that "under Vorster we (SADF) were on the shelf, now under PW we are being co-opted; I don't know which situation is worse!" In the course of his term as SSC secretary it was evident he had resolved the dilemma.

The general's problem was made easier by the fact that Mr. Botha and General Malan ("my Minister") were increasingly couching the main thrust of the reform program in terms that were instinctively grasped by this military professional. Within the framework of the management system SADF was tasked to spearhead the assault on the great redoubt of Afrikaner bureaucracy. "I am in a command position insofar as the internal unrest situation is concerned," Westhuizen confirmed. "The JMCs (Joint Management Centers) are reporting in from the country to me." He was not hesitant to note that "there have been the expected difficulties from both the Left and the Right in this regard," but was pleased with the progress to date. "The Security Management System is being developed from the bottom up—from 'the grass roots' as it were." Referring to the impending start-up of the Regional Services Councils (RSCs), he was confident they would be helpful "on the local welfare side. But in moving from 'stabilization' to 'normalization' we confront the central bureaucracy." The SSC secretary extolled the new impetus from the minister of Law and Order (Adriaan Vlok) in addressing this problem, but again—from a general officer—there was stress on "the overriding importance of 'the new sentiment in the country' being translated into a revived reform mandate for the National Party and State President." The assault on the bureaucracy must have the backing of ballots. It must in the final analysis be a political victory that is won. (Whether his emphasis on this point had any bearing on his reassignment in September 1987 will be taken up in chapter 7.)

It was manifest throughout a longer than planned interview[54] that Gen. J J (Jannie) Geldenhuys, chief of SADF, was reluctant to be drawn away from the borders. Geldenhuys, who with his predecessor (Constand Viljoen), warrants much of the credit for making SADF/ARMSCOR Africa's unrivaled military instrument, saw as his highest obligation maintaining the fighting potential of this force in the field. SADF, he contended, faces major conventional capabilities across the Republic's borders. In a prophetic observation he said that "at some point in the near future it may have to engage those forces— and most assuredly alone." (The heaviest conventional-war fighting in the history of southern Africa would occur in Angola in 1987–88.) The foundation premise of the officer corps had been articulated again— this time at the highest level. At the same time it was evident that the chief of SADF now had a more comprehensive grasp of the security problem facing the Republic (and the defense force) than when he was GOC Southwest.[55]

> Why is so much being made of the fact that SADF is engaged today in internal security? All of the military organizations have the "aid to civil" mission—none of them like it. We have always had under statute both the external and the internal mission; indeed, they are in actuality one. We are trained for both and that training goes on today.

(Parenthetically, in responding to a question about the recently completed "Geldenhuys Report,"[56] he noted that his committee had not been charged with looking at how the internal situation might bear on future force structure, doctrine, and training, but that "this did develop" in the course of things.)

Responding to the thesis of "negotiation (with Black leaders) only after discipline,"[57] General Geldenhuys displayed some perhaps recently acquired political sophistication along with some emotion. "This viewpoint comes from the Left—not the Right, the usual source of difficulty; it reflects a business viewpoint in search of a pro-business centrist government." The political ramifications of this viewpoint were clear to him: "If the government were required to administer 'salutary lessons' of discipline to Black leaders it would only result in a hardening of their positions, in which event it would be clear to all that the government would have to be reconstituted in order to have any negotiations with the now hardened Black leaders and," he emphasized, "this is what the proponents of the thesis bloody well understand and are seeking!" Warming to his subject South Africa's foremost combat leader declared that SADF was now deployed in the Great Undertaking of P W Botha—internally and externally—at the behest of the State President himself. "We shall stay within constitutional boundaries; we shall not resort to extraconstitutional means—as our 'enemies' hope." (He did not specify the "enemies.")[58] "Our clear emphasis is controlled reform with bargaining on the part of all interested parties beginning with local-level matters. What we are seeking *at all costs* is to avoid a hardening of positions."

General Geldenhuys then pointed to another factor in the equation— clearly a critical factor for the chief of SADF. "There must be no question as to the political leadership of the Republic, and no question that 'bloody-mindedness' is any part of it." Confirmation of this most fundamental of propositions would be obtained by electoral reaffirmation of Nationalist principles.

Stability within the Republic and stability in the region are not isolated factors in the South African security equation; they are reciprocals. RSA security officials are entirely persuaded that the achievement of one cannot be sustained without at the same time achieving the other. By mid-1989 for the first time in a generation there was, if not the full-scale realization, the very real promise of both. In the "security-cum-welfare" program in the townships the test issue of control had been decided. Ameliorative measures to "meet basic needs" now occupied center stage. In the region the Southwest Question (enmeshed with the Angolan Question since 1975) seemed no longer to require the ministrations of arms. Whether the Angolan aspects of the issue had moved safely into the anchorage of diplomacy was somewhat more problematic, yet there was promise here as well. In 1988 President Botha launched a new "African Diplomatic Initiative" to revive the flagging "spirit of N'komati" and perhaps in anticipation of his approaching end of term. The achievement of breakthroughs in the quest for regional stability in the very years when the "people's war" was reaching its peak within South Africa can be attributed to—and certainly will be claimed by—a number of sources. What cannot be overlooked, however, is the fact that when it was compelled to direct unprecedented effort inward the South African Defense Force scored

its greatest successes outside the Republic. The beginnings of regional
stability have been laid upon that foundation.

Notes

1. South Africa, Parliament, *Report on the Investigation into Education for
Blacks in the Vaal Triangle following upon the Occurrences of 3 September 1984
and Thereafter* (RP 88/1985). This report is from a commission chaired by Dr. D
van der Walt. When the author met with Dr. van der Walt in June 1988, he was
serving as Parliamentary officer for the director-general of the Department of
Manpower (Dr. Piet van der Merwe). The report is developed along the lines of
the 1979 Commission of Inquiry into the Riots of Soweto and other places from
June 16, 1976, to February 28, 1977. See section 2 of this chapter.

2. The center of gravity could be said to shift outside for the period August
1987/June 1988 when a final, full-scale conventional war rages in Angola. This
last resort to resolve the Namibian Question by arms on the part of
MPLA/FAPLA and its backers will fail as well. See chapter 6.

3. F Ackron and R D Henwood, "Anarchism and Ungovernableness with
Specific Reference to the RSA," *Strategic Review* (Pretoria) (December 1986):
31–32. Professor Ackron's experience extends from fieldwork in the Venda district to the Commission on Constitutional Planning and Development. The "strategy literature" aside, the literature on counterinsurgency, terrorism, and other
forms of contemporary warfare (and mayhem) upon which South African analysts
(both military and civilian) have drawn heavily in this period include: Paul Wilkinson, *Terrorism and the Liberal State* (London: Macmillan, 1977); Sir Robert
Thompson, *Defeating Communist Insurgency* (London: Chatto & Windus, 1966);
Brig. Frank Kitson, *Low Intensity Operations: Subversion, Counter-Insurgency
and Peacekeeping* (London: Faber & Faber, 1972); and J.J. McCuen, *The Art of
Counterrevolutionary Warfare: The Strategy of Counter-Insurgency* (London:
Faber & Faber, 1966, 1969). Attuned to the French experience in Africa there is
familiarity as well with an earlier genre that includes the writings of Marshals
Lyautey and Gallieni as well as the later French school ranging from Marshal
Bugeaud to General Catroux in the 1930s. See Jean Gottman, "Bugeaud, Gallieni,
Lyautey: The Development of French Colonial Warfare," in *Makers of Modern
Strategy,* ed. Edward Meade Earl (New York: Atheneum, 1967), 234–59. The
conjunction of politics and arms in all of this literature (appearing even in
Gallieni's "Madagascar Instructions") would be a troublesome point for SADF.
The major outlet for this analysis is the Institute for Strategic Studies of the
University of Pretoria under the direction of Prof. Michael Hough. Somewhat
scholastic in form and tone at times, the institute's publications are an invaluable
and unrivaled source of South African thought on revolutionary warfare. The
author's indebtedness will be evident throughout this book.

4. Longreach Report, *Short Term Forecast: South and Southern Africa*
(Sandton, RSA), and Africa-International Communications, *A/C Bulletin* (Johannesburg, RSA). Both monthlies are invaluable sources on current ANC activities.
Both appear to have a variety of intelligence sources. The official ANC monthly
is *Sechaba* (ANC: P.O. Box 31791, Lusaka). Billed as "a message to the people

of South Africa," the *Statement of the National Executive Committee of the African National Congress on the Occasion of the 76th Anniversary of the ANC Presented by President Oliver Tambo* (January 8, 1988) outlines the objectives of armed mass insurrection. If the initial June 1985 declaration was not wholly clear, President Tambo reiterated in an interview with BBC-TV correspondent Jonathan Dimbley (October 27, 1985, in London) that "we will go to every conceivable length to destroy the system. . . . It must be seen as a growing conflict that becomes deeper and more intensive, involving the use of guns."

5. For a brief discussion of the earlier period see section 1 of chapter 3, also n. 55 of chapter 2.

6. South African officials are persuaded of "orchestration" from various points at different times, but in this instance RSA Intelligence had been watching the Soviet Embassy in Maseru (Lesotho) grow to the largest in the region eclipsing Lusaka. The matter would not go unattended.

7. In retrospect a piece appearing in the *Johannesburg Star,* December 3, 1982, detailing incidents that the government stated were launched from Lesotho and Mozambique, should have served as a warning of what would come six days later. See Deon Geldenhuys, "Recrossing the Matola Threshold: The 'Terrorist' Factor in South Africa's Regional Relations," *South Africa International* 13 (January 1983): 152–71. This piece is instructive for the awkwardness it reveals on the part of the best of scholars in dealing with concepts such as terrorism, insurgency, destabilization, and militarization—not to mention "hawks" and "doves." In fairness it must be noted that some five years later conceptual clarification has moved apace.

8. In the course of remarks in Parliament in support of the N'komati Accord, Foreign Minister R F "Pik" Botha responded to criticism that prior to N'komati "members were accusing us of destabilization" and that the Ministry of Defense was largely responsible. "The hon members can take it from me that in the period during which we determined the strategy which was ultimately crowned with success at N'komati, I was in absolute agreement with all of the decisions taken." The foreign minister reminded his colleagues that it was he who sent the telegram following the May 1983 bombing in Church Street in Pretoria telling Maputo that if they persisted in allowing further ANC action retaliation would follow—as it did. See *Debates,* South Africa House of Assembly (May 9, 1984), cols. 6099–6102. Cited by Hough, *Selected Strategic Perceptions,* 112.

9. Ibid., 86. (*Debates,* February 1, 1983, cols. 136–37.)

10. For a sympathetic treatment of Botswana's plight, consult the work of Richard Dale, "Between Pretoria and Praetorianism: Crafting a National Security Establishment and Policy for Botswana," a paper presented to the 31st Annual Meeting of the African Studies Association, October 28–31, 1988, Chicago. While rejecting SADF offers to assist the Botswana Defense Force, President Masire was ready to entertain other offers. A U.S. Military Delegation headed by Brig. Gen. T. Richards (representing CINCEUR, then Gen. Bernard Rogers) visited Gaborone in March 1987. Announcement of the visit (*Cape Times,* March 11, 1987) contained the note that assistance for the BDF, which would be forthcoming, would not include weapons; this was part of an economic assistance program for frontline states. Whatever the case it was construed in certain RSA circles as smacking of U.S. State Department posturing. The author was told by a

senior official that he had encouraged the United States to do this some time ago because of "the alarming size of the Soviet contingent in Gaborone—now they start to do something!" The timing could only be seen as part of the heightened anti-Pretoria campaign then raging. As for the possibility of a U.S. Military Advisory Assistance Group (MAAG) advising the BDF on how to cope with SADF, no concern was evidenced. For confusion in the U.S. Security Assistance Program where Botswana is concerned, see "Commitment to Freedom-Security Assistance as a U.S. Policy Instrument in the Third World," a paper by the Regional Conflict Working Group submitted to the Commission on Integrated Long-Term Strategy (Washington, D.C., GPO, May 1988), 31.

11. Major du Toit was returned to South African officials in Maputo on September 7, 1987, in exchange for 133 FAPLA soldiers (captured by UNITA) and others. The remains of the two SADF soldiers killed in the Cabinda undertaking were returned as well. Almost the entire upper echelon of the RSA government received Major du Toit!

12. The description of an external operation against ANC as "the harsh killing of *anti-apartheid activists*" (italics mine) and as "an attack on Botswana" (*The Economist,* London, June 22–28, 1985, 16) was put alongside the British statement in the UN following the Sebokeng deployment the previous October that "the problems of South Africa could or should not be solved by repression, denial of civil and political rights or by violence." Statements of this sort coming from the Ulster Occupation Force, it was suggested, have to be the high-water mark of hypocrisy or so it would appear on the *voortrekkerhoogte*. Official British comment would moderate over time, especially when put alongside U.S. reaction to cross-border operations.

13. Robert Mugabe would equivocate on the question of providing assistance to relocated ANC elements, but with the passage of time the evidence that Zimbabwe might in fact become the major sanctuary would grow. For the difficulties at the Zimbabwe border preceding May 1986, especially the limpet mine incidents along the Limpopo, see chapter 4.

14. *South African Digest* (Pretoria: Bureau for Information, May 23, 1986), 440. The following day Mr. Louis Nel, deputy minister of Information (Ministry of Foreign Affairs) met the international press in Pretoria to provide, in excruciating detail, the brief for the May 19 raids. Ibid., 441. See also the address of minister of Law and Order, Mr. Louis LeGrange, to the National Party Congress in Durban, August 12–13, 1986. The British foreign secretary, Sir Geoffrey Howe, on a visit to the RSA at this time stated that "what is needed is that the South African government should agree to . . . unban the ANC and other political parties and to enter peaceful dialog—*against a matching commitment from the ANC to call a halt to violence and to enter peaceful dialog*" (italics mine). Statement to the press, Pretoria, July 29, 1986. (Sir Geoffrey's Prime Minister will describe the ANC as a terrorist organization rather than a political party. For Mrs. Thatcher's interview with the editor-in-chief of *Beeld* on this and related topics, see *South Africa Foundation Review,* 15 [April 1989], 4–5.) In either case the stipulation that there should be a matching commitment from the ANC was not heard in Washington. In testimony before the U.S. Senate Foreign Relations Committee on July 23, 1986 (the day after a "tough speech" on the same subject by the president of the United States), Secretary of State George Shultz would not

make unbanning of the ANC and peaceful dialogue contingent on the ANC forswearing violence. Implying that they had not already done so, he called upon the ANC to "avoid the easy descent into violence, terrorism, and extremism." The following January he would meet with ANC leader Oliver Tambo in Washington. The disarray in the U.S. government on the ANC issue reached its nadir in the final month of the Reagan administration with the publication by the Department of Defense of *Terrorist Group Profiles.* In a section on "African Terrorism" the ANC is the only organization to which an article is devoted. While the Department of State's Office of Counter-Terrorism joined in the DOD designation of ANC as a terrorist organization, the Bureau of African Affairs presumed to say that "the U.S. government has not determined that the ANC is a terrorist organization"! Mr. Herman Nickel, ambassador to the RSA for Mr. Reagan until mid-1986, has concluded that Washington does not have a coherent South African policy. See his "Promoting Change in South Africa," *SAIS Review* 8 (Winter/Spring 1988): 29–41.

15. General Malan's remarks in the House of Assembly on May 28, 1985, will suffice as a typical example of South African realism on this point. *Debates, House of Assembly* (May 28, 1985), cols. 6376–81, cited by Hough, *Selected Strategic Perceptions,* 112–15. The tension between Pretoria and Washington on this issue reached its peak in 1986. Mr. Roelf P Meyer, visiting the University of South Carolina in July (shortly before his appointment to the post of deputy minister of Law and Order), felt compelled to express his concern about the "hypocrisy" to the author—as he had expressed it in Washington on the same trip. Even the most recent writing of "Africanists" will include such sentences as "P W Botha . . . has always been one of the most enthusiastic supporters of the regional destabilization policy," and "the military believes that weak, and even unstable neighbors are the best guarantee of South Africa's security." At this point in an otherwise documented study (documentation from secondary sources) the author fails to provide sourcing. See Mark V. Kauppi, "The Republic of South Africa," in *The Defense Policies of Nations—A Comparative Study,* 2d ed., ed. Douglas J. Murray and Paul R. Viotti (Baltimore: Johns Hopkins Press, 1989). The author is indebted to Colonel Viotti for permitting him to read this chapter in galley proof. On the basis of more than ten years of association with the SADF officer corps, this writer contends that their position is *exactly opposite* that represented by Kauppi.

16. Tom Lodge, "Black Resistance Politics under the State of Emergency," *South Africa Foundation Review* 14 (September 1988): 4–5. Professor Lodge (University of the Witwatersrand), invariably sanguine in his expectations where the ANC is concerned, has nonetheless followed their affairs closely. See his *Black Politics in South Africa since 1945* (London: Longman, 1983). A fellow South African academic (Prof. Hermann Giliomee, University of Cape Town), after a meeting with ANC officials and Africanists from the Soviet Union in Leverkusen (FRG), had a number of questions about contradictions in the path (or paths) being followed by the ANC toward a political settlement. See his "The ANC, the Soviet Union and South Africa," in *South African Foundation Review,* 14 (December 1988): 4–5.

17. Some saw SAP with a particularly long reach in the spring of 1988 with the demise of ANC operative Dulcie September in Paris and the serious wounding

of Albie Jacks in Maputo, recalling the death of Ruth First in Dar es Salaam some years earlier. Then at the end of the year came revelations of a new "Forsyth Saga." Lieutenant Olivia Forsyth of the SAP (a British subject) had succeeded in infiltrating the ANC through Harare. Upon discovery of her mission she was put in the notorious Quatro prison, northeast of Luanda, where as one report has it she endured the "vilest of tortures." In May 1988 she escaped from a safe house in Luanda into the British Embassy from whence she made her way back to the RSA. Her disclosures would appear to have contributed substantially to SADF/SAP successes as well as the image of RSA intelligence prowess. The episode is reminiscent of the exploits of Mr. Craig Williamson approximately a decade earlier. A student activist in his university days, Williamson joined the International University Exchange Fund (IUEF). Upon leaving the country in 1976 for Geneva and elsewhere, he went underground for the SAP. Rising to the level of deputy director of IUEF, he was able to monitor the educational activities of ANC, SWAPO, and the Rhodesian Patriotic Front. This story broke in 1980. Today Mr. Williamson is a member of the President's Council, a connoisseur of South African wines, and a businessman who, along with other well-placed countrymen, has interests in Mozambique and the off-shore islands.

18. SADF has been reluctant to consider ANC as presenting anything but a low-scale military threat. "Make no mistake about it we are at war with the ANC, but the whole business is overplayed" was the 1985 view of a SADF officer. "For us it is primarily an external matter—that's where the (ANC) assets are (command and control, leadership, infrastructure, arms, etc.). It's a matter of good intelligence; when we have it we move against those assets. We are doing reasonably well although 'hypocrisy' in certain quarters (especially abroad) could be a problem." SADF officers find it noteworthy that their cross-border operations against ANC, which have much more of an intelligence collection and "commando raid" character (and much less of a "reprisal" character) than do Israeli air and ground strikes into Lebanon, bring down considerably greater opprobrium. As for the external orientation of SADF, a South African civilian observer told the author that "if the Defense Force people had their way they would draw a line around the country and announce that everything inside was the problem of the police and the politicians and that everything outside was their problem!" This view, to the extent that it obtained in SADF early on, would mature through the eighties.

19. Following a cabinet shake-up in November 1986, Mr. Adriaan Vlok, deputy minister of Defense, would replace Mr. Louis LeGrange as minister of Law and Order. (Mr. LeGrange would subsequently be elected Speaker of Parliament in the House of Assembly.) Mr. Roelf P Meyer would become deputy minister under Mr. Vlok. On July 31, 1987, the commissioner of Police, Gen. Johann Coetzee, retires to be replaced by Lt. Gen. Hendrik de Wit. Thereafter Lt. Gen. Johann van der Merwe takes command of Security Police. The new minister of Law and Order's declaration in connection with Dingaan's Day (December 16, 1987) that "we are not prepared to accept it any longer" would be a harbinger of the climactic year in the armed-struggle phase. On September 2, 1987, Mr. Vlok told the House of Assembly that more than five hundred ANC/PAC had been "eliminated" in the year preceding the National State of Emergency (July 1985–June 1986). *South African Digest* (September 11, 1987), 6.

20. In the nine-year period 1976–84 less than three hundred incidents of terrorism and sabotage are reported by RSA authorities. In the four "surge years" (1985–88), more than one thousand incidents are reported. The MK leadership is taken over by Chris Hani in this period. It will take credit for hitting "soft" targets increasingly concentrated in White areas as necessary to success in a "people's war." The Executive Committee, on the other hand, by late 1988 will back away from assuming responsibility for such incidents.

21. A brief statement of principles, thoroughly revolutionary in tone, the Freedom Charter was adopted by a so-called Congress of the People at Kliptown (Soweto) in June 1955.

22. See chapter 1 for a discussion of this meeting.

23. In a study for the minister of Justice, the South African Law Commission has looked at both the Freedom Charter and the new guidelines from the standpoint of possible incorporation in a future constitution. See South African Law Commission, *Group and Human Rights* (Working Paper 25/Project 58), Pretoria, 1989, 215 ff.

24. "Certain sources" indicate that this entails the removal of some six thousand ANC from seven camps, four of which are military training centers. See Deon Fourie, "The ANC Leaves Angola—Implications," *South Africa Foundation Review* 15 (May 1989): 6–7. Fourie, not inexperienced in these matters, is somewhat wary that mass action has replaced mass insurrection. For a somewhat more sanguine view, see Colin Legum, "The USSR and South Africa," in *The Red Orchestra*, ed. Bark, 103–17.

25. The "diplomatic accreditation drive," while global in scope, is aimed first at those African states aligned with the West. Kenya is the first of these to officially receive an ANC ambassador (Tami Sindelo).

26. It is no longer correct to refer to the military wing of PAC by the Xhosa term *Poqo* (alone). See Longreach Report, *Short-Term Forecast* (March 17, 1989), 22.

27. Visitors to the Voortrekker Monument on the heights outside Pretoria will know that it is on Dingaan's Day that a shaft of sunlight strikes the high altar through an aperture in the ceiling. As one observer noted "there is considerable emotional freight in all of this!"

28. Slovo, while traveling widely, is based in London. Liaison with ANC is to a considerable extent through Ron Kasrils, associated with MK as head of special operations and military intelligence and also based in London. A Latvian, Slovo has not been able to shake charges that he is KGB and a colonel at that!

29. *Debates,* South Africa House of Assembly (September 15, 1987), cols. 5907–11, cited by Hough, *Selected Strategic Perceptions,* 23–27.

30. South Africa, Parliament, *Report of the Commission of Inquiry into the Riots at Soweto and Other Places* (1979), vol. 1, 435. See also Michael Hough, "The Concept of Political Coercion and Intimidation with Specific Reference to the RSA," *Strategic Review* (Pretoria) (November 1987): 32–47. State President P W Botha addressed a joint sitting of the three houses of Parliament on June 12, 1986, in connection with his declaration of a National State of Emergency and later delivered a nationwide television address. Declaring his ongoing commitment to reform he emphasized that he would not neglect the task at hand, namely, "to totally exterminate violence and lawlessness." Mr. Botha's remarks were also

an expression of exasperation with the international community for its failure to recognize his reform measures, let alone assist in the reform program. See *South African Digest* (June 20, 1986), 539–41. On June 13, 1986, the South African newspaper the *Citizen* published excerpts from a document of the SACP Central Committee, acquired by RSA Intelligence, spelling out the objectives of the then raging "revolutionary onslaught" in the townships.

31. Taken from statistical data released by the Bureau for Information on June 11, 1987. For a subsequent discussion of this data, see "The Unrest Situation in South Africa: September 1984–May 1987," *Strategic Review* (Pretoria) (August 1987): 21–41; also Patrick Laurence, "Black Politics—1987," *South Africa Foundation Review* 14 (January 1988): 1–2. There was a precipitous drop in both unrest incidents and deaths in the first year of NSE (80 and 90 percent respectively). Deaths by burning (in most cases "necklacing"), which claimed nearly five hundred people between January 1986 and May 1987, had all but ceased by the end of 1987.

32. There are exceptions to this proposition. In a number of cases there were pleas for both SADF and SAP to stay in the townships to maintain the peace, namely to contain the intimidators. See the remarks of Mr. A B Williams in this connection in chapter 1. When the "Black upon Black" nature of most of the violence was made known to the international community it was often dismissed as "the inevitable concomitant of revolutionary struggle," or as simply "necessary suffering."

33. Reference n. 11 in chapter 4.

34. This section is based on a series of interviews in 1985. In attempting to sort things out with SAP, reference would be made to an article by then chief of the army, Lt. Gen. J J Geldenhuys, in which he attempted to confine himself to problems the army faced in dealing with "rural insurgency," implying, perhaps unintendedly, a rural/urban division of responsibilities between SADF and SAP. See his "Rural Insurgency and Counter-measures," in *Revolutionary Warfare and Counter Insurgency,* ed., Michael Hough (Pretoria: ISSUP, 1984), 40–45. No such division of labor would obtain.

35. A judiciary commission reported (in June 1985) that Uitenhage was not so much an ANC episode as a "disturbance" and that police procedures left much to be desired in coping with this new complexity. In part the problem would lie with police recruitment, but only in part. Today members of SAP (and SADF) may not belong to extreme organizations of the right or left, perhaps most notably the Afrikaner Defense League.

36. Interview, March 1987.

37. This section is based in part on an interview with Mr. Vlok in March 1987.

38. Both Police and Defense Force officers, upon exposure to the unrest situation in the townships, would express exasperation with the lack of attention on the part of civilian agencies. For the comments of a SAP officer on the failure of Education officials to attend to even minor matters such as textbooks and school bus fares, see Maj. Gen. A J Wandrag, SAP, "Political Unrest—A Police View," *Strategic Review* (Pretoria) (October 1985): 8–16. Today Lieutenant General Wandrag is head of Riot Control Police. SADF officers would venture the view that "we don't want to go back in there again only to find the same damn problems!"

39. For a discussion of the Joint Security Management Group and the National Joint Management Center (NJMC), see chapter 3.

40. Meyer would not be free of internal security matters himself. For his discussion of the role of SAP in monitoring the labor sphere, that realm of endeavor to which the new secretary-general of the South African Communist Party (SACP), Mr. Joe Slovo, had turned see *Debates, South Africa House of Assembly* (September 2, 1987), cols. 5066–69, cited by Hough, *Selected Strategic Perceptions,* 128–30. Within the year Mr. Meyer would become deputy minister for Constitutional Planning and Development.

41. See n. 29 above.

42. SADF's "civic action" programs provide basic medical, educational, and technical assistance to outlying population groups under the counterinsurgency rubric of "winning the hearts and minds of the people," and should not be confused with refurbishing the townships. Both undertakings are, of course, counterrevolutionary in thrust. Critics of SADF's civic action who, almost without exception, have not seen the programs attribute anything but altruistic motives to them. When the Directorate for Civic Action ventured into "psychological programs," it was abolished (1980) with its nonpsychological elements continuing under other branches today. Maj. Gen. Phillip Pretorius, originator of "psychological civic action," now serves as director of the South African National Museum of Military History. See also *White Paper on Defense, 1986,* 13–15.

43. This section is based largely on interviews with Mr. Steward in March 1987 and June 1988; see also, however, Colin Vale, "South Africa's Communications Crisis," *Strategic Review* (Pretoria) (October 1986): 1–16. Well known in Washington, Steward followed R F "Pik" Botha as RSA ambassador to the UN and then served as head of the Planning Division in the Ministry of Foreign Affairs. One of his last tasks in the Foreign Ministry was to journey to Washington in September 1985 as the result of a new offensive in Angola. His discussions led to the decision to provide military assistance to UNITA.

44. At the height of the "armed mass insurrection" phase (and the peak of unrest incidents) the Bureau of Information ordered foreign television crews out of the townships and otherwise restricted their coverage. Restrictions on the print press were imposed as well, however, without the same visual impact. (See chapter 2, n. 55.) Something of the tenor of the relationship between RSA government officials and the foreign press corps can be gathered from accounts of the Foreign Correspondents Annual Dinner on November 5, 1988, in Johannesburg. Responding to questions following his address to the assembly Mr. R F "Pik" Botha declared, inter alia, "You don't understand Africa. You don't understand African aspirations. You don't understand African history. I accuse you of glibly gliding over the African realities of which you know nothing, absolutely nothing." The foreign minister then recalled the opening words of a famous speech by Paul Kruger, " 'Friends, citizens, thieves, and enemies'—and that is how I look at you this evening." Lest one conclude that the foreign minister was suffering from after-dinner indigestion it must be reported that the chairman of the Foreign Correspondents Association resigned the following day in dismay over the raucous and uncivil behavior of his colleagues. Finally, and typically, in the AP dispatch reporting on the dinner there is a reference to President Paul Kruger (the most famous of all Boers) as "a nineteenth-century politician"!

45. Interview with Mr. Ecksteen, May 1985. Made director-general in 1983, Ecksteen is replaced following Mr. van der Merwe's elevation to minister of

Information and Culture. His successor is Wynand Harmse, deputy director-general for Finance. Harmse's promotion is not thought to stem entirely out of concerns to reduce spiraling operating costs.

46. Ellsworth Bunker, U.S. ambassador to Vietnam during the climactic years of the war, touched on this defeat in an interview with the *New York Times,* May 11, 1984: "I think experience has shown that in the age of television you have to have some sort of press control, as the British did during the Falklands war. Television, naturally enough, goes after the dramatic. And that's what the American people saw from Vietnam. After the Tet offensive in 1968, I reported back to Washington that we had won a military victory. But I feared a psychological defeat." Bunker's statement has been ringing in the ears of RSA officials ever since.

47. See his "La nouvelle politique de Pretoria entend tirer parti de la dépendance de fait des États voisins," *Le Monde,* November 20, 1979. Contrast this with the viewpoint of the political editor of *The Economist* (London) who found SADF generals "a stale and introverted oligarchy." (Simon Jenkins, "Destabilization in Southern Africa," *The Economist,* July 16–22, 1983: 19–28.) One must take account of differences in French and British perspectives, keeping in mind that Walter Bagehot, founder of *The Economist,* is purported to have complained that "I have a number of people who write well; the problem is they don't know anything!"

48. Interview with Brig. D J Mortimer, May 18, 1985.

49. See the discussion of "The Cardinal Thread" in chapter 1.

50. The reader is referred to the literature discussion in the introduction.

51. This from an English-speaking South African who has been a close observer of SADF. It was suggested by more than one source that the only conceivable basis for a crisis between the military and the political leadership in South Africa would be a return to power by the Right (*die verkrampte*) after the reform process had achieved many of its goals. Therefore, the suggestion by Frankel that SADF is conservative (the suggestion derives more from his study of the literature of military institutions than any direct analysis of SADF itself) is in almost all respects misleading. See introduction.

52. Not for direct attribution.

53. This section is based in part on interviews with General van der Westhuizen over a five-year period (1983–87). In September 1987 he was appointed RSA ambassador to Chile. (See chapter 7.)

54. Interview March 10, 1986. An aide, growing increasingly nervous as the interview went along, was reassured by the general that all would be well.

55. See n. 34 of this chapter.

56. The report is discussed in chapter 4.

57. See n. 21 of chapter 1.

58. With respect to the question of staying within constitutional bounds, the following is worth noting. State President F W de Klerk, responding to allegations circulating in the press at the end of 1989 to the effect that SAP had organized hit squads to eliminate opponents, established a Commission of Inquiry (February 1990) chaired by Justice L C Harms. After an investigation, focused on SAP's Civilian Cooperation Bureau, Justice Harms reported (in November 1990) that he found no evidence of state-sanctioned political murders. The internationally recognized integrity of the South African judiciary gave weight to his findings.

6 TOWARD REGIONAL STABILITY, 1985–1989

> South Africa is the stabilizer of the region and would like to expand this role.
>
> —Gen. Magnus Malan, RSA Minister of Defense,
> November 2, 1988

New Thinking and Heavy Fighting

In the ebb and flow of Soviet thinking about Africa, the Republic of South Africa is the constant factor.[1] The designs, ambitions, or opportunities of the Kremlin where the continent is concerned can be entertained only against the certainty of counterweight and counteraction from the "metropole power" at the Cape of Good Hope. By 1985 this contention had gained new cogency. In southern Africa the regional situation (as viewed from Moscow) was at a crisis point: the fortunes of national liberation and attendant socialist aspirations were in decline and those of the RSA in the ascendant. In the Soviet Union the Brezhnev era with its short Andropov/Chernenko epilogue is ended, and Mikhail Gorbachev is in power. While "new thinking" about Africa antedates Gorbachev's ascendancy—much of it had been instigated by him—the new premier and general secretary must now make decisions about investments in the African portfolio. Nothing in the putative pragmatism of Mr. Gorbachev—nothing in his ensuing adjustments of African policy and strategy—will do anything but underscore Pretoria's primacy in the region. Like other players on the periphery, Moscow in its post-Brezhnevian assessment of southern Africa will be constrained to give added credence to extraordinarily resistant "local

157

factors." Disappointment in ruling circles in Moscow with African polities as "seedbeds of socialism" is patent.[2] An ideological rout has occurred. However, this will not deter Mr. Gorbachev from moving to limit damage and, more significantly, to bring Soviet objectives in the region into sharper focus. The Gorbachev stamp on things will demonstrate (particularly for those who require instruction on the point) that more than socialist development and antiapartheid posturing define Soviet interests in this part of the world. The foundations of Soviet policy and strategy rest on more enduring realities.

In the ongoing competition with the West (viz., the United States of America), a competition that does not conclude with the Brezhnev era and that the new premier plainly understands as posing a challenge to Soviet credentials as a global power, Mr. Gorbachev will repair to classic norms of international relations. He will hoist the "geostrategic significance of southern Africa" as his guidon for Soviet actions in the region.[3] The resources and communications lines afforded by Africa are strategically important to Moscow in and of themselves, but above all as a fulcrum for leverage on Europe and the industrial democracies. In the pursuit of classic objectives both direct and indirect strategies will be employed.[4] A new team, utterly pragmatic, resolutely committed to results, and prepared to follow a variety of paths, however contradictory on their face, is put in place. An early indication of Mr. Gorbachev's determination to replace the expositors of socialist development with functionaries of a more conventional stripe is the prompt departure of Boris Ponomarev. As head of the CPSU Central Committee's International Department, Ponomarev had presided over "Brezhnevian expansionism" in Africa and other parts of the Third World. Anatoly Dobrynin, long-standing ambassador to the United States and presumably more of an "American specialist" than the less agreeable Georgy Arbatov, takes over but only for a brief period. Aleksandr Yakovlev, a source of much of Mr. Gorbachev's clarification of Soviet goals, is appointed head of a new Central Committee International Policy Commission displacing the International Department altogether. Andrei Gromyko, synonymous with the foreign policy of "old thinking," is required to move along to chairmanship of the Supreme Soviet to make way for Edward Shevardnadze whose foreign-policy credentials consist of the fact that he is the Georgia "party boss."[5] In addition to Yakovlev and Shevardnadze, the journalist Boris Asoyan (now with a Foreign Ministry portfolio) will have a prominent role in African affairs. His posting to Maseru (Lesotho) and the message he carries to southern Africa will contrast sharply with that of Vasilii Solodovnikov in Lusaka a decade earlier.[6] Another new star in the southern sky is Anatoly Adamishin, deputy foreign minister, who will act as cofacilitator with Mr. Chester Crocker (continuing in the second Reagan administration as assistant secretary of state for African Affairs) in negotiations aimed at a resolution of the Angola/Namibia Question.

The advent of the Gorbachev era in southern Africa will be bloody. In its new geostrategic calculus the USSR is not prepared to depart so critical a region: the Angolan (MPLA) and Namibian (SWAPO) accounts are not items for liquidation. Mr. Gorbachev, having been given to believe there was neglect if not erosion of U.S. support, decides to test the depth of Washington's commitment to Dr. Jonas Savimbi and his UNITA movement. There is a dramatic surge in Soviet arms shipments to MPLA/FAPLA for the year ending October 1, 1985.[7] The opening gambit is to improve the military situation of both MPLA/FAPLA and SWAPO/PLAN and, indeed, join the fortunes of the two parties in contravention of previously understood "rules of the game" in southern Africa. Pretoria, as we have seen (chapter 2), had noticed increased PLAN activity as soon as the ink was dry on the Lusaka Agreement (February 1984) and especially in the final stages of SADF withdrawal from Angola (April–May 1985). Just a month after withdrawal SADF announces (July 1, 1985) a "hot pursuit" operation back into Angola in which more than sixty "SWAPO boys" are killed. (A SWAPO propensity to step up activity in the wake of a formal agreement will surface again in April 1989.) Visiting the "operational area" at this time (Ondangwa, Oshakati, Eenhana, Rundu, Omega), one encountered "taut SADF kommandants."[8] While the disengagement of forces in the area in question (south-central Angola) was proceeding and while PLAN infiltrations were not particularly threatening (nine would be killed near Eenhana within hours of our departing for Omega), the assessment of our hosts was that neither the bush war (SWAPO/PLAN) nor the conventional war (MPLA/ FAPLA)—presumably separate wars in May 1985—were behind them. The attitude was sardonic rather than pessimistic: nothing will be settled until there is conclusive fighting. The "kommandants" would prove either prescient or in possession of excellent intelligence!

In August 1985 the conclusive phase of a long Angolan war opens.

The Gorbachev phase has new rules: MPLA/FAPLA and Cuban units *jointly* hit UNITA forces at Gazomba (Cazombo), driving them back upon Mavinga to the north of Dr. Savimbi's headquarters at Jamba. SADF reenters the area in question in September to cries from the usual sources that it is Pretoria that is violating the Lusaka Agreement! In heavy fighting around Mavinga, SADF encounters the new rules: Mi-24 (Hind) helicopters and MiG-23 fighters, flown by Soviet pilots, are in the fray. Cuban and Soviet advisers are in the field in stepped up numbers at brigade and battalion levels. At this point SADF is forced to commit a portion of its limited Mirage assets to save the day, downing one-quarter of the Hinds. As a South African Air Force pilot described it to the author: "The situation was very fluid with everyone milling around in the melee"—Cubans, Soviets, South Africans, assorted Angolans, and SWAPO.[9] The conventional and bush wars were linked up and Moscow was displaying an earnestness to bring them to a conclusion not seen before. The intensity of the 1985 offensive (starting late and terminated early by South African action—and by the rains) catches Washington by surprise and sets off an equally intensive review of the situation. The review will reveal rifts along the Potomac that had been developing for some time.

Jonas Savimbi arrives in Washington at year's end on a mission more urgent than any of his previous ones. (RSA Foreign Ministry officials will have preceded him with their own interpretations of Mr. Gorbachev's entry on the southern African stage and with their own recommendations.)[10] The UNITA leader is clear about his purpose: he must have direct and immediate military assistance for his embattled forces, which—he did not need to remind his listeners—already had the "rhetorical support" of the president of the United States. Nor, in light of a substantial U.S./RSA intelligence exchange, did he need to point out that a second surge of Soviet arms for Angola would follow in 1986. The necessity to make urgent choices concerning the Angola/Namibia Question further aggravated the relationship between the Department of State and the Central Intelligence Agency already made raw over the conflict in Central America. Reminiscent of 1975, "State" strongly opposes the Savimbi request. Secretary of State George Shultz in an exchange of correspondence (in October 1985) with House Republican leader Robert Michel puts himself and his department on record in the plainest of terms. In November, after a nearly yearlong hiatus (Luanda had failed to respond to Washington's inquiries concerning a Namibian timetable), State resumes talks with the MPLA with the claim that arms for Savimbi would complicate the task of Assistant Secretary Chester Crocker.[11] President Reagan, however, rejects State's position and orders arms assistance for UNITA: The "Reagan doctrine" remains in effect! Congress, *mirabile dictu,* had earlier (July 1985) come full circle on the Tunney and Clark amendments of 1975, which had shut off arms to Savimbi. Taking cognizance of the intelligence flow from southern Africa, Congress first repeals the amendments and subsequently votes an initial fifteen-million dollars of military assistance to UNITA.[12] This amount has been increased since.

The decision of the president and the turnabout of Congress represented a clear-cut victory for the director of Central Intelligence in what was now an acrimonious relationship with the secretary of state. The fall out was as much between Mr. Casey and Mr. Shultz as it was between their respective organizations. The secretary responded to his setback with a multipronged campaign to recapture the southern Africa account from the director. In December (1985) he appoints an Advisory Committee on South Africa, which, viewed in its most favorable light, is a public front for State's inbred propensities on the entire range of regional issues.[13] This was followed by establishment of a "Working Group on South and Southern Africa," defined by Assistant Secretary Chester Crocker as "an *interagency* office *in the State Department* whose purpose was to encourage a wider understanding of *our policy goals*" (italics mine).[14] State makes perhaps its most overt move in connection with the formation of a new Inter-Agency Committee on Covert Operations chaired by the deputy NSC advisor (the late) Donald Fortier. In time-honored Washington fashion, Mr. Shultz sets out to control this committee by loading it up with rank. He appoints both under secretary of state for Policy, Michael Armacost, and assistant secretary of state (Intelligence and Research), Morton Abramowitz, to the committee. The Department of Defense is represented by under secretary of defense for Policy, Fred Ikle, and the CIA by deputy director for Operations, Clair George. The director of Central Intelligence is anything but inactive following the Savimbi visit. In the early months of 1986 Pretoria confirms that there is another big push of material through the Soviet pipeline to Angola and that Luanda is hurrying the 1986 offensive, aiming at April–May instead of August to avoid the rains. In March press reports have it that Mr. Casey is in southern Africa personally expediting the flow of arms to Savimbi's troops. Be that as it may, in a public address the following month (a rare event in itself but now evidently deemed necessary) Mr. Casey notes that Cuban troops and Soviet advisers are "feverishly preparing for a campaign likely to be launched during the month (April) designed to wipe out the forces resisting the Marxist government of Angola."[15]

Whoever else might have been abroad in March 1986, the author was in the RSA and found the chief of SADF echoing the concerns of the Director of Central Intelligence. "We are clear," General Geldenhuys confirmed, "and we believe Washington is clear as to just what equipment (for UNITA) is required." Shoulder-fired Stinger ground-to-air missiles ("the weapon of choice of the Reagan doctrine") and TOW antitank missiles (not shoulder-fired) to respond to the rising air and armor threats were the critical items. As for the mechanics of how this equipment will be put in place, "there is no problem there"— and as to the issue of training and indoctrination of UNITA forces in the use of their new equipment "we, of course, are there."[16] Rather than go into details of the aid arrangement the SADF chief was anxious to express certain concerns. "I have one major worry: ever since it became known that Savimbi was going to Washington there has been a significant Soviet reaction." General Geldenhuys was anxious about the new material in the Soviet pipeline but even more that the promised Stingers and TOWs get into the hands of UNITA posthaste. He, too, was looking at April as the launch date for the 1986 offensive. Should this aid be delayed or not be forthcoming (the general was not yet prepared to entirely trust Washington on the Angolan account), "*we will be left to face the Soviet reaction.*" An awkward military situation is developing in Angola, he emphasized, with the Soviets not operating under earlier restrictions. Soviet pilots are not only in the Hinds but in the MiG-23s, which, incidentally, "have an interesting configuration." The general did not elaborate further. His concerns would be put in abeyance temporarily. The sharp, prompt, and perhaps unexpected response of Washington had its impact in Moscow: there would be no 1986 offensive. The last roll of the military dice would wait a year; in the interim Mr. Gorbachev would reconsider but not yet choose the political-settlement option.

The lure of the military option—the lure of overrunning Dr. Savimbi's headquarters at Jamba, in southeastern Cuando Cubango Province (Angolan Military Region Six), and thereby erasing the international symbol of UNITA resistance—continued to exert its hold over the cabinet of Eduardo dos Santos (see map 2). While Mr. dos Santos personally may have had doubts about the feasibility of the military option (the 1985 offensive was the fourth major offensive to fail), this was outweighed by Moscow's decision to try one more time and try on a level unmatched in the past. By March 1987 the buildup for a climactic effort was evident both in terms of what was again passing through the Luanda docks and by the stockpiling in both Region Six and Region Three. (Headquarters for the latter is at Luena, or Luso, on the Benguela Railway.) What was shaping up was a two-pronged offensive to be initiated by an advance on Mavinga from Luena and Lucusse. The Region Three thrust was intended to be diversionary in order to direct UNITA attention away from the main Region Six offensive that would jump off from Cuito Cuanavale, now an advance command post directly south of the Region headquarters at Menongue. The Region Three "feint" at Mavinga from the northeast was broken up entirely by UNITA elements, some of which had gotten behind the advancing columns to harass logistic lines, and by others that fought FAPLA head-on, forcing them back on Lucusse. This success enabled UNITA to deploy quickly the bulk of its troops (regular and reserve) east of Cuito Cuanavale. FAPLA had established a brigade on the east side of the Cuito River (the town, airfield, and command post were on the west bank) and was building up a bridgehead with four additional brigades. UNITA understood well the lines of advance this force must follow southwestward toward Mavinga, the lines being dictated in part by water sources. Mines were laid, highly motivated troops with Stingers and TOWs in hand were in place, yet the weight of the final offensive (launched August 14, 1987) was such that South African assistance would be required. Never had it been so clear that more than intra-Angolan rivalries were at stake.

Col. Deon Ferreira, SADF ("he has been in the bush too long to retire back to the Republic—he'll probably take up farming out here in Namibia"),[17] set off on his greatest campaign in August 1987 exactly twelve years after Jan Breytenbach first went into Angola. Earlier in his career he had succeeded Breytenbach as OC of Three-Two Battalion and had gone across the border with his men on numerous occasions. The contingent he would take into Angola this time would differ vastly from the little band that accompanied Breytenbach in 1975, except that in both cases the size of the force would be greatly exag-

Map 2. **Angola: The Military Regions of FAPLA**

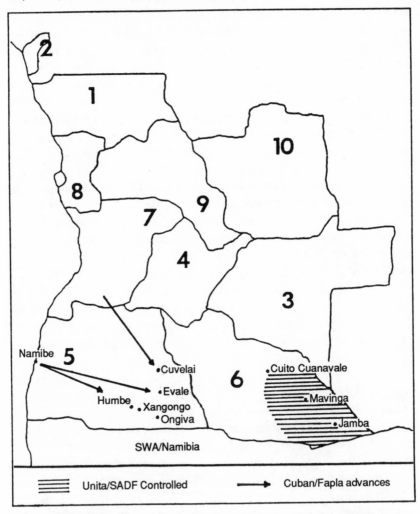

Source: "Short-Term Forecast: South and Southern Africa: Labour, Political and Security Developments," *Longreach Report* (Johannesburg: Longreach), June 18, 1988, p. 15.

gerated. At no time would his force exceed three thousand troops (the veteran Three-Two Battalion, SWATF battalions, mechanized infantry, and armored-car units).[18] The superlative forty-kilometer range 155-mm guns—both the G-5 towed and G-6 self-propelled systems—and *Valkiri* MARL systems (all compliments of ARMSCOR!) were included in the force and would soon reveal their lethality to the world. The FAPLA force was, on the other hand, a combined FAPLA/Cuban Soviet/PLAN[19] army with an unprecedented stock of tanks, armored vehicles, artillery, and supporting aviation. With a strength approaching twenty-five thousand (greatly exceeding combined SADF/SWATF/UNITA troops deployed above Mavinga), it was for the first time under the direct tactical control of a Soviet general. In the ensuing four months the two armies would engage in the heaviest fighting south of the Sahara in the history of Africa.

Ferreira's war aims were specific: in the first stage (*Operation Modular*) of what was to become a three-stage battle, he was to "halt and reverse" the FAPLA advance on Mavinga. In operational terms this meant that the lead brigade (Four Seven) must not be permitted to establish a bridgehead south of the Lomba River as it had done east of the Cuito. Fierce fighting occurred on September 13 and 14 and continued to October 3. "By then," as one account puts it, "the remnants of 47 Brigade had fled northward under cover of darkness . . . leaving all of their equipment behind in abandoned positions."[20] Ferreira had deployed his G-5s, G-6s, and *Valkiris* in fire-support positions out of range of enemy fire. Four Seven managed to cross the Lomba only to be decimated; consequently follow-on FAPLA units were smashed as they made repeated attempts to bridge the river. The retreat began. The instructions for stage two (*Operation Hooper*) were equally cryptic: "Inflict maximum casualties on the retreating enemy" (the Geldenhuys dictum). At this juncture—for the first time since World War II—South African tanks (the reconditioned *Olifants*) went into action. Throughout October and November there was heavy fighting particularly at the sources of the Chambinga and Hube rivers resulting, inter alia, in FAPLA's Two-One Brigade being removed from the field. As FAPLA continued to send reinforcements forward to stop the slaughter, it only added to the toll taken by Ferreira's "professional gunners." The colonel was determined that no force capable of launching a new offensive would be left intact east of the Cuito.

His final instruction "to attempt to force the enemy to retreat to the west of the Cuito River" marked the final stage (*Operation Packer*). By mid-October the SADF 155-mm guns had come within range of Cuito Cuanavale on the west bank and commenced a siege that would extend through February (1988). The fire—at times reaching two hundred rounds a day—took Cuito Cuanavale out of the war as a command post, an airfield, and as an element in the air-defense grid. In early December General Geldenhuys ordered a tactical disengagement as part of an ongoing operation in Angola. While the Cuban commander Gen. Arnaldo Ochoa Sánchez took note of this withdrawal, he was told by Havana that the fighting was not yet over. Heavy engagements would occur east of the Cuito in January and February. Having dispersed the entire enemy force, except for one battalion, "to beyond the Cuito River," Ferreira was later asked why he did not take the city itself. "We were east of the river, remember, and the town was on the west bank"; while it would have been possible, he continued, intelligent military strategy disallows "the placing of a *two-mile-wide* river between one's own forces and one's target" (italics mine).[21] The combined SADF/SWATF/UNITA force had inflicted the most massive defeat in the long Angolan war on their adversaries at the point of their maximum effectiveness. For Moscow the time had come "to settle this question." Luanda's pro-war cabinet faction gave way, although Havana would find the debacle more difficult to digest.

South African reticence to publicize either the extent or the outcome of the fighting gave credence in the usual circles to Luanda's forlorn claims of victory. In his wide-ranging press conference in Windhoek a year later, Colonel Ferreira told reporters of his government's decision "to operate under the pretense of limited assistance to UNITA" so as not to jeopardize the ongoing Brazzaville/New York talks aimed at an Angolan/Namibian settlement. Now following the signing of the Tripartite Agreement in New York (December 22, 1988), the SADF commander of operations *Modular, Hooper,* and *Packer* was ready to talk. The colonel, who can be at once amiable and blunt, stated, "If defeat for South Africa meant the loss of thirty-one men (SADF), three tanks, five armored vehicles, and three aircraft, then we'd lost. If victory for FAPLA meant the loss of forty-six hundred men, ninety-four tanks, one hundred armored vehicles, nine aircraft, and other Soviet equipment valued at more than a billion rand, then they'd won."[22] Aware of UNITA sensitivities about responsibility for the devastation of FAPLA, Ferreira pointed out that they had cleared the entire south of Angola of FAPLA and PLAN presence, laying the basis for "superfunctional" SADF logistic lines. The key to success was "the fine discipline and training" of SADF troops and "the massive artillery advantages" provided by the G-5s and G-6s. Ferreira did not minimize the air situation. He was frank in saying (as we recounted in chapter 4) that "the enemy's MiG-23s were the single most serious threat to our operations" and that Stingers in the hands of UNITA troops made the difference. Four months after he spoke, his concern was underscored at Calueque. The incidents of June 27, 1988, were striking evidence of what it means not to have Stingers in hand and of the fact that Fidel Castro was playing yet another hand.

It was evident from March onward through the spring and summer of 1988 that Havana—whatever the degree of ambivalence in Moscow and Luanda—was opening up Angolan Military Region Five as a potential new theater of operations. Fresh contingents of Cuban troops were arriving through the southern port of Namibe and deploying directly to launch points immediately above the Namibia border. (By this time earlier understandings, such as the Ruacana water scheme on the Cunene River being off limits, were a thing of the past.) Cuban/ FAPLA and Cuban/SWAPO integrated units were observed within a few kilometers of the border as were "Whites with long hair," which suggested to some that Soviet (or East German) *Spetsnaz* troops were in the area. More ominous was the MiG-23 buildup at Lubango (as would be confirmed on June 27) and the massive presence of tanks and other armored vehicles. Fully abreast of these developments, Pretoria advanced its deadline for SADF withdrawal from Region Six to September 1 (perhaps as much to regroup its forces as to expedite the negotiation process) and began to call up Citizen Force elements for duty at the border. An eyewitness who found himself on a Namibian highway on a July night told the author of "an endless column of tanks being trucked north." SADF was readying itself for the "all the chips on the table" kind of battle that General Earp spoke of over dinner in Washington that same month.

In what was described as a "cards on the table" briefing for correspondents at Oshakati on October 12, 1988, Gen. J J Geldenhuys and the new GOC for the Southwest, Maj. Gen. Willie Meyer, put Cuban strength in Angola at nearly seventy thousand—an all-time high and an increase of some fifteen thousand over the previous year.[23] In the month following SADF withdrawal from Angola (September), Cuban forces had not redeployed to the Line of the Benguela, as called for in the New York Principles,[24] but had in fact deployed farther southward. The Cuban 50th Division was now at Cahama as the centerpiece of the self-styled Namibian army. Working in closer conjunction than at any time in the Botha years, RSA Defense and Foreign Ministry officials (the latter were in attendance for the Oshakati briefing) agreed on strategy. Confronting the concurrent realities of a negotiation process that was gaining momentum and a Cuban buildup in southern Angola that was also gaining momentum, their decision was to look upon the latter as "Parthian shots" from Fidel Castro (while preparing for the worst) and to seize the diplomatic initiative.[25] Not only Defense but Foreign Affairs held the view that the victory at the Lomba River was a rich bed to be mined through negotiations. Moreover, the time had come to take up a wide-ranging diplomatic agenda going well beyond the Southwest Question.

Diplomatic Paths to Normalization in the Region

The Reagan–Gorbachev summit in Moscow (April 1988) marks the beginning of the final phase of a negotiation process that up to this point had been characterized by notable diligence on the part of the Bureau of African Affairs of the U.S. State Department and an equally notable contrast in the behavior of the other parties. Only now—three years after taking power and with the results from the battlefield in—is Mr. Gorbachev disposed to follow a diplomatic path where the fortunes of MPLA and SWAPO are concerned. Only now is Assistant Secretary of State Chester Crocker (accompanying Mr. Reagan and Mr. Shultz to Moscow) able to formulate with Deputy Foreign Minister Anatoly Adamishin mutually acceptable guidelines for conducting what will be severely constrained negotiations. Mr. Crocker had been determined all along (this would be particularly evident in the latter stages of the second Reagan administration with time running out) to confine himself to an international agenda, to the exclusion of either Angolan or Namibian domestic issues. What both he and Adamishin sought, once Guidelines (April) and a Statement of Principles for a Peaceful Settlement in Southwestern Africa (July) were in hand, were international agreements. The first of these was the Tripartite Agreement (Angola, Cuba, and South Africa) in which the parties pledged themselves to begin to implement United Nations Security Council Resolution 435/78 as of April 1989. The second was the Bilateral Agreement (Angola and Cuba) "for the conclusion of the internationalist mission of the Cuban military contingent."[26]

   The Tripartite Agreement merely puts into force the preordained provisions of UNSCR 435 for ensuring "free and fair elections" leading to an independent Namibian state. In its original 1978 formulation it was entirely unacceptable to Pretoria, and only as the result of intervening agreements and understandings did it become an acceptable framework for a treaty a decade later. South Africa's consistent argument that "435" implicitly incorporated General Assembly Resolutions 311 and 31/146 (December 1973), establishing SWAPO as "the sole and authentic representative of the Namibian people," was summarily rejected until 1982. During the course of that year informal impartiality undertakings on the part of the secretary-general established the following:

> —When Resolution 435 is implemented, all parties will be subject to equal treatment by the Administrator-General and the UN Special Representative.
> —All UN support to SWAPO will cease as from that day. No other party may receive aid from the UN either.
> —The UN Council for Namibia will cease involvement in any public affairs.
> —The Commissioner for Namibia will suspend all political activities for the duration of the transitionary period.
> —SWAPO will voluntarily forego its preferential treatment by the UN General Assembly.[27]

The provisions, while not part of the language of the Tripartite Agreement itself, are part and parcel of the "Settlement Plan."

Pretoria was determined that what had been won in a protracted bush war in Namibia, namely, the elimination of SWAPO/PLAN as an effective fighting force and its removal from Ovamboland bases in Namibia, would not be lost in any settlement plan. Again in 1982 an understanding was reached that a United Nations Transition Assistance Group (UNTAG) deployed to the area in connection with the implementation of UNSCR 435 would assume responsibility for monitoring SWAPO bases in Angola and Namibia. SWAPO/PLAN having long since been flushed from the latter, Pretoria insisted upon the further understanding that SWAPO be confined to positions north of the sixteenth parallel in Angola during the sensitive transition period. The intimidatory impact of ZANU and ZAPU in Rhodesia during the post–Lancaster House electoral process was very much on South African minds. Such an understanding was obtained, but as we shall see, it broke wide open on the day the implementation process was to begin (April 1, 1989).[28] Similarly, the provision in the Tripartite Agreement (and in the New York Principles) that the parties "shall ensure that their respective territories are not used by any state, *organization*, or person in connection with any acts of war, aggression or violence, against the territorial integrity, inviolability of borders, or independence of any state of southwestern Africa" (italics mine) was originally put forward as *not applicable* to the African National Congress. The point was obtained that it did apply to the ANC, but this required a corollary precluding RSA assistance to UNITA with the effective date of the treaty. Accompanied by much bravado from Kabwe, ANC initiated a process of dismantling bases in Angola in January 1989.

Fundamental principles concerning the Constituent Assembly (to be elected November 1, 1989) and fundamental principles concerning the Constitution of Namibia to be drafted by that assembly likewise required clarification in advance. On November 26, 1985, the secretary-general of the UN announced that the electoral system best designed to "ensure fair representation in the Constituent Assembly to different political parties which gain substantial support in the election" would be based on proportional representation (PR).[29] An assembly so constituted would formulate a constitution and adopt it "as a whole by a two-thirds majority of its total membership." Pretoria took the conjunction of PR and "two-thirds to adopt" as meeting (as far as could be expected) their concerns about SWAPO dominance of the Constituent Assembly.[30] In the run-up to the November elections the issue was posed with precision: could SWAPO-controlled candidates win a commanding two-thirds of the seats?[31] The importance with which this question was regarded underlined the importance RSA officials attached to the precise manner in which UNTAG would monitor the run-up between April 1 and November 1. As for the constitution itself, the principle that "Namibia will be a *unitary,* sovereign and *democratic* state" (italics mine) was a prickly one in view of the outcome in Zimbabwe following Lancaster House. Against all that this implies by way of a "one-party state," there is the offset stipulation that executive and legislative branches of government "will be constituted by periodic and *genuine elections* which will be held by secret vote" (italics mine). Stipulations such as a "democratic state" and "genuine elections" can easily be understood as precluding a one-party state; however, during the run-up not all principles had been fully clarified. Much would be left to the good faith of the parties.

The "advance group" of the United Nations Transition Assistance Group (UNTAG) arrived in Windhoek in late February 1989. Under the command of veteran Indian army officer Lt. Gen. Prem Chand (who had been designated for the post in 1980!),[32] UNTAG was to build up a military component of 4,650 (rather than the originally specified 7,500), a civilian administration of 1,000, and a police monitoring force of 500. (The latter would be doubled following the SWAPO incursion in April.) General Chand was not in command of a peacekeeping force; his charge was to assist the UN special representative (Martti Ahtisaari) in ensuring the achievement of UNSCR 435 goals. UNTAG consequently was an observer or monitoring group with no police or military functions as such.[33] Its civilian component is to assist the special representative in each stage of the election process. It also has responsibilities for "arrangements for the release of all political prisoners and detainees."[34] The civil police contingent's duties include "the prevention of *intimidation* or interference with the electoral process, and accompanying the existing police forces in the discharge of their duties" (italics mine). The larger military contingent has a number of specific if somewhat restricted duties:

—supervise the cessation of hostilities,

—restrict SADF and SWAPO forces to base (Angola and Zambia for SWAPO),

—supervise the withdrawal of all but one thousand five hundred SADF troops from Namibia, restricting those remaining to specified locations (Grootfontein and Oshivelo),[35]

—patrol Namibia's international borders and prevent infiltration, and

—demobilize SWATF and Southwest Citizen Force units.

UNTAG was prepared neither psychologically nor militarily for what occurred on the day formally marking the beginning of the independence process. Throughout the month of March SADF Intelligence had been reporting to Mr. Ahtisaari, General Chand (and the administrator-general for Southwest Africa/Namibia, Mr. Louis Pienaar[36]) that significant elements of SWAPO/PLAN strength, perhaps 40 percent, were well below the sixteenth parallel in contravention of the Geneva Accord. On April 1, 1989, some twelve to fifteen hundred PLAN troops, in groups ranging from twelve to thirty, equipped with AK-47 rifles, mortars, and rocket-propelled grenades (and, indeed, SAM-7s) crossed over into Namibia from bases in Angola. The biggest incursion in the twenty-two-year history of the bush war, it was at the same time the greatest miscalculation in the long career of Sam Nujoma. The SWAPO leader managed in one action to alter (if only temporarily) the roles of "oppressors" and "oppressed" in the minds of world opinion. Now the United Nations had bungled; now the U.S. State Department issued a legal analysis condemning SWAPO! Even leaders of frontline states demanded from Mr. Nujoma an explanation for his "shortsighted action." At first denying that there had been an incursion, Mr. Nujoma then stated that "a peaceful regrouping" was taking place inside Namibia. The explanation was not accepted in the capitals of the world and most assuredly not by the security forces still under the control of GOC/Southwest.

SADF had begun the massive logistic effort entailed in a complete withdrawal from Southwest Africa/Namibia, but neither it nor SWATF (nor the police forces) had as yet substantially reduced troop strength. Together they met the SWAPO incursions with a fierceness born out of years of never having brought large numbers of the enemy to battle. The opportunity was not missed: some three hundred SWAPO were killed, most in the initial response. In contrast to this purposefulness the civilian side (UN officials and a Joint Monitoring Commission, including representatives of the United States and the USSR) scrambled to salvage the incipient implementation process. A hastily contrived Mount Etjo Declaration prescribed ground rules by which SWAPO/PLAN personnel would be delivered back to north of the sixteenth parallel. Over the objections of the UN secretary-general, the RSA insisted that troops released from their holding positions to deal with the incursion would not return until the special representative and the administrator-general had verified that SWAPO was in full compliance with the Geneva Accord. Accommodations on all sides became the order of the day once it was clear that a repetition of "Mr. Nujoma's biggest blunder"[37] was not a likely prospect. Huge caches of arms would be found subsequently—vestiges of SWAPO's "peaceful regrouping"—and the special representative and the administrator-general would quarrel over police monitoring responsibilities. Nonetheless, as the Botha era came to a close the process of bringing

Namibia to independence had reached its farthest point; the ultimate destination point, to be sure, was still unknown.

The Reagan administration's seizure of the "peaceful settlement in southwestern Africa" negotiation process early on in its first term was prompted by two considerations. The first was the belief that *rapprochement* with Pretoria could best be initiated by an equitable disposition of the Southwest Question, long outstanding as a stumbling block between the RSA and the West. UNSCR 435/78, along with subsequent understandings required by South Africa, provided an acceptable framework for bringing Namibia to independence. However, and this is the second consideration, the implementation of UNSCR 435 could not go forward without regard to the ongoing conflict in Angola. Without picking up the threads of the long-discarded Alvor Accord (which would entail "national reconciliation" and "free and fair elections" inside Angola), the Reagan administration did commit itself to maintaining the viability of Dr. Jonas Savimbi and his UNITA movement. It did determine to preclude a military solution imposed by the Soviet Union and its adventuresome proxy, Cuba, in behalf of the MPLA. In short, it considered any settlement plan in southwestern Africa as having two intertwined elements that must go forward hand in hand: (1) independence for Namibia accompanied by (2) the forswearing of a military solution in Angola and the withdrawal from the country of, specifically, Cuban troops. The challenge both to Mr. Crocker and to Mr. Adamishin, even after the Moscow Summit in April 1988 when Mr. Gorbachev at last turned away from the military option, was to firmly link Cuban withdrawal from Angola with milestones along the path to Namibian independence. It was when they turned to the second treaty "for the conclusion of the internationalist mission of the Cuban military contingent" that they (in the words of one of the principal negotiators) "reached 'rock face'."[38]

The "rock face" would not prove to be granite, but the mining would take longer than anticipated and would all the while be carried out against a backdrop of menacing Cuban troop movements in southern Angola.[39] In order not to lose the withdrawal agreement altogether, the cofacilitators of the negotiations (Washington and Moscow) extended its length (the period allowed to complete the withdrawal) and narrowed its span. Following an initial removal of three thousand troops prior to April 1989, Cuba would have twenty-seven instead of twelve or eighteen months to remove the balance. The redeployment-northward schedule called for all Cuban forces to be north of the fifteenth parallel by August 1, 1989, and north of the thirteenth parallel by October 31, 1989. This schedule was devised effectively to remove Cuban military presence as a factor in the Namibian electoral process. The withdrawal schedule had a front-loading factor requiring the departure of 50 percent of "the internationalist mission" by election day in Namibia (November 1, 1989). Then, however, another 25 percent had eleven months to withdraw, with the balance not required to leave until July 1, 1991. Inevitably, major questions of verification arose. As put in the New York Statement of Principles, redeployment and withdrawal would proceed "on the basis of an agreement between the People's Republic of Angola and the Republic of Cuba and *the decision of both states* to solicit on-site verification of that withdrawal by the Security Council of the United Nations" (italics mine). In short, South Africa was dropped from the verification process: verification would lie with parties allied on one side of the Angolan conflict. With the signing of both agreements on December 22, 1988, the Security Council in response to a request from Havana and Luanda placed a UN Military Observer Team in Angola. The team, or "verification mission," consisting of only seventy personnel drawn from ten nations, was initially under the command of a Brazilian, Brig. Gen. Pericles Ferreira Gomes. Equipped with a knowledge of Portuguese and an obvious sense of realism, General Ferriera Gomes was frank to say that in verifying the redeployment and withdrawal of some fifty thousand troops from so vast a country as Angola with a contingent of seventy, he would "rely on the word of Angola and Cuba."[40] While no major problems had come to his attention in the early months of his tour, matters outside his purview indicated that peace was not yet at hand in southwestern Africa.

There can be no gainsaying the progress achieved should the onset of the nineties be accompanied by Namibian independence and Cuban withdrawal from Angola. This having been said, the war continues in Angola—a war by no means sanitized of its international dimension.[41] Nothing in either of the New York treaties speaks to the question of continuing Soviet assistance to MPLA/FAPLA ("the People's Republic of Angola" in the parlance of diplomacy) or continuing assistance to UNITA from Washington. Prior to the signing of the agreements (in October 1988) Mr. Eduardo dos Santos journeyed once again to Moscow to be assured that the October 8, 1976, Treaty of Friendship and

Cooperation between his government and the Soviet Union would in no way be impacted by the new treaties and that another one billion dollars worth of military aid was en route. Having required South Africa to forego further military assistance to UNITA, the United States "took up the slack" by doubling its annual fifteen-million-dollar outlay. As the fighting in Angola continued through 1989, President Mobutu Sese Seko of Zaire convened eighteen member states of the Organization of African Unity (OAU) in his native village of Gbadolite in northwestern Zaire in late June. (Although the new Bush administration in Washington was slow in organizing itself, it is no doubt fair to suggest that there was some U.S. prompting of Mobutu.) No longer regarded as a mere puppet of Pretoria by his OAU colleagues, the Zairean leader's purpose (in which they now joined) was to establish a new milestone in the Angolan war: the first ever face-to-face meeting of Jonas Savimbi and Eduardo dos Santos. The meeting and the "handshake" of June 22, 1989, was far more of an achievement for the UNITA leader than it was for anyone else present that day.[42] Now recognized by a growing number of his fellow African leaders as "a given" in any process that held a promise of reconciliation in Angola, Jonas Savimbi had succeeded where Sam Nujoma had failed. He came to Gbadolite not "in a UN bus, disarmed and in civvies," but as commander of a guerrilla army that had achieved its objective. This essential fact explained the gathering of African leaders in a remote Zairean town.

Authorized by an OAU committee to organize a cease-fire in Angola, President Mobutu has found that what has eluded others might also elude him. (Mr. dos Santos on returning to Luanda could not prevail on the merits of a cease-fire.) Positive in terms of broad African support, the Gbadolite initiative underscored a second essential fact about the Angolan war: it had long since been taken from the regional to the East–West agenda. The conclusion of the New York agreements was the beginning of a task that would be completed when Washington and Moscow settled their accounts in southwestern Africa. In a settlement plan for Angola, UNITA will have a role in the governing of the country. That much has been established. From that much, P W Botha at the end of his public career could take no little satisfaction.[43]

If 1989 would prove to be anticlimactic in the long public career of P W Botha, it would again underscore 1988 as the climactic year. As the negotiation process leading to the two New York agreements gained momentum in the last three quarters of 1988, the State President launched yet another diplomatic offensive on another front. The revival of a flagging "spirit of N'komati" would be only part of a broader African Diplomatic Initiative that would contain within it an appeal to Europe as well. The death of Samora Machel of Mozambique in an airplane accident on South African soil[44] (October 20, 1986) and the advent of Joaquim Chissano called attention to the fact that little had been realized from the breakthrough at Komatipoort in March 1984. At the same time the change of leadership in Maputo offered a new opportunity. Contrary to standardized perceptions (so frequently substituted for detailed analyses where southern Africa is concerned), Pretoria has consistently taken Mozambique as an issue primarily for diplomatic rather than military disposition. If the diplomats in addressing a Mozambique agenda of seemingly intractable problems of political and economic development could enlist the South African business sector, all to the better. In the intervening years since N'komati, neither the public nor the private sector had found much on which to focus its attention or involvement.[45] However, by the spring of 1988 there was renewed vigor on Pretoria's part to press ahead. Discussions on the Cabora-Bassa Scheme looking to the development of a southern Africa electricity grid indicated that the Trilateral (Cape Town) Agreement of May 1984 between the RSA, Mozambique, and Portugal was still intact and that South Africa had returned to a concept of regional development. These talks were led by Mr. Ian McRae, chairman of the Management Board of the Electricity Supply Commission (ESCOM). His message was that "economic growth" (this concept was now preferred to that of earlier "economic development" phrasing) has numerous prerequisites, not the least of which is infrastructure. To the rail-highway-ports system created throughout the region under the auspices of South African Transport Services (SATS) must now be added an electricity grid engineered by ESCOM.[46]

Following preliminary talks in the Joint Liaison Committee, the Joint Security Commission (both entities established at N'komati) met for the first time in three years in Pretoria in July 1988. By this time there had been some considerable clarification of positions on the status of the Mozambique National Resistance Movement (MNR or RENAMO), the activities of the Beira Corridor Group (although it was not entirely clear just what the purposes of Lonrho's British CEO, Mr. "Tiny" Rowland, might include), and the shape of the Maputo–Moscow relationship. All of this laid the groundwork for President Botha's first official visit to a frontline state. On September 12, 1988, he visited President Chissano in Maputo and on the following day President Hastings Banda of Malawi in Lilongwe.[47] More significantly in terms of a broader African initiative, Mr. Botha met with President Mobutu Sese Seko on October 1, 1988, at the latter's own village of Gbadolite. Then in mid-October the State President returned to Europe for the funeral of Franz Joseph Strauss who had visited the Republic as recently as January. This trip included meetings with bankers and industrialists in Switzerland as well as conferences with Chancellor Helmut Kohl of West Germany and Prime Minister Anibal Cavaco Silva of Portugal, with a return via the Ivory Coast and a meeting with President Felix Houphouet-Boigny. This diplomatic debouchment exceeded anything John Vorster had achieved through his détente diplomacy of the early seventies whether in terms of its public, formal nature or in terms of substantive issues discussed. It marked the breakout from the diplomatic isolation endured by Pretoria for much of the Vorster and Botha tenures. (The "isolation," it must be noted, was purely formal, the RSA having enjoyed private lines to a large number of African states throughout this period and an even larger number of clandestine trading relationships.)

By the end of 1988, relations between Mozambique and RSA were normalizing rapidly. The flow of migrant workers into South African agriculture and mining had resumed; South African businessmen were looking harder at investment opportunities; and incredibly, "nonlethal military aid" for protection of the Beira Corridor was arriving on the Beira docks from the Republic.[48] It was the Botha–Mobutu meeting at Gbadolite, however, that was reverberating through Africa at the end of the year. This meeting prepared the way for Mobutu's initiative with the OAU concerning a cease-fire and an internal settlement in Angola and set the stage for the introduction of Jonas Savimbi to OAU leaders at Gbadolite nine months later. The long-term ramifications of the October 1, 1988, meeting are undoubtedly more important. Pretoria has long sought an opening to Zaire, formally and publicly, as an offset to "Nigerian pretensions" in central Africa and as a venue for cooperative African undertakings with Kinshasa and Washington. (Zaire has been the venue for "informal undertakings" as among Washington,

Pretoria, and Kinshasa since the days of Patrice Lumumba and Moise Tshombe, that is to say, since independence.) Strategically, it vaults southern Africa's regional powerhouse into Central Africa. Only in the most embryonic form at the end of the Botha term, the "opening to Zaire" becomes a priority item on the agenda of a successor regime in Pretoria.

The African diplomatic initiative of P W Botha contained both an invitation and a warning for Robert Mugabe. It bespoke the special position of the RSA in southern Africa at a time when the Zimbabwean leader was fast approaching a turning point in the future direction of his own country. Wooed by Moscow since coming to power in 1980 Mugabe made his first official visit to the Kremlin in 1985 following the accession of Mikhail Gorbachev. (It will be a rather nondescript Third World leader who will not have been invited to Moscow in the immediate aftermath of the leadership change.) Pretoria's renewed appeal for African solidarity at the end of the eighties when placed alongside a dismal Soviet African record could not be ignored by Harare as it considered the merits of a relationship with Moscow that, hitherto, it had by and large rejected. Pretoria, always holding the Zimbabwe relationship seminal in its security concerns, could only trust that Mr. Mugabe's quest for primacy of place in Black Africa would in the final analysis require him to reject Kremlin overtures. Should that in fact be his decision it will again confirm for Moscow the centrality of the RSA in its African endeavors. On the other hand, should Mr. Mugabe choose a Moscow or semi-independent Leninist option he will ensure Zimbabwe's place in South Africa's defense concerns in the nineties.

Mr. Botha had traveled to Europe in the summer of 1984 after the successes of Lusaka and N'komati and was more successful in his presentations on southern Africa (especially with Mrs. Thatcher) than either the press or European chancelleries were prepared to acknowledge. When he returned to Europe in November 1986, ostensibly to dedicate a South African War Memorial at Delville Wood, the French, as they had two years earlier, maintained an awkward pose. (However, this visit produced a highly favorable reception on the Portuguese island of Madeira that would be something of a portent of things to come.) Elections in 1987, both in Portugal and France (especially the former), contained elements of promise for Pretoria. A substantial victory for center-right Social Democrats appeared to end the turbulence and drift set off in Portugal in 1974. The new Prime Minister, Mr. Anibal Cavaco Silva (a practical-minded economist in the mold of Mexico's Salinas de Gortari), has effectively engaged his country in the quest for normalization in southern Africa. While keeping lines open to UNITA, Cavaco Silva hosted Eduardo dos Santos for the first visit of an MPLA leader to Portugal since 1975. There was the suggestion that the promise of Alvor might yet be redeemed. Moreover, the presence in the RSA of some six hundred thousand Mozambique émigrés adds to the commonality of interests between Pretoria and Lisbon in the region. The reelection of François Mitterrand, likewise, may serve to restore a relationship that had languished in the eighties. President Mitterrand, reportedly, has a "passion for geography" that, in turn, may explain his interest in "the dramatic situation in the Third World" (an interest he sought to underscore on the occasion of republican France's bicentennial). In any case French realism, today more centrist than in the recent past, does not countenance schemes for southern Africa that do not have the metropole power at the Cape as the hub.

The essential foundation stones for normalization in southern Africa had been laid by the conclusion of the Botha term. The breaking of diplomatic ground by Pretoria throughout 1988 was made possible by vision, by determined "demonstrations at arms," and by a resultant pragmatism on the part of frontline leaders and for that matter Moscow. It consisted of "openings" in the region and of a new appeal to Europe with attention directed to Portugal, France, and Italy—a kind of frontline of its own with respect to Africa—as well as to the "inner group" of the United Kingdom, the Federal Republic, and Switzerland. At the end of the eighties Pretoria could consider each of the foregoing European governments as favoring the concept of regionally devised measures for political settlement and economic growth in which the RSA played a role commensurate with its position in the region. A basis had been established for linkages between Europe (both frontline and inner-group states) and southern Africa to grow apace with regional progress and movement toward a new dispensation within the Republic. More problematical is the contention that "the American flag flies high"[49] in southern Africa at the conclusion of the Reagan–Botha era (diligent contributions to the New York agreements notwithstanding). We turn last to this vexing issue.

Agreement among the People's Republic of Angola, the Republic of Cuba, and the Republic of South Africa

The Governments of the People's Republic of Angola, the Republic of Cuba, and the Republic of South Africa, hereinafter designated as 'the Parties',

Taking into account the 'Principles for a Peaceful Settlement in Southwestern Africa', approved by the Parties on 20 July 1988, and the subsequent negotiations with respect to the implementation of these Principles, each of which is indispensable to a comprehensive settlement,

Considering the acceptance by the Parties of the implementation of United Nations Security Council Resolution 435 (1978), adopted on 29 Sepember 1978, hereinafter designated as 'UNSCR 435/78',

Considering the conclusion of the bilateral agreement between the People's Republic of Angola and the Republic of Cuba providing for the redeployment toward the North and the staged and total withdrawal of Cuban troops from the territory of the People's Republic of Angola,

Recognizing the role of the United Nations Security Council in implementing UNSCR 435/78 and in supporting the implementation of the present agreement,

Affirming the sovereignty, sovereign equality, and independence of all states of southwestern Africa,

Affirming the principles of non-interference in the internal affairs of states,

Affirming the principle of abstention from the threat or use of force against the territorial integrity or political independence of states,

Reaffirming the right of the peoples of the southwestern region of Africa to self-determination, independence, and equality of rights, and of the states of southwestern Africa to peace, development, and social progress,

Urging African and international cooperation for the settlement of the problems of the development of the southwestern region of Africa,

Expressing their appreciation for the mediating role of the Government of the United States of America,

Desiring to contribute to the establishment of peace and security in southwestern Africa,

Agree to the provisions set forth below.

(1) The parties shall immediately request the Secretary-General of the United Nations to seek authority from the Security Council to commence implementation of UNSCR 435/78 on 1 April 1989.

(2) All military forces of the Republic of South Africa shall depart Namibia in accordance with UNSCR 435/78.

(3) Consistent with the provisions of UNSCR 435/78, the Republic of South Africa and the People's Republic of Angola shall co-operate with the Secretary-General to ensure the independence of Namibia through free and fair elections and shall abstain from any action that could prevent the execution of UNSCR 435/78. The Parties shall respect the territorial integrity and inviolability of borders of Namibia and shall ensure that their territories are not used by any state, organization, or person in connection with acts of war, aggression, or violence against the territorial integrity or inviolability of borders of Namibia or any other action which could prevent the execution of UNSCR 435/78.

(4) The People's Republic of Angola and the Republic of Cuba shall implement the bilateral agreement, signed on the date of signature of this agreement, providing for the redeployment towards the North and the staged and total withdrawal of Cuban troops from Angola, and the arrangements made with the Security Council of the United Nations for the on-site verification of that withdrawal.

(5) Consistent with their obligations under the Charter of the United Nations, the Parties shall refrain from the threat or use of force, and shall ensure that their respective territories are not used by any state, organization, or person in connection with any acts of war, aggression or violence, against the territorial integrity, inviolability of borders, or independence of any state of southwestern Africa.

(6) The Parties shall respect the principle of non-interference in the internal affairs of the states of Southwestern Africa.

(7) The Parties shall comply in good faith with all obligations undertaken in this agreement and shall resolve through negotiation and in a spirit of cooperation any disputes with respect to the interpretation or implementation thereof.

(8) This agreement shall enter into force upon signature.

Signed at New York in triplicate in the Portuguese, Spanish and English language, each being equally authentic, this 22nd day of December 1988.

Agreement between the Government of the Republic of Cuba and the Government of the People's Republic of Angola for the conclusion of the internationalist mission of the Cuban military contingent

The Government of the Republic of Cuba and the Government of the People's Republic of Angola, hereinafter referred to as 'the Parties',

Considering

That on 1 April the implementation of United Nations Security Council resolution 435 (1978) on the independence of Namibia will commence,

That the question of the independence of Namibia and the safeguarding of the sovereignty, independence and territorial integrity of the People's Republic of Angola are closely interlinked and closely linked to peace and security in the southwestern region of Africa,

That, on the same dat as the present Agreement, a tripartite agreement between the Government of the Republic of Cuba, the Government of the People's Republic of Angola and the Government of the Republic of South Africa, containing the essential elements for the achievement of peace in the southwestern region of Africa, is to be signed,

That, with the acceptance of and strict compliance with the aforementioned, the causes that gave rise to the request made by the Government of the People's Republic of Angola, in legitimate exercise of its rights under Article 51 of the United Nations Charter, for the dispatch to Angolan territory of a Cuban internationalist military contingent to ensure, together with FAPLA, its territorial integrity and its sovereignty in the face of the invasion and occupation of a part of its territory,

Taking into account

The agreements signed between the Governments of the Republic of Cuba and the People's Republic of Angola on 4 February 1982 and 19 March 1984, the platform of the Government of the People's Republic of Angola approved in November 1984 and the Brazzaville Protocol signed by the Governments of the Republic of Cuba, the People's Republic of Angola and the Republic of South Africa on 13 December 1988.

Now therefore hold it to be established

That the conditions have been created which permit the commencement of the return to its homeland of the Cuban military contingent now present in Angolan territory, which has· successfully fulfilled its internationalist mission,

And accordingly agree as follows:

ARTICLE 1
The redeployment to the fifteenth and thirteenth parallels and the phased and total withdrawal to Cuba of the 50,000-man contingent of Cuban troops dispatched to the People's Republic of Angola shall commence, in accordance with the pace and time-limits established in the annexed

time-table, which shall form an integral part of this Agreement. The total withdrawal shall be concluded on 1 July 1991.

ARTICLE 2
The Governments of the People's Republic of Angola and the Republic of Cuba reserve the right to modify or alter their obligations arising out of article 1 of this Agreement in the event that flagrant violations of the tripartite agreement are verified.

ARTICLE 3
Both Parties, through the Secretary-General of the United Nations, request the Security Council to carry out verification of the redeployment and the phased and total withdrawal of the Cuban troops from the territory of the People's Republic of Angola, and to that end the corresponding protocol shall be agreed upon.

ARTICLE 4
This Agreement shall enter into force upon signature of the tripartite agreement between the Governments of the Republic of Cuba, the People's Republic of Angola and the Republic of South Africa.

DONE on 22 December 1988 at United Nations Headquarters, in duplicate in the Spanish and Portuguese languages, both texts being equally authentic.

Appendix
Timetable annexed to the Agreement between the Government of the Republic of Cuba and the Government of the People's Republic of Angola on the conclusion of the Internationalist Mission of the Cuban military contingent

In compliance with article 1 of the Agreement between the Governments of the Republic of Cuba and the People's Republic of Angola on the conclusion of the internationalist mission of the Cuban military contingent now present in Angolan territory, both Parties establish the following timetable for withdrawal:

TIME-LIMITS:

By 1 April 1989   3,000 troops
(day of the commencement of the implementation of resolution 435 (1978))

Total duration of the timetable starting from 1 April 1989   27 months

Redeployment northwards:
To the 15th parallel   1 August 1989
To the 13th parallel   31 October 1989

Total troops to be withdrawn:

By 1 November 1989	25,000	(50 per cent)
By 1 April 1990	33,000	(66 per cent)
By 1 October 1990	38,000	(76 per cent)
By 1 July 1991	50,000	(100 per cent)

Taking as a basis a Cuban force of 50,000 troops.

Notes

1. It is possible to date this from the inception of the Republic (or more precisely December 16, 1961) when the African National Congress and the South Africa Communist Party join forces for the express purpose of waging armed struggle against the RSA. This undertaking is seen in South African quarters as a declaration of war continuing in effect to this day.

2. The literature of Africanists (both Soviet and Western) is full of Soviet disenchantment with Africa and the effort to develop socialist-oriented clients. For comprehensive discussions of this genre see Francis Fukuyama, *Moscow's Post-Brezhnevian Reassessment of the Third World* (Santa Monica: Rand, 1988), also his "Patterns of Soviet Third World Diplomacy," *Problems of Communism* 37 (September–October, 1987): 1–13. S. Neil MacFarlane, "The Soviet Union and Southern African Security," *Problems of Communism* 38 (March–June, 1989): 71–89, represents more the Africanist perspective than the strategic perspective of Fukuyama. Today Mr. Fukuyama's perspective extends even unto "The End of History?" *National Interest* 16 (Summer 1989): 3–19. For a current South African appreciation of the Soviet reassessment of Africa, see P du T Botha, "The USSR and Some Third World Realities," *Strategic Review for Southern Africa* (Pretoria) 11 (May 1989): 1–26.

3. Regrettably, Zbigniew Brzezinski (formerly national security advisor to President Carter) gives little attention to this theme in his otherwise commendable study of declining Soviet fortunes. See *The Grand Failure: The Birth and Death of Communism in the Twentieth Century* (New York: Scribner's, 1989). He does note, however, that in the Gorbachev era the USSR begins to concentrate on "key targets of strategic opportunity" such as Angola and Ethiopia, adding that these are "related more to the geo-political competition with the United States than to a wider expectation of a continental ideological triumph" (215). For a fuller explication of this theme, see Colin Gray, *The Geo-Politics of Super Power* (Lexington: The University Press of Kentucky, 1988).

4. Intelligence services in the West are taking increasing note of the multidimensionality of the "new thinking" in Moscow. Attention is being drawn in particular to the fact that Soviet foreign-policy goals are served not just by "openness" and "convention" but by a wide array of options including "indirect means" for the continuation of conflict. While ostensibly the USSR is working toward stabilization of southern Africa and above all else seeks to avoid conflict with the United States over such regional issues (a portrayal avidly advanced in the Africanist literature today), it is simultaneously increasing arms shipments to selected Third World clients and notably stepping up a broad array of "active measures" under the auspices of an enlarged and ever more active KGB. The KGB, for example, in conjunction with the now defunct East German service, sought to expand the security-police capabilities of both Angola and Mozambique in anticipation of the needs of the respective governments following a political settlement. For an elaboration of this argument see James Hansen, "The War of Manipulation (Soviet Capabilities for Indirect Conflict Today)," a Conference Paper prepared for the 30th Annual Convention of the International Studies Association, London, March 28–April 1, 1989. This theme will be expounded at

greater length in his forthcoming book, *Indirect Conflict*. In Mr. Bush's Department of Defense the under secretary of Defense for Policy, Mr. Paul Wolfowitz
suggests that "new thinking" notwithstanding there is a lot of "old policy" on the
regional-conflicts front. See his "Glasnost in Order on Regional Clashes," *Wall
Street Journal*, November 7, 1989.

5. Approximately a year before his appointment as foreign minister (May
1984), hard on the heels of the Lusaka and N'komati accords and the death of
Andropov, Mr. Shevardnadze met with Sam Nujoma of the Southwest Africa
People's Organization in Algiers to reassure him of continuing firmness in
Moscow's support. (Mr. Nujoma will repay the visit in October of that year.) There is
evidence for the view that Mr. Shevardnadze was already speaking for Mr. Gorbachev
who had assumed a commanding position in foreign policy during "the year of
Chernenko" and who had already determined upon the unprecedented step of bring-
ing a non-Slav to the post of foreign minister. See Peter Clement, "Moscow and
Southern Africa," *Problems of Communism* 34 (March–April 1985): 29–50; also,
Seweryn Bialer, *The Soviet Paradox* (New York: Random House, 1987).

6. General Malan, referring to Solodovnikov as "the unrelenting opponent of
the RSA," took note of his appearance in a new guise at the Leverkusen (FRG)
meeting with South African scholars in 1988 (chapter 5, n. 16). See his "The
Contemporary Strategic Situation in Southern Africa," 12 ff.

7. One estimate of Soviet military assistance to Angola in the decade 1978–
88, using NATO sources, puts the amount in excess of eight billion dollars peaking in the early Gorbachev years 1985–87. See W. Martin James III, "Cuban
Involvement in the Angolan Civil War" and Alexander R. Alexiev, *UNITA and
US Policy in Angola* (Santa Monica: Rand, 1987). Alexiev calls the Soviet shipments to Angola at this time among the largest arms transfers in history signaling
a commitment to a military solution. He further suggests that the 1985 Angolan
offensive was probably "ordered" in a March meeting in Moscow.

8. For his visit to "the border" in late May 1985 the author wishes to acknowledge the hospitality of Kommandants W H Welgemoed (101 Battalion,
Southwest Africa Territorial Force), Johann Jooste (54 Battalion, SADF), Brian
Adams (201 "Bushmen" Battalion, Southwest Africa Territorial Force), and the
redoubtable Sector 20 commander, Col. Deon Ferreira, who would play such a
vital role in the heavy fighting that lay ahead. Under a series of "GOCs Southwest" (J J Geldenhuys, 1977–80; Charles Lloyd, 1980–83; George Meiring,
1983–86; and today Willie Meyer) the Southwest Africa Territorial Force
(SWATF) has steadily assumed the burden of fighting in the counterinsurgency
bush war against SWAPO/PLAN and in the conventional war against
MPLA/FAPLA. In 1980, when General Geldenhuys handed over command to
General Lloyd, SWATF was formally established as an entity independent of the
RSA Department of Defense although remaining under operational control of
GOC Southwest. Built on formations that go back to 1915, SWATF, unlike
SADF, also rests on universal conscription of all ethnic groups. In 1980 approxi-
mately one-fifth of the troops available to GOC Southwest was provided by
SWATF. At the end of 1988 SWATF was providing three-quarters of the total. A
force of some forty thousand, which was to be the basis of an independent Nami-
bia Defense Force, it would be disbanded under terms of the December 1988 New
York Tripartite Agreement. See *Paratus* 40 (May 1989), 32–34.

9. Interview not for direct attribution. The further observation was offered that "shooting up 'Hinds' was not a maximal use of 'Mirage' assets." The new air situation in Angola was clearly a worry. At least part of the problem—if only the helicopter problem—must be dealt with from the ground.

10. See chapter 5, n. 43.

11. For a blistering critique of this approach "based on an unrealistic assessment of Angolan reality and therefore doomed to failure from the beginning," see Alexander R. Alexiev, "The Soviet Stake in Angola," in *The Red Orchestra*, ed. Bark, 140–57. See also his "U.S. Policy in Angola: A Case of Nonconstructive Engagement" (Rand Corporation Paper, 1986) and Constantine C. Menges, *Inside the National Security Council* (New York: Simon and Schuster, 1988), chapter 9. For an excellent recent account, see Peter Vanneman, *Soviet Strategy in Southern Africa* (Stanford, Hoover Institution Press, 1990).

12. Congressman Lee Hamilton (D-Ind), chairman of the House Select Committee on Intelligence, unlike the majority of his counterparts on the House and Senate Intelligence committees, could not reconcile himself to this turnabout. In September (1986) he seeks a vote in the House to rescind UNITA aid and is defeated by a 220–187 vote. Menges, *Inside the National Security Council*, 249.

13. Department of State, *A U.S. Policy toward South Africa*. The secretary's committee comes as close to opposing the established policy of the U.S. government as a sitting secretary of state can permit with its recommendation that "the President take note of the complications for U.S. policy in South Africa created by U.S. military assistance to UNITA in Angola" (15).

14. Testimony by Mr. Crocker before the Subcommittees on Africa and International Economic Policy and Trade, House Foreign Affairs Committee, March 12, 1986, Washington, D.C. Mr. Douglas Holloday of the National Security Council staff is given the rank of ambassador and brought over to State to head the Working Group. Ambassador Holloday, after "good faith" efforts to reflect the president's thinking as well as that of his officials, concluded the circumstances were not propitious and resigned after eighteen months. See Constantine Menges, "Sanctions '86—How the State Department Prevailed," *National Interest* (Fall 1988): 65–77. Menges himself resigned from the NSC at this point.

15. Speech to the American Israel Public Affairs Committee. Washington, D.C., April 16, 1986.

16. Interview with Gen. J J Geldenhuys, Chief, SADF. Cape Town, March 10, 1986.

17. An observation to the author from one of his officers. Rundu (Namibia), May 1985.

18. The Angolan foreign minister, Alfredo Van Dunem, put the SADF contingent in Angola at nine thousand troops, six hundred artillery pieces, and five hundred tanks and armored cars! Associated Press Dispatch, Johannesburg, April 18, 1988. Accounts of 1987–88 fighting in Angola drawn upon for this chapter include numbers of Longreach Report. *Short-Term Forecast* (Johannesburg); *American Review* (Tenth Anniversary Edition, 1989), Johannesburg; statements to the press by Gen. J J Geldenhuys, Chief, SADF, on November 11, 1987, and April 18, 1988; information briefing for the press by Col. Deon Ferriera (Windhoek), reported in *Paratus* 40 (March 1989): 14; and personal interviews not for attribution.

19. The South African military analyst William Steenkamp writes that, "for

help received, about 85 percent of PLAN's manpower assets are serving full-time with FAPLA against UNITA." See his "The War in Angola," *South Africa Foundation Review* 14 (January 1988): 3–4. This development is also due to a total loss of military effectiveness in Namibia and a consequent consolidation of resources for the 1987–88 Angolan offensive. For a detailed account of the demise of PLAN see the April 1987 number of *ISSUP Bulletin* (Pretoria), "The War in Southwest Africa/Namibia."

20. Carl Noffke, "Southwestern Africa—The Myths and the Realities," in *American Review* (Tenth Annual Edition, 1989): 31. Immediately after the fighting at the Lomba River a SADF officer noted that "UNITA used up much of its 'TOW' stock and needs to have it replaced now." Interview not for attribution.

21. Information briefing, Windhoek (February 1989).

22. Ibid. FAPLA losses have been revised upward since to approximately five thousand killed, fourteen aircraft and eight helicopters lost, and nearly five hundred armored and logistic vehicles destroyed. A significant portion of the Soviet tanks were recovered intact by SADF. One report has SADF taking more than a dozen complete Soviet SAM-8 systems with them when they retired. General Malan would put great stress on the RSA's technological superiority in explaining the victory: "As the conflict increased in technological complexity, the participants that could not control technology fell by the wayside." "The Contemporary Strategic Situation in Southern Africa" (15). Those who were promulgating "perceptions" of South African defeat at this time invariably did so without specifications as must necessarily be the case about "perceptions." In this connection see the account of Simon Barber in *Business Day,* July 27, 1989, reprinted in *Paratus* 40 (September 1989): 16–17. For a definitive account of SADF achievements in Angola in 1987–88 (under considerable political constraints imposed by Pretoria) see Helmoed-Romer Heitman, *War in Angola: The Final South African Phase* (Johannesburg: Ashanti, 1990).

23. FBIS-AFR-88-201 (October 18, 1988), from *The Citizen* (Johannesburg), October 13, 1988. See also Map 2 this chapter.

24. See U.S. Department of State, *Principles for a Peace Settlement in Southwestern Africa* (Washington, D.C.: GPO, July 20, 1988). Principle number three calls for "redeployment toward the North and the staged and total withdrawal of Cuban troops from the territory of the People's Republic of Angola." This principle was agreed to upon the basis of a two-nation (Cuba and Angola) agreement to solicit UN verification of the withdrawal. Between July and December when the final agreements were signed Pretoria would seek, unsuccessfully, to include the United States and the USSR in the verification process.

25. It would be more appropriate to suggest that Pretoria was now prepared to cooperate with Washington at least insofar as the Angola/Namibia agenda was concerned, the "initiative" having passed to the Americans during the first Reagan term. (See our discussion chapter 2.) The State President's African Diplomatic Initiative of 1988 would be another matter, however. On Castro's "Parthian shots" see Barber, *Business Day,* July 27, 1989.

26. The texts of the two agreements will be found at the end of this chapter. See also U.S. Department of State, *Southwestern Africa Regional Brief,* Tripartite Agreement on Southwestern Africa: Blueprint for Peace and Namibian Independence (Washington, D.C.: GPO, December 1988).

27. "Some Observations Regarding the Settlement Plan for Namibia," *ISSUP Bulletin* (February 1989), 3. See also Sean Cleary, "The Impact of the Independence of Namibia on South Africa," *South Africa International* 19 (January 1989): 117–29. Geoffrey Berridge, on the other hand, is apparently unaware of the understandings reached prior to 1988 on the status of SWAPO. See his "Diplomacy and the Angola/Namibia Accords," *International Affairs* 65 (Summer 1989): 463–79 (especially 472).

28. The Geneva Protocol signed by Angola, Cuba, and South Africa on August 5, 1988, states that "Angola and Cuba shall use their good offices so that, once the total withdrawal of South African troops from Angola is completed, and within the context also of the cessation of hostilities in Namibia, SWAPO's forces will be deployed to the north of the sixteenth parallel." This protocol was not made public and had to be released to the press by the RSA following the SWAPO incursion. The U.S. State Department's *Regional Brief* (n. 26) does not include the protocol but does publish the Brazzaville Protocol of December 13, 1988, which refers to "understandings" reached at Geneva on August 5 "that are not superseded by this document." While vitiated by diplomatic language, the Geneva Protocol clearly placed Pretoria on "the high ground" following the SWAPO incursion.

29. "Some Observations Regarding the Settlement Plan," 4–8.

30. Sean Cleary, a former associate of Neil van Heerden who headed the RSA negotiating team, reflects the concerns of many of his colleagues when he asks whether "the balanced compromises so essential to national (Namibian) unity and stability after independence . . . ought to be drawn up *by the victors* in an electoral campaign conducted under UN supervision" (italics mine). "The Impact of the Independence of Namibia on South Africa," 121. Cleary's concerns stem on the one hand from the fact that Namibia has been "a focal point of the struggle to exact retribution from South Africa for its refusal to bow to the collective weight of internationally accepted political wisdom" (118), and on the other from the fact that political leadership both in the Republic and in Southwest has never agreed upon "a coherent policy towards the territory" (120). On the security ramifications of an independent Namibia see H de V du Toit, "The Strategic Implications of an Independent Namibia," in *Namibia: Current and Future Perspectives,* ed. M Hough and M van der Merwe (Pretoria: ISSUP, October 1989), 40–49.

31. SADF has played no political role in the territory. A SADF officer did, however, observe to the author that the required demobilization of the Southwest Africa Territorial Force would result in forty thousand new civilian voters who had not developed any particular affinity for SWAPO.

32. General Chand came with the best of credentials, having commanded the UN contingent in the Congo in 1962–63 and in Cyprus in 1974. Appointed as UN Special Representative for Rhodesia in 1977, he was not posted in view of the fact that the UN Settlement Plan was not implemented.

33. In this section we rely in part on "The Role of UNTAG in the Namibian Independence Process," *ISSUP Bulletin* (March 1989), Pretoria.

34. Ibid., 8. By far the most serious issue to arise in this regard was the question of disaffected SWAPO members held as detainees in camps in Angola and Zambia. The International Society for Human Rights presented its *Report on Human Rights Violations in SWAPO Camps in Angola and Zambia* to the United Nations high commissioner for Refugees at the end of 1988. Mr. Herman Cohen,

REGIONAL STABILITY, 1985–1989   187

successor to Mr. Chester Crocker as assistant secretary of state for African Affairs, expressed the hope that the high commissioner would see to it that "all detainees held by SWAPO" would be accounted for inasmuch as the implementation process had now moved beyond an "irreversible threshold." See Longreach Report, *Short-Term Forecast,* December 9, 1988, 14, and July 17, 1989, 16; also "The Role of UNTAG," 11.

35. In the relocation the legendary Three-Two Battalion would be moved from its Omega base camp at the entrance to the Caprivi Strip to a new base in the northern part of the Cape Province at Pomfret. This would be its first domicile in the Republic.

36. On March 1, 1989, in accordance with provisions of the Settlement Plan, the Transitional Government of National Unity (TGNU), established in Windhoek in June 1985, relinquished governance of the territory to the administrator-general, that is to say to the RSA. The AG would govern Southwest Africa/Namibia until after the November elections. In the interim he would also cooperate with the special representative in preparing for those elections. Controversies between the two would arise however. The TGNU was based on the Multi-Party Conference formed in 1983 out of a coalition of parties rather than a coalition of ethnic groups as had the Turnhalle Alliance of 1978. Some observers saw the "party basis" of the TGNU as eventually leading to an internally fashioned political solution for the territory. However, the outbreak of the 1985 offensive in Angola just two months after its installation aborted such hopes.

37. Brian Pottinger, quoting the old African saying: "Only a fool tweaks the tail of the lion when it is leaving the kill" (*Sunday Times,* Johannesburg, April 9, 1989), asks the question, Why did he do it? His answer is one that has wide acceptance among close students of such matters. SWAPO had waged one of the worst military campaigns in the annals of guerrilla warfare—a sour legacy to bequeath to an independence government. "Imagine," he writes, "the position of the PLAN fighter who, asked in years to come by his grandchildren what he did in the great war, is obliged to answer that we waited—disarmed and in civvies—for the UN bus to take him back to the motherland (from the exile to which he had been banished by SADF)." Then there was SADF, not without pride at what it had achieved and what it had made possible. SWAPO might well have the eventual political victory, but the military victory—never. Mr. Nujoma had to go one last time at the lion. His ensuing disaster deprived SWAPO/PLAN of any "intimidatory" role in the electoral process. It foreclosed any exalted role of successful freedom fighters. What bearing this will have on the future of Namibia is for the future to reveal.

38. Cleary attributes the term to Mr. Neil van Heerden, leader of the RSA delegation (125); see also n. 25 above.

39. It is difficult to determine whether Cleary feels that Cuba had the RSA under some kind of military duress in the months leading up to the New York treaties. At one point he argues that there had been "an objective shift in the balance of power in southern Angola, after Fidel Castro's decision to introduce some twelve thousand troops. . . ." (123), and then at another point that "by any objective measure (SADF was) superior to any military force, or combination of forces, in the region" (126). He adds to the confusion by writing that "the continuing claims by Minister of Defense Magnus Malan and the Chief of SADF, Gen. Jan Geldenhuys that SADF successes in Angola and against SWAPO have contributed materially to the agreements now being negotiated, are quite accurate."

But he then concludes that "the underlying reason for the search for a political solution is, however, Gorbachev's desire to eliminate unimportant points of friction between the USSR and the USA" (129). This is a striking manifestation of the diplomatist mind-set. It appears impossible for Mr. Cleary to imagine that the two factors may be related and that the latter may be a consequence of the former. Mr. Gorbachev's underlying reason to search for a political solution comes from the banks of the Lomba and the Cuito rivers. Moreover, in turning belatedly to negotiations it is not over "unimportant points." One does not make the investments Mr. Gorbachev and his predecessors have made in Angola over "unimportant points" in the Soviet scheme of things. The negotiations, from Moscow's standpoint, are all too evidently designed to eliminate friction with the United States on precisely "important points" where military solutions have not availed.

40. Longreach Report, *Short-Term Forecast,* January 17, 1989, 18. Havana at no time provided the interested parties with a definitive count on the "internationalist mission." The basis figure of fifty thousand used in the bilateral treaty could be as much as 20 percent short of the actual figure.

41. Berridge begins his article with the extraordinary contention that the agreements signed in New York in December 1988 "brought to an end over two decades of fighting in southwestern Africa," "Diplomacy and the Angola/Namibia Accords," 463. The statement is inexplicable: neither of the New York agreements undertake to settle the Angolan war!

42. The Portuguese journalist Jaime Nogueira Pinto in an extended interview with Savimbi following the Gbadolite meeting stressed the strength of the UNITA position—and that of its leader—going into any "internal settlement" negotiations. See "The Angola Handshake, According to Jonas Savimbi," *Wall Street Journal,* July 17, 1989.

43. There is one caveat. Pretoria, ever ready for treachery from Washington where Angola is concerned, will act in behalf of its own interests should UNITA be abandoned by others. This will be a matter for Messrs. de Klerk and Savimbi.

44. An International Commission, including Mr. Frank Borman of the United States, absolved South Africa of complicity charges that had been leveled from the first hour.

45. President Joaquim Chissano provides such statistics as the following: six hundred to seven hundred thousand dead in a country of fifteen million, between one and two million "refugees"; twenty-six hundred primary schools and more than eight hundred rural clinics destroyed. The problem of rebuilding Mozambique is "a problem of a generation." See the *New York Times,* August 6, 1989.

46. For an account of ESCOM's plans and the role of Mr. McRae, see "Current Affairs," *Leadership* 7 (1988): 127–35.

47. Mrs. Elise Botha, wife of the State President, made her own follow-up "state visit" to Malawi the following month.

48. *Paratus* 39 (December 1988): 6–11 ff.

49. Lecture by Mr. Chester Crocker (formerly U.S. assistant secretary of state for African Affairs) to the Royal Institute of International Affairs (Chatham House), London, April 25, 1989. Quoted by Berridge, "Diplomacy," 468. For a self-congratulatory piece, not free of paternalistic overtones, by the principal assistant to Mr. Crocker, see Charles W. Freeman, Jr., "The Angola-Namibia Accords," *Foreign Affairs* 68 (Summer 1989): 126–41.

7 THE FAR HORIZON

South Africa could serve as a key southern support both for European engagement in African development and security for the United States' interest in developing powerful regional allies throughout the Southern Hemisphere.

—R F Botha,
Minister of Foreign Affairs,
September 17, 1981

A Faulty Connection

For anyone who observed the hopefulness with which the government of P W Botha greeted the Reagan administration, it remains a vivid impression to this day. The American presidential election of 1980 was seen, first, as providential rejection of Teddy Kennedy (and, to be sure, Jimmy Carter) and, second, as creating an opportunity with a country highly regarded, whatever mishaps had occurred in the past, that hitherto most South Africans had not dared anticipate. Warned at the time that, while the new administration—or more particularly the new president himself—would be inclined to review the South Africa Question, South Africans would be well advised to keep in mind the perils inherent in "conducting foreign policy the American way"—it was not the moment for such advice. Hope—ultimately a theological virtue—is a powerful ingredient in the affairs of nations as well as men. Holding promise of that which is much sought after, it contains all the while at its core a volatile potential should it be unrequited. By anticipating the fruition of bitterness the effects can be ameliorated, if only in modest degree. However, in the face of excessive hope, if there is little or no mitigation of inevitable disappointment—little or no attempt, for example, to maintain comity between two governments—there is secular failure. The relationship between South Africa and the United States at the close of the Reagan–Botha era constitutes secular failure—as much the result of obtuseness on the part of Washington as of illusion on the part of Pretoria.[1]

The remarks of Mr. Botha's foreign minister, which introduce this chapter, exemplify the hopefulness of that early day (not yet a year into the first Reagan term) and the characteristic propensity of his government to think strategically about secular reality.[2] Mr. R F Botha's discursive speech on South Africa's position in Africa and the Southern Hemisphere suggests bases for "strategic concurrence" between the RSA and the United States. (Americans, incidentally, were being advised at this point to disregard occasional fulminations on the subject of "neutralism" from the Prime Minister. P W Botha would be receptive to "an opening to Washington" for some years yet.) The appeal to the new U.S. administration to join with Pretoria in thinking strategically about the southern continent and hemisphere, as it would turn out, could not have been more misdirected. Implicitly calling upon the Reagan administration to build a relationship with a "seconding middle power"[3] at Africa's southern cape on the basis of geopolitical, geostrategic realities,[4] there was at the same time a request—not always implicit—to treat quite different realities (those bearing on the RSA's internal order) as items for South Africa's domestic agenda. In pressing an eminently practical distinction upon Washington, Pretoria could point to innumerable precedents in the post–World War II foreign policy of the United States. Precedents not withstanding, the appeal—implicit and explicit—fell victim to the processes of contemporary U.S. foreign policy.

No major capital is as disinclined to think strategically as the city on the Potomac.[5] In this riparian realm the "policy process" dominates, however torrential the flood of studies purportedly strategic in character that pour from its enclaves. The foreign-policy process presumptively aimed at defining national purposes and setting national goals, which, presumably, represent national interests, only rarely reaches this exalted level. What it does succeed in accomplishing year in and year out, irrespective of the political coloration of an administration, is keeping options open, thereby making closure on any issue the least likely of outcomes. (As one highly placed participant in the process during the eighties is reported to have remarked: "Nothing in this city is ever over!")[6] Politicians—official and otherwise—who draw their oxygen from Washington's ambient air instinctively understand that strategy entails closure. (It cannot be expected that they will understand anything else about strategy.) A strategic choice is a commitment to a course of action—invariably the result of hard intellectual activity and some rectitude of will. Such choices can only be made with reference to clearly articulated policy goals, however. Thus, the first and greatest obstacle to thinking strategically in Washington is the failure of the policy process to provide agreed-upon and settled foreign-policy objectives.[7] A second and equally damaging impediment makes itself felt when the necessity for making a strategic choice—however great the policy disarray—becomes inescapable: the choice is then made in the modalities of the policy process itself, that is, through an accommodation reached among attentive (invariably disparate) interests. (Those observers not wholly traumatized by this spectacle would concede that hard intellectual activity and rectitude of will are essentially absent at this point!) Strategies devised in this fashion are hostage to domestic factors in foreign-policy making, but at the same time can serve the purposes of an administration not prepared to formulate a strategy on the basis of objective factors.[8]

Not long into the first Reagan term it was evident to highly placed South Africans (both in and out of government) that the president of the United States was not personally seized of the South Africa Question. Rather than the turn of events they had hoped for, what they saw was "State" working its own purposes (this would be clearer once George Shultz succeeded Alexander Haig) and that this did not include responding to appeals—either visionary or practical—from Pretoria. Under the guise of "constructive engagement," Messrs. Shultz and Crocker were inserting the United States into southern Africa as principal broker of regional issues. Such an undertaking necessarily foreclosed a bilateral relationship, strategic or otherwise, with "the apartheid regime" in Pretoria.[9] Constructive engagement, anything but a policy, was a platform from which—keeping all options open—Washington would address broad African interests. (To the extent that there was a strategy contained in all of this, it consisted merely of opening up and maintaining an ongoing process.) Couching African interests for the most part in the idiom of "Third Worldism," constructive engagement could not wholly discount the proclivities of Ronald Reagan on regional issues. An accommodation of sorts was struck on one point, namely, the removal of the Cuban "internationalist contingent" from one country in Africa (Angola) in return for initiation of the independence process in another (Namibia). Accommodation could not be made to extend, however, to the question of military assistance to Jonas Savimbi and his UNITA movement. On this divisive point the imperatives of the Reagan doctrine had to be superimposed on constructive engagement and its State Department advocates. Mr. Reagan's positive response to Dr. Savimbi at the end of 1985 (in the wake of the first Gorbachev offensive in Angola) was a fillip to those South Africans whose hopes for a Reagan policy on southern Africa had not entirely vanished. As it happened there were elements in both Washington and Pretoria who now saw one last opportunity to strengthen direct, bilateral ties between the leader of the Western world and Africa's southern regional power. Mr. Reagan's first ambassador to South Africa (a political appointee) may have been one such.

In a speech to a group of Afrikaner businessmen in Johannesburg on February 21, 1985, Mr. Herman Nickel spoke as very much the ambassador of his president. "Let me assure you here this evening: the Reagan administration will do all in its power to defeat punitive measures designed to damage the South African economy." Calling sanctions the self-indulgence of elitists, he warned his audience that it would be difficult, nonetheless, to stay the hand of Congress. Nickel then went on to say that "it is not my role, *nor that of my government,* to define change in South Africa . . . the principal impetus for change must come from within South Africa. Ours is a *supportive role . . . whatever it is in our power to assist you with the direction of reform and change that you have chosen, we will do*" (italics mine). He concluded by telling his audience that "the promise and vision of a strong, peaceful, and economically active South Africa . . . leading the vital struggle against disease, hunger, and underdevelopment on the continent of Africa" was there for all to see, but that in any case their real object was "not to please the outside world but to create a new South Africa that can satisfy the aspirations of all of the people of this beautiful land."[10] Four months later Ambassador Nickel was recalled to Washington for an extended home stay (three months), returning in September 1985 with the task of explaining his government's adoption of limited sanctions. A year later he would be replaced by career officer Edward Perkins, and Congress, over the veto of the president, would pass the Comprehensive Anti-Apartheid Act of 1986. A portion of what transpired in the interim can be related here.[11]

On a number of occasions as 1985 turned into 1986, the Director of Central Intelligence engaged the president of the United States in conversation on the subject of South Africa, quite apart from the matter of Angola. (South Africa was on a shortlist of perhaps a half-dozen countries that Mr. Casey felt, on the one hand, were of growing importance from the standpoint of U.S. interests and about which, on the other, we knew too little.) The paucity of hard information on the Republic and particularly a lack of understanding of what principals in that country were thinking—and were prepared to do—was a growing problem that needed to be turned around. Mr. Casey did not need to point out to "his boss" (but reportedly did so nonetheless) that the traffic coming through the formal channels was more indicative of a rising temperature level in the RSA/U.S. relationship than anything else. One result of this development was that conventional intelligence efforts were as effectively locked down in the RSA as anywhere in the world.[12] The DCI did not bring this matter to the attention of the president without at the same time bringing recommendations for new courses of action. Long a proponent of the view that intelligence collection must be considered in the broadest possible terms and that U.S. access to intelligence worldwide was extensive (especially if one was not too parochial in his thinking about "collection"), Mr. Casey proposed new undertakings to remedy the communications gap between the United States and South Africa. He was searching for options to deal with the Soviets in the Third World as well as options for dealing with southern Africa (beyond those contained in constructive engagement—a process tightly held by State). New options would entail alternative channels, which is to say the use of alternative assets or "knowledgeables," to the extent that they could be identified, with direct lines to key contacts. Such "direct message links," it was expected, might well be able to open up and broaden agendas. While other instances of the Casey style of doing intelligence have gained some notoriety, the South African case has not. The undertaking was short-lived: a bitter struggle would occur over the South African account in which the president would ultimately concede the ground to State. In the brief span of the Reagan-approved Casey initiative, expectations in South Africa would be raised high and then sent crashing.

Mr. Casey's initiative could not have come at a more opportune moment in the thinking of at least some members of an inner circle of advisers that P W Botha was now drawing more closely around him with each passing week.[13] With the onset of 1986 the Botha government was caught up in a rapidly developing internal situation of armed mass insurrection on the part of the African National Congress and of more or less spontaneous unrest in the townships. While the decision to provide arms to UNITA had been welcomed, the rising drumbeat of the sanctions movement (in both Europe and the United States) was now the dominating concern. Within the inner circle there was one imperative as far as the United States was concerned: determine, as a matter of urgency, what is possible during the next two years in the way of critical reinforcement of the reform process from Washington. ("After that, once you are into the presidential campaign, it will be too late.") In March 1986 one of this group conceded with commendable candor, "there are some developing telltale signs of paranoia here— morale needs a boost." The best remedy, he was quick to add, would be a breakthrough in the relationship with Washington. Highly attuned to what he called the psychological dimension in the relationship between the two countries and conscious of the fact that "opportunities had been missed in the past," he made no effort to conceal his anxiety that a corner be turned *soon:* "The future of southern Africa is in the hands of two men only—Ronald Reagan and P W Botha."

South Africans, who need not be identified except to note that their access to the State President was immediate, responded with alacrity to the concept of "alternative channels," which they hastened to describe as "complementing formal channels," as a means for establishing direct linkage between the two presidents. The underlying, and indeed, urgent objective of those searching for new options (on both sides) was in the end a Reagan–Botha summit. Anything short of this admittedly "one in a thousand possibility" would not produce the necessary breakthroughs. It was axiomatic that such an undertaking would be stillborn if recourse was had to formal, diplomatic channels.[14] What was required were talks described in such terms as "exploratory," "totally private," or "unofficial" that would not engage the prestige or commitments of either side and would be mercifully free of posturing. Consequently, they must be carried out by fully trusted, highly knowledgeable, private individuals who can readily identify critical elements in the situation for priority consideration. Private initiatives to formulate the mechanics by which a breakthrough agenda could be achieved (relating to reform assistance, the embargo,[15] and related matters) were authorized at the highest level on each side. As proposals were beginning to be exchanged—that is passed from totally private to official hands in both capitals—and as the meeting began to take on some semblance of the possible, abrupt word arrived in Pretoria from Washington.

The Casey initiative to develop new options in the U.S./RSA relationship through alternative channels did not come to flower in the spring of 1986 but died with a decision to confine such matters to formal channels. The decision eliminated all possibility of breakthroughs, and most particularly that of direct talks between the two presidents. More than that, it brought the bilateral relationship to its lowest ebb in the decade. The closedown came just as a highly placed South African "private individual" was to meet with the State President to apprise him of progress being made toward his prized objective. Word arrived "just in time as I was due to see *the person concerned* within the next day or so. I canceled the appointment explaining that *the matter which would have been the subject of our discussion*, had now been altered by events" (italics mine).[16] Accounts of the explosive reaction of Mr. Botha come from private individuals within earshot: "The bloody Americans will see Buthelezi and Tambo but not the State President of South Africa!" (A second report puts it as follows: "The bloody Americans can meet with Oliver Tambo and other terrorists but not with the State President of the Republic!") In any case it was entirely clear that Mr. Botha was not only exceedingly disappointed that a face-to-face meeting would not be part of the Reagan–Botha era, but personally offended by the Washington decision to override a "back-channel effort" that had become too successful too quickly.[17] Trying to salvage something from the collapsed effort, certain members of the inner circle proposed to Mr. Botha that he accept a private invitation to visit the United States, "which would lead inevitably to 'a private meeting' with Mr. Reagan." This was pouring gasoline on the fire. Some months later with the tension subsiding Mr. Botha observed (this time with a melancholy noted earlier softening his words), "It is a personal disappointment to me what has taken place in America." A listener suggested that what had taken place did not represent the views of Ronald Reagan. "That is true," came the rejoinder, "he has been badly used by his advisers—but it is the American people who have let us down." No amount of additional suggestion that the American people had precious little involvement in what had transpired appeared to assuage a shaken president.

Africa's State of the Future

A year later (March 1987) in a last meeting with the secretary to the State Security Council (SSC) before his assignment to Santiago as RSA ambassador to Chile, Lt. Gen. Pieter van der Westhuizen was anything but his ebullient self.[18] "What you are doing is incomprehensible," he exclaimed, "the posture adopted by Washington in the past year is not just a mistake in *tactics;* it is a mistake in *principle!*" His visitor was again exposed to a mind thoroughly geostrategic in cast, thoroughly outward in its orientation (however demanding the internal agenda):

> The RSA is "Africa's State of the Future"—never mind mineral resources, never mind strategic location—South Africa has the dynamic peoples of Africa, black and white. There will be a new dispensation here, which *we* shall work out, and then our position in Africa will bear no relationship to what it is even today: *cannot Washington understand that?*

The disaster, heretofore inconceivable in the mind of Mr. Botha's SSC secretary, which he now foresaw was "an estrangement between us in the future because you will have been perceived here as having done nothing but place obstacles in the way of achieving a new order." South Africa would have a new order in any event, he reiterated; it can come sooner or it can come later depending in part on what role you choose to play. "One thing you *have* done," he noted parenthetically, "is assist Black leaders in coming around to the view that we South Africans must sit down together and solve our own problems. Your sanctions have put Blacks on the unemployment lines, but more importantly they alienate Blacks on the issue of American help." The *verlig,* internationalist officer was clearly worried that he must now confront the possibility that he could not persuade his fellow SADF officers that they could look forward to anything but a solitary future.

Implicit in the impassioned words of one of the most influential members of the Botha coterie is a paradigm for a relationship between the primary global power and the primary regional power. That paradigm warrants explication if a relationship valued at the highest level on each side (the prospects for which seemed shattered at the end of the eighties) might yet be established. The explication is entirely our own, but framed in terms set forth a generation ago and requiring today only minor modification.[19] The imperial (order-maintaining) task that falls to the United States can only be effectively discharged through relationships (informal rather than formal, but rooted in shared substantive interests) with relatively major middle powers. The latter, Liska points out, largely sharing in the objectives of the center *imperium*, will yet be anxious to supplant them to a degree and exploit center mistakes. The result, however, is that the middle power will assume some of the burdens and facilitate some of the tasks of the global power. The regional power is able to take on initiatives locally that the central power is unable to take on with comparable effect. The critical issue is that of candidates for primacy or paramountcy in a particular region. Has a middle power emerged (in Southern Africa) demonstrably capable of and desirous of establishing a normal, autonomous regional order whose initiatives the United States can realistically second and who, in turn, can second the American *imperium*? It was one of Liska's cardinal assumptions, nearly a quarter of a century ago (open to refutation by events), that Africa had not so far produced "an indigenous regional power even remotely capable of doing more than fend for itself on a day-by-day basis." General van der Westhuizen is hardly alone in his affirmation that that day has passed. Africa's "state of the future" is now identified.

The relationship envisaged in this analysis is one in which the purposes of the center are served by the advance toward regional primacy of a seconding middle power. While identifying with the imperial power, the seconding middle power must retain the key attribute of independence, yet not pursue a local imperialism of its own. ("Pergamum must serve Rome!") The relationship is delicate, informal, and complex inasmuch as it consists of a mix of competitive and cooperative elements. Greater political leeway (and uncertainty) will characterize relationships of this kind than normally obtain between formal allies. This requires "a measure of detachment from critical local issues": the underlying premise is that (in the instant case) the United States cannot *precisely* determine local or regional issues in southern Africa and must in any event focus on "manifest threats to international order" as they may emerge in the region. If a relationship can be

attained of "ultimate dependability" combined with "manifest independence" on the part of both, it can over time reduce the imperial responsibilities of the center.

The basic *external* problem for the United States is "to apportion
critical instrumentalities of control or influence so as to conform to the
genius loci." In Europe these would appear to have shifted from the
military to the economic spheres and from the center to the local sectors. By contrast with Europe they remain primarily politico-military in
the Third World. In Africa, generally, economic instrumentalities are
in themselves incapable of generating a stable new order based on
local responsibility. (An adaptation of the argument must now be made
in the case of South Africa.) The basic *internal* requirement for the
United States "is to blunt the bitterness and enhance the intellectual
significance of the more or less academic debate" engaging Americans
on the utility of apportioning instrumentalities of control or influence
abroad. In part, this can be accomplished by separating the ideological
factor (whether anticommunism or antiapartheidism) from that of long-
range policy, that is, promoting gradual transformations toward largely
autonomous regional orders in conditions of practical independence—
and blocking contrary approaches. Severe questions are posed for the
U.S. polity. Does the United States possess the temperamental qualifi-
cations for detached order maintenance in outlying regions? Can it
resist "communal overinvolvement" in peripheral conflicts that do not
raise imperial issues? Is Washington capable of insulating the economy and the society from the recurrent traumas that will accompany
such a role? The questions are at the heart of U.S. national-security
policy but bear heavily as well on the security of candidate "seconding
middle powers" (i.e., South Africa in the present instance). They suggest that a profound U.S. foreign-policy determination must precede
any discussion of strategic concurrence with outlying middle powers.
For the balance of this discussion we make a cardinal assumption of
our own (likewise open to refutation by events) that Washington cannot choose at the end of the twentieth century—anymore than it could
at mid-century—to eschew the "imperial obligation."

At the beginning of the century the regional-order paradigm employed by Great Britain and its dominion to address, inter alia, the
question of Germany in Africa (successfully done) was the 1910 Union
of South Africa. The end-of-century paradigm conceptually outlined
here, while lacking the formalities of an earlier era, is yet analogous. It

is analogous in its informing quest for regional order and in the requirement thereby imposed on both center and locality for reciprocal sustenance. Departures from this standard, modish fin de siècle transmutations, such as a southern Africa cooperative-development venture, must be guarded against. It is not promising (the new era has not yet arrived) to have the administrator of the U.S. Agency for International Development suggest to the Southern Africa Development Coordination Conference (SADCC) that *it* is the forum within which "regional development" is to be realized and that frontline (SADCC) states should seek ways to *lessen* their dependency on the primary regional power.[20] Insofar as economic instrumentalities might be apportioned in support of regional order, they are most likely to be effective to the degree that they directly enhance the power of the regional partner and as called for by that partner. In somewhat less visionary language than his minister, the RSA director-general of Foreign Affairs makes the point that southern African states are interdependent and their future peace and stability indivisible. In this regard, he underscored two factors in particular: first, his country ("a mature regional power") must inevitably lead the regional-development effort and that "South Africa is an ally (of regional states) against foreign invasion." In the execution of these regional leadership roles "the international isolation of South Africa is contrary to African interests."[21]

The exasperation of one of South Africa's leading businessmen was as palpable as that of one of its most influential general officers. The retreat of American business and American investment from the country represents, he feared, "American commercial pressure in connivance with the State Department—no matter what the latter might say publicly."[22] The contingency that could "easily and quickly develop" was one where U.S. presence, commercial and strategic, in Africa's state of the future would be eliminated with Europe and the Far East occupying the ground. In any apportionment of instrumentalities by the United States for purposes of regional order maintenance below the Sahara (or for that matter below the Zambezi), those falling strictly within the commercial-financial category will not have the highest priority in the near-term. However, it must be emphasized that to the extent that these are utilized (merely by including technology assets[23] among economic instrumentalities, the case for such apportionment becomes compelling), they must be essentially directed to increasing the performance of the established engine of regional growth. Thus, the argument of the director-general of Foreign Affairs, Mr. van Heerden, that the mature regional power must play the lead role in the stabilization of southern Africa is at the very heart of the argument for the imperial paradigm. This requires a U.S. economic presence that is strategic in its reinforcement (its "seconding") of Pretoria's regional programs. (That it also be unobtrusive is, perhaps, to ask too much!)

Liska reminds us that "the key word and concept distinguishing a multiregional imperial order" is *access.* In those Third World areas where the military instrument has greater significance than economic instrumentalities, even here "the requirements of political access will have to take increasing precedence over requirements of military logistics."[24] Where the two might come in conflict the *"mot d'ordre"* will have to be *indefinite access* rather than permanent bases." Second, *access* must be to the regional middle power for its own sake (as far as this is possible) rather than to "the real" great power adversary through the regional partner. Such a strategy will prove optimal over the widest range of regional-conflict scenarios. The report of the Regional Conflict Working Group (Commission on Integrated Long-Term Strategy), *Supporting U.S. Strategy for Third World Conflict,*[25] resonates with many of the intonations of the center-region paradigm short, to be sure, of formal adoption. The group (and the commission) seek to avoid "direct (imperial) intervention" in outlying regions except in unavoidable cases. The report goes into considerable detail (employing its own terminology) on "the apportionment of critical instrumentalities" to friends and allies, giving highest priority to security assistance. What it does not do—and cannot do—is address the question of political access or identify salient regional powers. It delineates few if any criteria for security-assistance recipients except to leave the strong impression that they are, for the most part, anything but middle powers. Constrained by a paucity of policy/strategy guidance the authors of the report must necessarily confine themselves to the realm of "ways and means."[26] In our analysis of maintaining international order (the phrasing is preferred to that of "maintaining international peace"), we are not similarly constrained.

The imperial issues of access, of security assistance, and of bases must take precedence in the bilateral agenda of the nineties between the United States and South Africa. The issue of bases, reduced to a set of ritualistic incantations on both sides when taken up between Washington and minor powers, is a straightforward agenda item when dealing with middle powers (NATO–Japan). It will be precisely such in discussions of *imperium* with middle-power South Africa. Today the United States has perhaps one-quarter of the overseas bases (with the bulk of these in the NATO region) that it possessed in 1947. A significant decline in dependence upon advance bases has been compensated for—to a degree—by equally significant gains in the strategic mobility of sea/air strike forces. How much farther this inverse correlation can be carried is an emerging question. An irreducible number of bases, their distribution over critical areas of the world, and the specific identity of host countries are far more pressing issues today than a decade ago as Washington must now consider the downsizing of the military establishment. (The U.S. Seventh Fleet, for example, cannot be forward deployed in the western Pacific on a continuing basis deprived of bases in Subic and Tokyo bays. Any adjustment of the base situation must entail adjustments in the deployment pattern.) The response of the Gorman group to the declining availability of bases is an almost frantic search for an "alternative way of performing the functions for which U.S. forces have heretofore depended upon terrestrial facilities (sic) in the Third World."[27] The possibilities envisaged (archetypally American) are largely of a technological character, at the level of "ways and means," and can be expected to supplant terrestrial facilities only to a point![28]

The First World base complex available at Africa's southern cape on one of the world's critical maritime routes or SLOCs (sea lanes of communication) has been well described in other places no less by Americans than by South Africans.[29] Its utilization by the center is indispensable to any concept of U.S./RSA strategic collaboration in the region. No less critical is the question of casting off self-defeating arms embargoes and addressing specific areas in which technology transfer from the United States to South Africa can best enhance a joint *imperium*. The areas are not difficult to identify. In stressing that the direct involvement of the United States (use of U.S. combat forces in the Third World) should be "an exceptional event" and that it should complement earlier-provided security assistance, the Gorman group is assuredly correct.[30] Again this points to U.S./RSA agenda items for the nineties. The issues can be taken up in practical, straightforward terms once the question of political access has been resolved. This is the policy challenge.

A Concluding Note

America's communal overinvolvement in South Africa's continuing historic transformation of its constitution has served to obscure commanding issues of international order to which it alone can attend. Our indulgence in the domestic agenda of a sovereign nation struggling to stay on the path of reform while under siege serves also to obscure a fundamental lesson of the American experience. It is apposite to recall that lesson particularly as it is so cogently related to the world—and to ourselves—by Daniel Boorstin.[31] The American people, he concludes, are bound together not by any "explicit political theory" but by "a fact of life," that is to say, by our common experience, by the uniqueness of our lives and institutions. Boorstin is plain as to the lesson: "If we have learned anything from our history it is the wisdom of allowing institutions to develop *according to the needs of each particular environment*" (italics mine). It is demonstrable folly that institutions can readily be transferred from one setting to another; at any rate, "the principles on which we approach politics and have succeeded in building our own institutions, deny such a possibility."[32] We shall be true to ourselves to the extent that we permit this fact of life to go abroad and embargo any doctrine—any theory—however efficacious in this environment.[33] The peoples of South Africa will devise in our time institutions (political, social, and economic) in accordance with the genius loci; in so doing they will emulate our example. Our recognition of this will signify maturity at the imperial center required for international order.

In the period 1975–89 South Africa dedicated its security resources to reducing specific, external military threats in the region and to "assisting the civil" in eliminating revolutionary war formulas for a new internal order. These goals were achieved in relative isolation under growing international constraints. In the nineties South Africa presents itself as the predominant regional power ready to join with the predominant global power (in competitive-cooperative interaction) to build pillars of international order in Africa. South Africa stands prepared to enter a new era. If the United States is to respond to this end-of-century opportunity to extend the realm of order in the Third World, it will do so only on the conscious adoption of the imperial obligation. Washington's South African policy at the conclusion of the eighties, based neither on American nor African *experience* and overtaken by hostility, is a mistake.[34] Delivered today into the hands of "compassion" and "expediency," the policy is debilitating. Mistakes in foreign policy can be corrected. Where adolescence gives way to maturity they are corrected and obligations discharged.

Notes

1. The New York agreements of December 1988 do not go to the direct, bilateral relationship between Washington and Pretoria. While Mr. Crocker may initially have seen the process that ultimately led to a Namibian settlement as establishing a basis for *rapprochement* between Washington and Pretoria, this process soon became dedicated to serving ostensible U.S. international objectives. In many respects the Namibian settlement plan and the removal of Cuban forces from Angola, both welcomed by Pretoria, have come at the expense of an improved bilateral relationship between the United States and the Republic of South Africa.

2. Major extracts from the speech were published as a special supplement to *South African Digest,* October 9, 1981, then published by the Department of Foreign Affairs and Information, Pretoria. Much disparaged by analysts within the U.S. government at the time, Mr. Neil van Heerden, currently director-general of Foreign Affairs, reiterates many of its themes in a recent commentary. See his "South Africa and Africa: The New Diplomacy," *ISSUP Bulletin* (April 1, 1989), Pretoria.

3. See n. 19.

4. The rediscovery if not the renascence of the geostrategic perspectives of Sir Halford Mackinder, Alfred Thayer Mahan, and Nicholas Spykman is evident in the eighties although there is little evidence as yet of its permeating the highest level of the U.S. government. The Report by the Regional Conflict Working Group of the Commission on Integrated Long-Term Strategy, *Supporting U.S. Strategy for Third World Conflict* (Washington, D.C.: GPO, June 1988), may be seen as a limited attempt in this regard. For a discussion and summary of the recent geopolitical literature, see Colin Gray, *The Geo-politics of Super Power* (Lexington: The University of Kentucky Press, 1988). See especially chapter 1 and notes.

5. The South African foreign minister was perhaps thinking of those few years following World War II when Washington in fact conducted foreign/national security policy in strategic terms, which, as Charles Burton Marshall has put it, "is a business of maintaining coherence among perceived threats, recognized opportunities, defined interests, and acknowledged and accepted costs." This posture of practical realism in dealing with the world at large in accordance with a "quite plausible code of norms" was short-lived. As Marshall laments, "(This) epoch of strategic concern seems to have been a parenthesis in national experience. The non-strategic operational code of our longer past seems to have endured without having been more than temporarily affected." See his "Continuity and Discontinuity: Dour Reflections on the National Security," *Journal of Politics* 38 (August 1976), 265. On the theme of the unpredictability of U.S.

foreign policy see Raymond Aron, *The Imperial Republic: The United States and the World, 1945–1973* (Cambridge: Winthrop, 1974). However, Aron, while finding the United States often unpredictable, often flagging, often divided, reiterates that it stands alone as the banner carrier. Therein lies the painful dilemma for would-be "seconding middle powers."

6. The remark has been attributed to Secretary of State George Shultz. Professor Marshall suggests that the foreign-policy slough in Washington stems from an acquiescence in, if not commitment to, "indeterminate results"—a view, he adds, not shared by our adversaries! "Continuity and Discontinuity," 274.

7. The inflection (and the anguish) is that of Walter Lippmann. In his *U.S. Foreign Policy: Shield of the Republic* (Boston: Little, Brown, 1963), he laments the spectacle of a great nation that does not know its own mind and cannot form a foreign policy. In our own day, leaving aside the South African case, the disaster at the level of courses of action to take in support of the Democratic Resistance in Nicaragua (strategy) flows inexorably from the disaster of failing to define our purposes in Central America (policy).

8. In a revealing self-study of his term as assistant secretary of state for African Affairs, Mr. Chester Crocker testifies, no doubt inadvertently, to this point. He chides Pretoria for jejunely failing to understand the (domestic political) limits under which the United States government had to act with respect to South Africa. Pretoria's suggestion of hypocrisy—of the Department of State using this pretext to disguise its real purposes in the region—must be put on the scales as well. See "Southern Africa: Eight Years Later," *Foreign Affairs* 68 (Fall 1989): 144–64. Like the article of his principal deputy in the preceding issue of the same journal (see n. 49, chapter 6), Crocker's assessment of the RSA/U.S. relationship during the Reagan years supports our contention of secular failure. Moreover, the steady deterioration "at the formal level" between Washington and Pretoria does much to explain efforts through "alternative channels" to develop a stronger bilateral relationship.

9. The fact that Congress had thoroughly "domesticated" foreign-policy questions relating to southern Africa was enormously convenient to the Department of State, permitting it to "keep options open" with respect to the RSA in particular and even to join in the rituals of the U.S. antiapartheid movement.

10. Remarks delivered by U.S. Ambassador Herman Nickel before the *Johannesburger Afrikaanse Sakekamer* on February 21, 1985. *South Africa Digest* (March 1, 1985), 182–83.

11. At no time during the writing of this book has the author had access to classified information, nor is he required to have the text cleared by any government agency. Nonetheless, in what follows it will be necessary to take account of the requests of sources.

12. At this juncture the author was told at the highest level of the U.S. Defense Intelligence Agency that "we have a HUMINT (Human Intelligence Collection) problem in southern Africa—we need collectors." On this same subject a source in South Africa noted that "the handling of (defense) attachés is hurting both sides—State is almost in a frenzy on this point!" Once the arms were in the pipeline to Savimbi, intelligence sharing, particularly between DIA in Washington and CSI (Defense Force) in Pretoria, improved markedly. However, it was described to the author as "roughly a 70–30 arrangement with 70 percent coming

into Washington and only 30 percent going out." The 1987–88 fighting in Angola, thanks to CSI cooperation with DIA, was an intelligence bonanza for Washington on how one fights the Russians and the Cubans. Since that time, as a result of congressional action, the exchange has been reduced to a trickle.

13. This dwindling group consisted of a few key individuals in government (not necessarily the most senior) and as one of them put it, "those few—outside of government—who can call him 'Piet.' " Periodic access in the late eighties to members of this group makes this section possible.

14. Ambassador Nickel, personally anxious to achieve some kind of breakthrough in the bilateral relationship, was aware of the back-channel effort and lodged objections. While his objections would ultimately win out, his objectives would not. Subsequently, Mr. Nickel would speak openly of having to withstand the ire of Mr. Botha in his last months in South Africa!

15. See the final pages of chapter 4.

16. From private correspondence with the author. The correspondent would add the plaintive hope that "the steps *now being taken* will improve the relationships, which are so important to the future" (italics mine).

17. The suspension of this particular special activity would be among the factors that would lead Mr. Casey to write a letter to the president of the United States requesting that he ask for the resignation of the secretary of state. See Menges, *Inside the National Security Council,* 247, also interviews not for direct attribution.

18. The announcement, September 18, 1987, by the RSA Foreign Ministry that General van der Westhuizen had been appointed ambassador to Chile (to be succeeded as State Security Council secretary by Lt. Gen. Charles Lloyd) was of more than passing interest in Washington. Long regarded as a vital asset of the regime by Mr. Botha, the point may well have been reached where it was deemed best to send the energetic general abroad for a time. The latter was particularly keen to capitalize on the reform impetus of the May 1987 elections and establish new lines to the West. The State President on the other hand, all too conscious of the constraints operating in both matters, may have wanted something more muted from his SSC secretary. It will be of interest to South Africa watchers to note what role, if any, General van der Westhuizen will have in a de Klerk government.

19. Here we follow the elegant conceptual argument of George Liska (perhaps not always elegant in its presentation!) offered in his *Imperial America: The International Politics of Primacy* (Baltimore: Johns Hopkins University Press, 1967) and especially in chapter 7. Liska writes of an America prone to deny any imperial purpose (presumably freeing itself, thereby, for discrete acts of intervention) that cannot, however, escape the imperial tasks of maintaining minimum order in an unorganized world. In the discharge of these tasks the methods "may or must be often indirect (acting through relatively, ostensibly, or up to a point really independent local friendly powers, within limits set by the possibility of a real divergence of their own and American interests)." See preface. This is to outline a relationship between an order-maintaining center and regional outposts similarly committed, immensely challenging in its sophistication for all parties. Quotations are from chapter 7.

Mr. Lee Kuan-yew (Prime Minister of Singapore) appears to have no problem with the United States as an imperial power. He suggested recently that "America is the only major power in recent history that has used its military might to sustain a system that enables all participants to equally benefit without her, as the provider of security, taking royalties . . . we are willing to share the political burden of being host to America, *an imperial power.* We think it isn't such a great burden, that it carries no stigma, and we are prepared to do it" (italics mine). *Wall Street Journal,* November 1, 1989.

One must take account of the fact that the much maligned and elegant Latin term *imperium* creates problems when introduced into American discourse. Charles Howard McIlwain, unsurpassed scholar of Western constitutional thought, wrote fondly of *imperium.* It strikes "a constitutional attitude toward politics," he maintained, inasmuch as it is the very concept of lawful authority as opposed to authority *de facto. The Growth of Political Thought in the West* (New York: Macmillan, 1932), 133. Leonard Mosley writes that on the eve of the Second World War Walter Lippmann, self-confessed Wilsonian, would find that the issue of imperial obligation could be put off no longer. On a June evening in 1939, a touring Lippmann dined with Winston Churchill in London. Already morose over the portent of ongoing Polish negotiations, Churchill earlier that day had listened to the conjectures of Ambassador Joseph Kennedy that Britain would be defeated in the war looming on the horizon. The soon-to-be wartime Prime Minister was not prepared to concede this outcome, but he told his American dinner guest that, should the dread contingency nonetheless come to pass, "it will be for you *to think imperially* which means always of something higher and more vast than one's own national interests" (italics mine). See *On Borrowed Time* (New York: Random House, 1969), 258. For the argument that American anti-imperialism is based upon a completely "irrational dogmatic feeling" see the remarkable discussion between John Courtney Murray and Reinhold Niebuhr in *Foreign Policy and the Free Society,* ed. Walter Millis and John Courtney Murray (New York: Oceana, 1958), 95–102. See, finally, Lewis Feuer, *Imperialism and the Anti-Imperialist Mind* (Buffalo: Prometheus, 1986).

20. Address by M. Peter McPherson, Gaborone, Botswana, February 5, 1987 (U.S. Department of State, Bureau of Public Affairs, Washington, D.C., Current Policy No. 919). In support of the argument for the fundamental unity of the regional economy of southern Africa and against utopian strategies for disengaging Black African states from their economic ties with the regional powerhouse, see Ronald T. Libby, *The Politics of Economic Power in Southern Africa* (Princeton: Princeton University Press, 1987).

21. Neil van Heerden, "South Africa and Africa," 7–8.

22. Interview, March 1987. The discrepancy between State Department rhetoric to the effect that U.S. business should "carry on" in South Africa and action on the part of Washington to sustain that presence does not go unnoticed and gives rise to conspiratorial theories.

23. In his review of "The Contemporary Strategic Situation in Southern Africa," the minister of Defense, General Malan, sketches the posture of the region's middle power and alludes to developing attitudes in no small part the result of isolation from prospective partners. In his analysis he stresses the technological prowess of South Africa, arguing that this factor goes far in explaining his country's regional primacy. Certainly this is correct to a degree, but there is

something of a "brave front" here as well. Business sector leaders are more prepared to discuss this critical factor with candor. The apportionment of technology assets to the RSA will have to be part of any center-regional association of the future if it is to meet its objectives. See "The RSA's Role and Influence Must Increase," *Paratus* 39 (December 1, 1988): 12–13ff.

24. *Imperial America*, 97.

25. U.S. Department of Defense (Washington, D.C.: GPO, 1988). Funded at the end of the Reagan administration, the work of the commission has carried over into a general strategic review by the incoming Bush administration. No major strategic departures are anticipated in spite of growing pressures for downsizing of the U.S. military establishment. In the case of the instant report (*Supporting U.S. Strategy for Third World Conflict*), it was written largely under the influence of Gen. Paul Gorman, USA (Ret.), who, in turn, was largely under the influence of his concluding active-duty tour as CINCUSSOUTHCOM (Commander in Chief, U.S. Southern Command). General Gorman expresses the hope that the report will help develop consensus where consensus does not as yet exist.

26. Ibid., 1.

27. *Supporting U.S. Strategy for Third World Conflict*, 40.

28. Throughout the report there is an "Army argument" for inclusion in Third World scenarios that raises strictly internal issues for Washington.

29. For an early—and premature—discussion, see my "Beyond Limpopo and Zambezi: South Africa's Strategic Horizons," in *The Indian Ocean*, 267–81.

30. *Supporting U.S. Strategy*, 25.

31. *The Genius of American Politics* (Chicago: University of Chicago Press, 1963).

32. Ibid., 185–87. Americans have had the salutary experience of late of being reminded (by a Peruvian source) that "rule-making procedures" and "property rights" are the cornerstones of the American experience, not such banalities as "one man–one vote." Hernando de Soto, *The Other Path: The Invisible Revolution in the Third World* (New York: Harper & Row, 1988). Mr. A B Williams of Cape Town (chapter 1) would concur with Mr. de Soto's priorities for his own constituents.

33. In noting that "we have taken for granted that God Himself drew the plans of our career and marked its outlines in our history and on our very ground" (161), Boorstin links Afrikaners and Americans perhaps more closely than he would anticipate. Former South African Prime Minister Daniel F Malan contended in similar accents that "it is through the will of God that the Afrikaner People exist at all. In His wisdom He determined that on the southern point of Africa, the dark continent, a People should be born who will be the bearer of Christian culture and civilization. In His wisdom He surrounded this People by great dangers." Quoted by T. Dunbar Moodie, *The Rise of Afrikanerdom* (Berkeley: The University of California Press, 1975), 247–48. Whether this commonality obtains in a less religious age is another question.

34. The reader will recall that Talleyrand, upon hearing the excesses of the Terror described as crimes, suggested that they were far worse—they were mistakes! On the point that mistakes with far-reaching policy implications will be made in all seasons but that governments are permitted, indeed required, to change their minds, the career of Disraeli may be more instructive than French

maxims. In his splendid biography *Disraeli* (New York: St. Martin's Press, 1967), Robert Blake offers the following:

> When Disraeli took office in 1874 it is doubtful whether he had any clear ideas on foreign policy other than doing something—it did not matter much what—to reassert Britain's power in Europe (571).

And this:

> Disraeli did not want war. He wished to preserve as much of Turkey as he could, stop the Russians from entering Constantinople . . . if possible without war, though he did not flinch at war if there were no alternative. . . . Of course he made mistakes, the worst being total failure to feel and therefore comprehend the indignation caused by Bulgarian atrocities. . . . It meant that anything like a national consensus was unobtainable, and by stimulating the fury of the Opposition he put unnecessary difficulties in the way of his own chosen course. . . . Nonetheless, Disraeli's foreign policy was an undoubted success (653).

SELECT INTERVIEW LIST

Ackron, F.
Adams, B.
Adler, J.
Barnard, L.
Barratt, J.
Bosman, P.
Breytenbach, W.
Castle, R.
Chettle, J.
de Lange, P.
deVilliers, J.
du Plessis, W.
du Toit, H.
Earp, D.
Ecksteen, R.
Ferreira, D.
Fourie, D.
Fraser, M.
Geldenhuys, D.
Geldenhuys, J.

Gleeson, I.
Golden, S.
Grimbeek, H.
Holmes, O.
Hough, M.
Irwin, M.
Jooste, J.
Louw, M.
McLean, I.
McRalston, D.
Maree, J.
Meyer, R.
Mortimer, D.
Mudge, D.
Myburgh, T.
Noffke, C.
Opperman, D.
Potgeiter, A.
Putter, A.

Rindel, F.
Sole, D.
Sorour, J.
Spicer, M.
Steward, D.
Swanepoel, L.
van der Merwe, P.
van der Walt, D.
van der Westhuizen, P.
van Heerden, N.
van Hirschberg, M.
van Rooyen, S.
Viljoen, G.
Vlok, A.
Vorster, T.
Willers, D.
Williams, A.
Williamson, C.
Worrall, D.

Note: Many were interviewed on more than one occasion.

GLOSSARY

ACDA	Arms Control and Disarmament Agency (U.S.)
ANC	African National Congress
APLA	Azanian People's Liberation Army
ARM	African Resistance Movement
ARMSCOR	Armaments Corporation of South Africa, Ltd.
ASW	Antisubmarine warfare
AWB	*Afrikanerweerstandsbeweging* (Afrikaner Defense League)
BOSS	Bureau of State Security
CCM	*Chama Cha Mapinduzi*
CF	Citizen Force
COIN	Counterinsurgency
COSATU	Congress of South African Trade Unions
CSI	Chief of Staff for Intelligence
DONS	Department of National Security
DP	Democratic Party
DPC	Defense Planning Committee
EPG	Eminent Persons Group
ESCOM	Electricity Supply Commission
FAPLA	Popular Forces for the Liberation of Angola
FNLA	National Front for the Liberation of Angola
FRELIMO	Revolutionary Front for the Liberation of Mozambique
FTF	Full-time Force
GOC	General Officer Commanding
IDC	Interdepartmental Committee

IP	Independent Party
ISSUP	Institute for Strategic Studies, University of Pretoria
IUEF	International University Exchange Fund
JMC	Joint Management Center
JMC	Joint Monitoring Commission
JSMG	Joint Security Management Group
K	Commandos
KP	Conservative Party
MFA	Armed Forces Movement (Portugal)
MK	*Umkhonto we Sizwe,* "Spear of the Nation"
MNR	Mozambican National Resistance Movement "RENAMO"
MPLA	Popular Movement for the Liberation of Angola
NDM	New Democratic Movement
NGK	*Nederduits Gereformeerde Kerk;* Dutch Reformed Church
NIE	National Intelligence Estimate
NIIB	National Intelligence Interpretation Branch
NIS	National Intelligence Service
NJMC	National Joint Management Center
NJMS	National Joint Management System
NP	National Party
NSE	National State of Emergency
NSM	National Servicemen
NSMS	National Security Management System
NUM	National Union of Mineworkers
NUSAS	National Union of South African Students
OAU	Organization of African Unity
OC	Officer Commanding
PAC	Pan-African Congress
PF	Permanent Force
PFP	Progressive Federal Party
PLAN	People's Liberation Army of Namibia
PTF	Part-time Force
RENAMO	See MNR
RSA	Republic of South Africa; name since 1961
RSC	Regional Service Council
SAAF/SALM	South African Air Force/*Suid-Afrikaanse Lugmag*
SABC	South African Broadcasting Corporation

SACC	South African Cape Corps
SACP	South Africa Communist Party
SADF/SAW	South African Defense Force/*Suid-Afrikaanse Weermag*
SAF	South Africa Foundation
SAL	South African Army/*Suid-Afrikaanse Leer*
SAMIL	Military Vehicle Division (ARMSCOR)
SAN/SAV	South African Navy/*Suid-Afrikaanse Vloot*
SAP	South African Police/*Suid-Afrikaanse Polisie*
SAS	Special Air Service
SASOL	South African Coal, Oil and Gas Corporation, Ltd.
SATS	South African Transport Services
SCAA	Special Committee against Apartheid (UN)
SSC	State Security Council
SWAPO	Southwest Africa People's Organization
SWATF/SWAGM	Southwest Africa Territorial Force/*Suidwes-Afrika Gebiedsmag*
TAZARA	Tanzania-Zambia Railway Authority
TGNU	Transitional Government of National Unity (Namibia)
UDF	United Democratic Front
UNITA	National Union for the Total Independence of Angola
UNTAG	United Nations Transition Assistance Group
ZANLA	Zimbabwe African National Liberation Army
ZANU	Zimbabwe African National Union
ZAPU	Zimbabwe African People's Union
ZIPRA	Zimbabwe People's Revolutionary Army
Aanslag	onslaught, refers to multidimensional attack on RSA
Askari	Black African soldier, European trained and equipped
Bantu	main family of peoples and languages in southern Africa
Hoofbestuurder	(with "*Uitvoerende*") General Manager
Indaba	council; coming together of different groups or peoples
Inkatha	extraparliamentary Zulu organization in RSA
KwaZulu	self-governing state within Natal province

Laager	camp within encircled wagons
Sechaba	monthly magazine of ANC
Spetsnaz	Russian contraction denoting Soviet special forces
Uhuru	freedom
Uitlander	outlander, used by Afrikaners to refer to White English-speakers
Ujamma	brotherhood, associated with communal projects at national level
Veldt/Veld	central plateau or grassy highlands in RSA
Verkrampte	rendered as "staunch" but used to describe political conservatives in RSA
Verlig	enlightened
Volk	people, refers exclusively to Afrikaners
Voortrekkerhoogte	describes heights around Pretoria; site of *Voortrekker* monument, political redoubt of Afrikanerdom
Voorsitter	chairman

SELECT BIBLIOGRAPHY

Adam, Heribert, and Kogila Moodley. *South Africa without Apartheid: Dismantling Racial Domination*. Cape Town: Longman, 1986.

Alexiev, Alexander R. *UNITA and U.S. Policy in Angola*. Santa Monica: Rand, 1987.

Aron, Raymond. *The Imperial Republic: The United States and the World, 1945–1973*. Cambridge: Winthrop, 1974.

Barber, James, and John Barratt. *South Africa's Foreign Policy: The Search for Status and Security 1945–1988*. New York: Cambridge University Press, 1990.

Bark, Dennis L., ed. *The Red Orchestra*. Vol. 2, *The Case of Africa*. Stanford: Hoover Institution Press, 1988.

Beaufre, Andre. *Introduction to Strategy*. London: Faber & Faber, 1965.

———. *Strategy of Action*. London: Faber & Faber, 1967.

Blake, Robert. *Disraeli*. New York: St. Martin's Press, 1967.

Boorstin, Daniel. *The Genius of American Politics*. Chicago: University of Chicago Press, 1963.

Bozeman, Adda. *Conflict in Africa: Concepts and Realities*. Princeton: Princeton University Press, 1976.

Breytenbach, Jan. *Forged in Battle*. Cape Town: Saayman & Weber, 1986.

Bridgland, Fred. *Jonas Savimbi: A Key to Africa*. London: Coronet, 1987.

Brzezinski, Zbigniew. *The Grand Failure: The Birth and Death of Communism in the Twentieth Century*. New York: Scribner's, 1989.

Butts, K.H., and P.R. Thomas. *The Geopolitics of Southern Africa: South Africa as Regional Superpower*. Boulder: Westview, 1986.

Campbell, R K. *Sea Power and South Africa*. Pretoria: ISSUP, 1984.

Chaliand, Gerard. *The Struggle for Africa: Conflict of the Great Powers*. New York: St. Martin's Press, 1982.

Chanock, Martin. *Unconsummated Union: Britain, Rhodesia, and South Africa, 1900–1945*. Manchester University Press, 1977.

Cilliers, J.K. *Counter-Insurgency in Rhodesia*. London: Croom Helm, 1985.

Coker, Christopher. *The United States and South Africa, 1968–1985: Constructive Engagement and Its Critics*. Durham, N.C.: Duke University Press, 1986.

Davidow, Jeffrey. *A Peace in Southern Africa: The Lancaster House Conference on Rhodesia, 1979.* Boulder: Westview, 1984.

Dowdy W.W., and R.B. Trood, eds. *The Indian Ocean: Perspectives on a Strategic Arena.* Durham, N.C.: Duke University Press, 1985.

Earl, Edward Meade, ed. *Makers of Modern Strategy.* New York: Atheneum, 1967.

Falwell, Byron. *The Great Anglo-Boer War.* New York: Harper & Row, 1976.

Feuer, Lewis. *Imperialism and the Anti-Imperialist Mind.* Buffalo: Prometheus, 1986.

Flower, Ken. *Serving Secretly: An Intelligence Chief on Record, Rhodesia into Zimbabwe, 1964 to 1981.* London: John Murray, 1987.

Frankel, Philip. *Pretoria's Praetorians: Civil-Military Relations in South Africa.* Cambridge: Cambridge University Press, 1984.

Fukuyama, Francis. *Moscow's Post-Brezhnevian Reassessment of the Third World.* Santa Monica: Rand, 1988.

Gann, Lewis, and Peter Duignan, eds. *Colonialism in Africa, 1870–1960.* 5 vols. London: Cambridge University Press, 1969–75.

Gann, Lewis, and T.H. Hendricksen. *The Struggle for Zimbabwe: Battle in the Bush.* New York: Praeger, 1981.

Geldenhuys, Deon. *The Diplomacy of Isolation: South African Foreign Policy Making.* New York: St. Martin's Press, 1984.

Gray, Colin. *The Geo-Politics of Super Power.* Lexington: University Press of Kentucky, 1988.

———. *Strategic Studies and Public Policy.* Lexington: University of Kentucky Press, 1982.

Grundy, Kenneth. *Soldiers without Politics: Blacks in the South African Armed Forces.* Berkeley: University of California Press, 1983.

———. *The Militarization of South African Politics.* Bloomington: Indiana University Press, 1986.

Hall, Richard, and Hugh Peyman. *The Great Uhuru Railway.* London: Victor Gallancz, 1977.

Hanf, T., H. Weiland, and G. Vierdag. *South Africa: The Prospects of Peaceful Change.* London: Rex Collings, 1981.

Hanford, John. *A Portrait of an Economy under Sanctions 1965–75.* Salisbury, Rhodesia: Mercury Press, 1976.

Heitman, Helmoed-Romer. *War in Angola: The Final South African Phase.* Johannesburg: Ashanti, 1990.

———. *South African War Machine.* Greenwich, Conn.: Bison Books, 1985.

Horowitz, Donald L. *A Democratic South Africa? Constitutional Engineering in a Divided Society.* Berkeley: University of California Press, 1991.

Hosmer, Stephen T., and Thomas A. Wolfe. *Soviet Policy and Practice toward Third World Conflicts.* New York: D.C. Heath, 1983.

Hough, M, ed. *Contemporary Maritime Strategy.* Pretoria: ISSUP, 1982.

Hough, M., and M van der Merve, eds. *Selected South African Strategic Perceptions.* Pretoria: ISSUP, 1988.

Howard, Michael. *Studies in War and Peace.* New York: Viking Press, 1970.

Hyam, Ronald. *Britain's Imperial Century; A Study of Empire and Expansionism, 1815–1914.* London: Macmillan, 1976.

Jaster, Robert. *South Africa in Namibia: The Botha Strategy.* Lanham, Md.: University Press of America, 1985.

Kirkpatrick, Jeane. *Dictatorship and Double Standards: Rationalism and Reason in Politics.* New York: Simon & Schuster, 1982.

Kitchen, Helen, and Michael Clough. *The United States and South Africa: Realities and Red Herrings.* Washington: CSIS, 1984.

Kitson, Frank. *Low Intensity Operations: Subversion, Counter-Insurgency and Peacekeeping.* London: Faber & Faber, 1972.

Klerk, Willem de. *The Second Revolution: Afrikanerdom and the Crisis of Identity.* Johannesburg: Jonathan Hall, 1984.

Klinghoffer, Arthur J. *The Angolan War: A Study of Soviet Policy in the Third World.* Boulder: Westview, 1980.

Kruger, D W. *The Age of the Generals.* Johannesburg: Dagbreekpers, 1961.

Legum, Colin, and Anthony Hodges, eds. *The War over Southern Africa.* New York: Africana, 1976.

Lehmann, Joseph. *The First Boer War.* London: Buchan & Enright,1985.

Lewis, William R. *Great Britain and Germany's Lost Colonies, 1914–1919.* London: Oxford University Press, 1967.

Libby, Ronald T. *The Politics of Economic Power in Southern Africa.* Princeton: Princeton University Press, 1987.

Liddell Hart, B.H. *Strategy.* New York: Praeger, 1968.

Lijphart, Arend. *Power-Sharing in South Africa.* Berkeley: University of California Press, 1985.

Lippmann, Walter. *U.S. Foreign Policy: Shield of the Republic.* Boston: Little, Brown, 1963.

Lipton, Merle. *Capitalism and Apartheid.* London: Smith/Gower, 1985.

Liska, George. *Imperial America: The International Politics of Primacy.* Baltimore: Johns Hopkins University Press, 1967.

Lodge, Tom. *Black Politics in South Africa since 1945.* London: Longman, 1983.

Louw, Michael H H. *National Security: A Modern Approach.* Pretoria: ISSUP, 1978.

McCuen, J.J. *The Art of Counter-Revolutionary Warfare: The Strategy of Counter-Insurgency.* London: Faber & Faber, 1969.

McIlwain, Charles Howard. *The Growth of Political Thought in the West.* New York: Macmillan, 1932.

Mackinder, Sir Halford. *Democratic Ideals and Reality.* New York: W. W. Norton, 1962.

MacMillan, W.M. *Bantu, Boer and Briton: The Making of the South African Native Problem.* Rev. ed. Oxford: Clarendon Press, 1963.

Marais, N. *The Political Dimension of the Settlement Phase during a Revolutionary War.* Pretoria: ISSUP, 1982.

Marcum, John. *The Angolan Revolution.* Vol. 2, *Exile Politics and Guerilla Warfare, 1962–76.* Cambridge: MIT Press, 1978.

Menges, Constantine C. *Inside the National Security Council.* New York: Simon & Schuster, 1988.

Middlemas, Keith. *Cabora-Bassa: Engineering and Politics in Southern Africa.* London: Weidenfeld & Nicolson, 1975.

Millis, Walter, and John Courtney Murray, eds. *Foreign Policy and the Free Society.* New York: Oceana, 1958.

Moodie, T. Dunbar. *The Rise of Afrikanerdom.* Berkeley: University of California Press, 1975.

Morris, Max. *Armed Conflict in Southern Africa.* Cape Town: Jeremy Spence, 1974.

Mosley, Leonard. *On Borrowed Time*. New York: Random House, 1968.

Murray, Douglas J., and Paul R. Viotti, eds. *The Defense Policies of Nations—A Comparative Study*. 2d ed. Baltimore: Johns Hopkins Press, 1989.

Neuhaus, Richard John. *South Africa: The Religion Factor*. Washington, D.C.: Foundation for Africa's Future, 1988.

Oliver, B.J. *The Strategic Significance of Angola*. Pretoria: ISSUP, 1984.

Pakenham, Thomas. *The Boer War*. New York: Random House, 1979.

Plessis, A de. *South Africa and the South Atlantic Ocean: Maritime-Strategic Analysis*. Pretoria: ISSUP, June 1987.

Pottinger, Brian. *The Imperial Presidency: P.W. Botha—The First Ten Years*. Johannesburg: Southern Books, 1988.

Rees, M., and C. Day. *Muldergate: The Story of the Information Scandal*. London: Macmillan, 1980.

Roherty, James M., ed. *Defense Policy Formation: Towards Comparative Analysis*. Durham, N.C.: Carolina Academic Press, 1980.

Schmokle, Wolfe. *Dream of Empire*. New Haven: Yale University Press, 1964.

Schreuder, D.M. *The Scramble for Southern Africa, 1877–1895*. London: Cambridge University Press, 1980.

Shackley, Theodore. *The Third Option: An American View of Counterinsurgency Operations*. New York: Reader's Digest, 1981.

Sincere, Richard E., Jr. *The Politics of Sentiment*. Washington, D.C.: Ethics and Public Policy Center, 1984.

Sinclair, Michael. *The Strategic Significance of Tanzania*. Pretoria: ISSUP, 1979.

Soto, Hernando de. *The Other Path: The Invisible Revolution in the Third World*. New York: Harper & Row, 1988.

Spinola, Antonio de. *Portugal and the Future*. Johannesburg: Perskor, 1974.

Stiff, Peter, and Ron Reid Daly. *Selous Scouts: Top Secret War*. Alberton: Galago, 1987.

Stockwell, John. *In Search of Enemies*. New York: W.W. Norton, 1978.

Summers, Harry G. *On Strategy: The Vietnam War in Context*. Carlisle Barracks: U.S. Army War College, 1981.

Sunter, Clem. *South Africa and the World in the 1990s*. Johannesburg: Argus, 1987.

Thompson, Sir Robert. *Defeating Communist Insurgency*. London: Chatto & Windus, 1966.

Vanneman, Peter. *Soviet Strategy in Southern Africa*. Stanford: Hoover Institution Press, 1990.

Venter, A.J. *The Zambesi Salient: Conflict in Southern Africa*. London: Robert Hale, 1975.

Villiers, D de, and I de Villiers. *P.W.* Capetown: Tafelberg, 1984.

Villiers, H H W de. *Rivonia—Operation Mayibuye*. Johannesburg: Afrikaanse Pers-Boekhandel, 1964.

Villiers, L E S de. *Secret Information*. Cape Town: Tafelberg, 1980.

Wassenar, Ad D. *Squandered Assets*. Cape Town: Tafelberg, 1989.

Wiarda, Howard J. *Transcending Corporatism? The Portuguese Corporative System and the Revolution of 1974*. Columbia: University of South Carolina Institute of International Studies, 1976.

Wilkinson, Paul. *Terrorism and the Liberal State*. London: Macmillan, 1977.

Wiseman, Henry, and Alastair Taylor. *From Rhodesia to Zimbabwe: The Politics of Transition*. New York: Pergamon, 1981.

INDEX

Operation Mayibuye, 70–71
Operation Modular, 106, 165
Operation Packer, 106, 165
Operation Protea, 47
Operation Savannah, 27, 37, 73, 93
Opperman, Daniel, 90*n.34*
Organization of African Unity (OAU), 175, 177
Ovambo (tribe), 46, 47
Ovimbundu (tribe), 35

PAC. *See* Pan-African Congress
Packard, David, 32*n.17*
Pan-African Congress (PAC), 71, 133, 136
Partition, 12, 13
Part-time Force (PTF), 95, 97, 101
People's Liberation Army of Namibia (PLAN), 46, 47, 70, 127–28, 133, 159, 169–72, 185*n.19*
People's Republic of China (PRC), 51, 54, 55
Perkins, Edward, 193
Permanent Force, 94, 96, 105
PFP. *See* Progressive Federal Party
Pienaar, Louis, 171
Pike–Church Hearings, 36
Pirow, Oswald, 88*n.11*
PLAN. *See* People's Liberation Army of Namibia
Podgorny, Nikolai, 55
Political instability in Africa, 39, 59–60*nn.11, 12*
Ponomarev, Boris, 39, 158
Popular Forces for the Liberation of Angola (FAPLA), 36, 38, 47, 106, 129, 159–60, 163, 165–67, 185*n.22*
Popular Movement for the Liberation of Angola (MPLA), 34–35, 36, 46, 73, 159–60
Portugal, 10, 34–38, 49, 51, 56, 176, 177, 178–79
Portuguese Armed Forces Movement (MFA), 34, 35
Potgieter Commission, 72
PRC. *See* People's Republic of China
Press. *See* Print media
Pretorius, Phillip, 155*n.42*
Print media, 67–68*n.55*, 155*n.44*
Progressive Federal Party (PFP), 8*n.3*, 17–18, 29*n.7*, 101, 120*n.4*

PTF. *See* Part-time Force
Putter, A P, 84, 89*n.25*, 92*n.53*, 110, 111

Races. *See* Blacks, Coloureds; Indians; Whites
Radio. *See* Broadcast media
Railroads, 53, 66*n. 48*, 66–67*n.50*
Rationalization, 43, 79
Reagan, Ronald, 15, 48, 49, 125*n.66*, 130, 151*n.14*, 161, 168, 173, 189–90, 192, 193, 195
Recces. *See* Reconnaissance Commando
Reconnaissance Commando, 75–76, 129
Religion, 6
Relly, Gavin, 20, 21
RENAMO. *See* Mozambique National Resistance
Revolutionary Front for the Liberation of Mozambique (FRELIMO), 54–56, 66*n.49*, 68*n.57*
Revolutionary war in Africa, combating. *See* Internal security; *specific countries*
Rhodes, Cecil, 49, 50, 66*n.50*
Rhodesia, 50, 51–52, 55, 169
Rhodesian Rail System, 53
Roberto, Holden, 35
Rocket launchers, 113–14
Rosholt, Mike, 32*n.16*
Rowland, "Tiny," 177
Ruacana Scheme, 106
Russia. *See* Soviet Union

SAAF. *See* South African Air Force
SABC. *See* South African Broadcasting Corporation
Sabotage Act, 87*n.7*
SACP.*See* South Africa Communist Party
SADCC. *See* Southern Africa Development Coordination Conference
SADF. *See* South African Defense Force
SAF. *See* South Africa Foundation
SAMIL. *See* Military Vehicle Division
SAMS. *See* South Africa Medical Service

SAN. *See* South African Navy
Sánchez, Arnaldo Ochoa, 166
SAP. *See* South African Police
SATS. *See* South African Transport
Services
Savimbi, Jonas, 35, 48–49, 159,
160–61, 173, 175, 177, 192
Schoeman, B J, 31n.12
Schwarz, Harry H, 101
Security Police. *See* South African Police
Shagari, Shehu, 60n.12
Shevardnadze, Edward, 158, 183n.5
Ships, naval, 108–11, 116, 123n.43.
See also Submarines
Shultz, George, 150–51n.14, 160, 161,
191, 204n.6
Simonstown Agreement, 10, 110
Sisulu, Walter, 87n.7
Slovo, Joe, 133, 153n.28
Smuts, Jan, 49–50, 67n.52, 88n.11,
120n.1
Solodovnikov, Vasilii, 159, 183n.6
Sorour, Peter, 20, 21
South African Broadcasting
Corporation (SABC), 139, 141
South Africa Communist Party
(SACP), 71, 133, 182n.1
South Africa Foundation (SAF), 20,
21, 31n.16
South Africa Medical Service
(SAMS), 122n.29
South Africa Question
political and corporate leadership,
16–24
reopening, 11–14, 28, 41
U.S. failure to understand, 14–16,
191
South African Air Force (SAAF), 99,
106, 107–8
South African Defense Force (SADF)
Angolan operations, 10, 13, 27, 37,
38, 48, 51, 76, 101, 106,
121n.11, 129, 159–60, 162,
163–68, 184nn.18, 22
ARMSCOR, relationship to, 112–19,
124n.55
basic role, 120n.2
Botha's early use of, 27–28
civilians, role regarding, 141–48
conscription, 95, 96, 120nn.4, 7

South African Defense Force (SADF)
(continued)
"coup" theory regarding, 4–5
doctrine development, 101–11,
121n.20
dual role of, 27, 33nn.23, 24, 26
intelligence section, beginnings of,
70, 74–75
Junior Leader Program, 105
in Mozambique, 55–56, 68nn.56, 57
in National Security Management
System, 86–87
Southwest insurgency, 46–47,
127–34, 152n.18, 172
structure, 94–101, 120n.6, 121n.13
township insurrections, 136–37, 139,
154n.38, 155n.42
Zimbabwe/Botswana border
surveillance, 99–100
South African Development Bank, 21
South African Military Academy, 105
South African Navy (SAN), 108–11,
116, 123n.49
South African Police (SAP), 25, 46,
70–71, 72, 77, 87n.4, 127, 131,
137, 151–52n.17, 154nn.34, 35,
38
South African Transport Services
(SATS), 53, 56, 176
South America, 78, 90n.35
Southern Africa Development
Coordination Conference
(SADCC), 199
Southwest Africa, 46–47, 98. *See also*
specific countries
Southwest Africa People's
Organization (SWAPO), 46,
47–48, 70, 127–28, 133, 134,
159, 169–72, 183n.5, 186nn.28,
31, 34, 187n.37
Southwest Africa Territorial Force
(SWATF), 105, 183n.8, 186n.31
Soviet Union
Angolan independence, 35, 36,
39–40, 47, 48, 73
Gorbachev era in southern Africa,
157–60, 162, 168, 173, 174–75,
182–83nn.3, 4, 183n.7
Mozambique involvement, 55, 56,
57, 177

van der Merwe, Johann, 152*n.19*
van der Merwe, Stoefel, 30*n.7*, 139
van der Westhuizen, Pieter, 75,
89*n.25*, 92*n.57*, 121*n.12*, 143,
144–46, 196, 205*n.18*
van Deventer, Andre J, 82–83, 85,
91*nn.39, 42*, 92*n.57*
van Heerden, Koos, 37
van Vuuren, Johan, 117, 124*n.56*
van Wyk, Alex, 89*n.29*
van zyl Slabbert, Frederick, 18
Verwoerd, Hendrik, 15, 30*n.11*,
31*n.12*, 35, 71, 88*n.12*, 111
Vietnam war, 141, 156*n.46*
Viljoen, Constand J, 103, 104,
121*n.19*, 122*n.37*
Viljoen, Gerrit, 32*n.19*
Vlok, Adriaan, 25, 86, 133, 137–38,
145, 152*n.19*
Vorster, B J
 Angolan independence, 36, 49, 73
 diplomatic isolation, 177
 relationship with van den Bergh,
  74
 resignation of, 30*n.11*, 74
 Rhodesian situation, 51, 52
 SADF, restrictions on, 143
 security system foundations
  established by, 69–72
 talks with Mondale, 32*n.18*
 term in office, 10, 16–17
 UNITA, role in, 35

Watson, Robert, 88*n.9*
Wessels, Leon, 86
West Germany, 177

Whites. *See also* Afrikaners
 National Party contingent, 7, 13, 21,
  24–26
 Partition of 1895 benefit to, 12–13
 in SADF, 95, 96
 working class, 69, 87*n.1*
Williams, A B, 24–25
Williamson, Craig, 152*n.17*
Wolpe, Harold, 87*n.7*
Worrall, Denis, 18, 31*n.14*

Yakovlev, Aleksandr, 158
Young, Andrew, 52

Zaire, 35, 36, 53, 175, 177–78
Zambia, 35, 46, 51, 53, 128, 130
ZANLA. *See* Zimbabwe African
 National Liberation Army
ZANU. *See* Zimbabwe African
 National Union
ZAPU. *See* Zimbabwe African
 People's Union
Zimbabwe, 51, 53–55, 99–100, 130,
 133, 150*n.13*, 170, 178
Zimbabwe African National
 Liberation Army (ZANLA), 51,
 55
Zimbabwe African National Union
 (ZANU), 51, 53, 55, 169
Zimbabwe African People's Union
 (ZAPU), 51, 169
Zimbabwe People's Revolutionary
 Army (ZIPRA), 51, 100
ZIPRA. *See* Zimbabwe People's
 Revolutionary Army
Zulu (Tribe), 12, 26